Photoshop® CS5
Top 100

Simplified®

TIPS & TRICKS

by Lynette Kent

Visual

WILEY

Photoshop® CS5: Top 100 Simplified® Tips & Tricks

Published by
Wiley Publishing, Inc.
10475 Crosspoint Boulevard
Indianapolis, IN 46256
www.wiley.com

Published simultaneously in Canada

Copyright © 2010 by Wiley Publishing, Inc., Indianapolis, Indiana

Library of Congress Control Number: 2010929308

ISBN: 978-0-470-61265-1

Manufactured in the United States of America

10 9 8 7 6 5 4 3 2 1

Trademark Acknowledgments

Contact Us

For general information on our other products and services contact our Customer Care Department within the U.S. at 877-762-2974, outside the U.S. at 317-572-3993 or fax 317-572-4002.

For technical support please visit www.wiley.com/techsupport

Permissions

Photospin

Wiley Publishing, Inc.

U.S. Sales

Contact Wiley at
(800) 762-2974 or
fax (317) 572-4002.

CREDITS

Executive Editor
Jody Lefevere

Sr. Project Editor
Sarah Hellert

Technical Editor
Dennis R. Cohen

Copy Editor
Scott Tullis

Editorial Director
Robyn Siesky

Business Manager
Amy Knies

Sr. Marketing Manager
Sandy Smith

Vice President and Executive Group Publisher
Richard Swadley

Vice President and Executive Publisher
Barry Pruett

Sr. Project Coordinator
Lynsey Stanford

Graphics and Production Specialists
Andrea Hornberger
Jennifer Mayberry

Quality Control Technician
Jessica Kramer

Proofreader
Mildred Rosenzweig

Indexer
Slivoskey Indexing Services

Media Development Project Manager
Laura Moss

Media Development Assistant Project Manager
Jenny Swisher

Media Development Associate Producer
Marilyn Hummel

Screen Artists
Ana Carrillo
Jill A. Proll
Ron Terry

ABOUT THE AUTHOR

Lynette Kent (Huntington Beach, CA) studied art and French at Stanford University, where she received a Master's degree. She taught at the high school and community college level before becoming an unconventional computer guru when she adopted the Mac in 1987. As a photographer and artist, Lynette writes books and magazine articles on digital imaging and photography. She also teaches and presents graphics-related hardware and software for technology companies, including Wacom, Adobe, G-Technology, and Digital Foci. Lynette enjoys traditional and digital painting and often blends these techniques with her photographs to create images. Lynette has written the *Top 100 Simplified Tips & Tricks* titles for Photoshop CS2, CS3, and CS4, *Teach Yourself VISUALLY Adobe Photoshop Lightroom 2, Teach Yourself VISUALLY Mac OS X Leopard,* and *Teach Yourself VISUALLY Digital Photography*, 3rd Edition. In her non-existent spare time, Lynette helps run the Adobe Technology Exchange of Southern California, a professional organization for photographers, graphic designers, and fine artists.

HOW TO USE THIS BOOK

Who This Book Is For

This book is for readers who know the basics and want to expand their knowledge of this particular technology or software application.

The Conventions in This Book

① Steps

This book uses a step-by-step format to guide you easily through each task. Numbered steps are actions you must do; bulleted steps clarify a point, step, or optional feature; and indented steps give you the result.

② Notes

Notes give additional information — special conditions that may occur during an operation, a situation that you want to avoid, or a cross reference to a related area of the book.

③ Icons and Buttons

Icons and buttons show you exactly what you need to click to perform a step.

④ Tips

Tips offer additional information, including warnings and shortcuts.

⑤ Bold

Bold type shows text or numbers you must type.

⑥ Italics

Italic type introduces and defines a new term.

⑦ Difficulty Levels

For quick reference, these symbols mark the difficulty level of each task.

DIFFICULTY LEVEL — Demonstrates a new spin on a common task

DIFFICULTY LEVEL — Introduces a new skill or a new task

DIFFICULTY LEVEL — Combines multiple skills requiring in-depth knowledge

DIFFICULTY LEVEL — Requires extensive skill and may involve other technologies

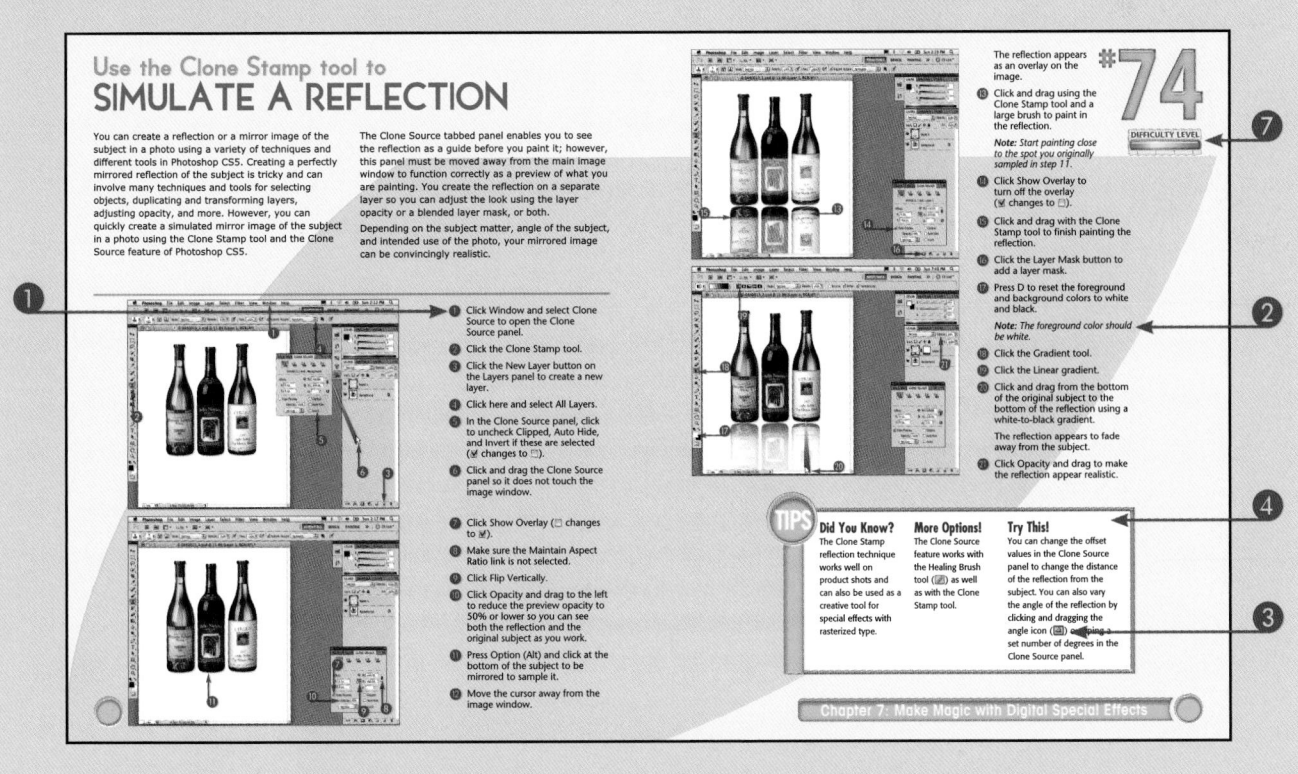

Table of Contents

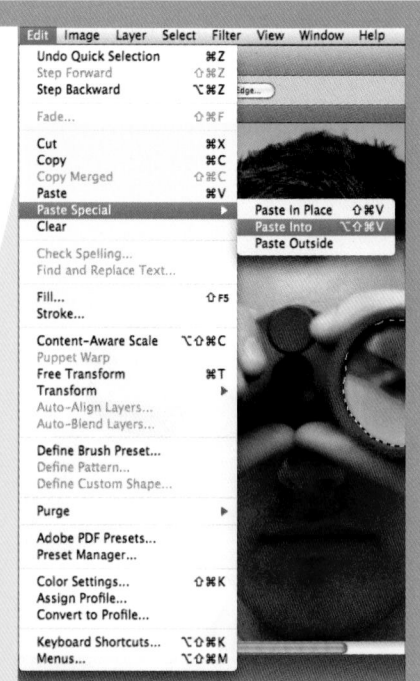

③ Straighten, Crop, and Resize

④ Retouch Portraits

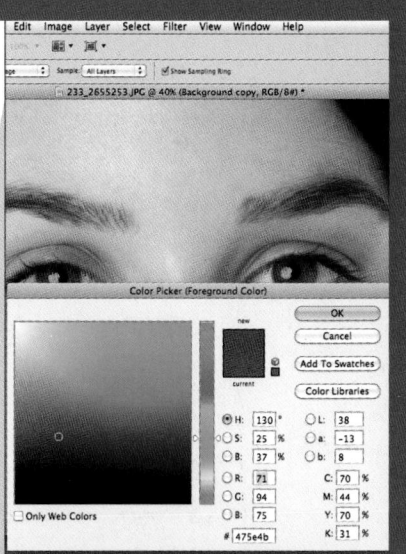

Table of Contents

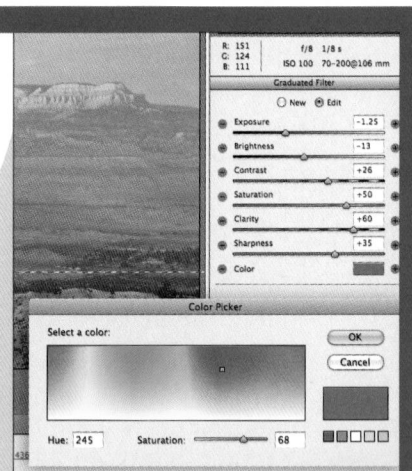

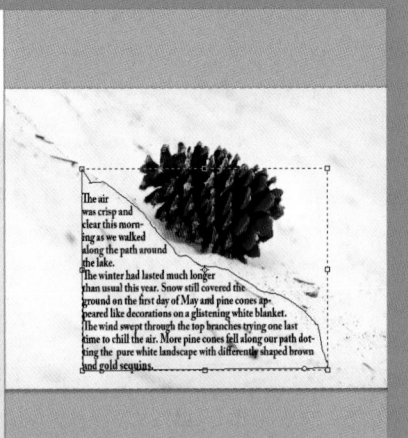

Table of Contents

Plug In to Photoshop CS5

Customize Photoshop for Your Projects

Photoshop is the core application for many different types of projects from graphic design to digital photography. You can perform many different types of tasks with Photoshop, and you can use multiple methods to complete each project.

Photoshop includes so many tools and panels that your screen can become cluttered, not leaving you sufficient room to work on an image. You may prefer to see only some panels and not others. You may also prefer certain tool settings to others. Customizing Photoshop's menus and tools to work your way makes you more productive, the program more useful, and everything you do with Photoshop much more fun.

With Photoshop CS5, Adobe has improved the interface and given you new ways to customize your settings. You can close some panels and open others to simplify your screen and keep only the tools you need available. You can make your own gradients, set up your own shortcuts, and design your own brushes. You can not only set up your workspace with only the panels and the tools you want for one project, you can also set up multiple workspaces, each with different tools for different projects, and switch between workspaces with one click.

These may seem like boring or simplistic steps, yet by learning to customize Photoshop, you gain familiarity with the program and become more efficient as you try different projects.

Top 100

SELECT THE COLOR SETTINGS
for your projects

Using Photoshop CS5 you can improve photographs, repurpose them, or start with a blank canvas to create original designs. Because printed images and Web images have different limits on the range of colors that they can represent, you need to set the working color space for your project.

Photoshop's default color space is set to sRGB, a limited color space intended for Web images to be viewable on even the lowest-quality monitor. sRGB is a much smaller color space than what printers can actually produce. Designers and photographers

generally prefer to work in the larger color space called Adobe RGB (1998) for working with projects intended for printing to inkjet printers.

In Photoshop CS5, you can easily choose your working color space and save it. To make your printed colors look much better, set your color space to the North America Prepress 2 settings and Adobe RGB (1998). So you can use the widest color gamut for photographic editing, you can instead select the ProPhoto working space.

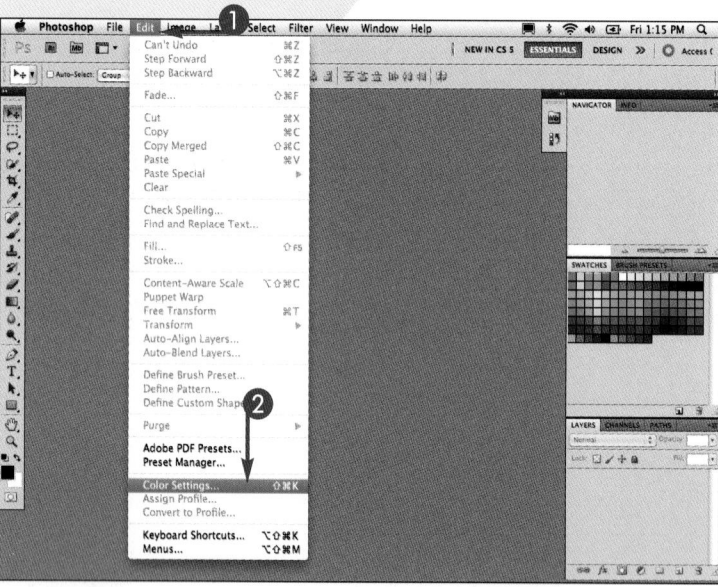

① Click Edit.

② Click Color Settings.

The Color Settings dialog box appears.

③ Click here and select North America Prepress 2.

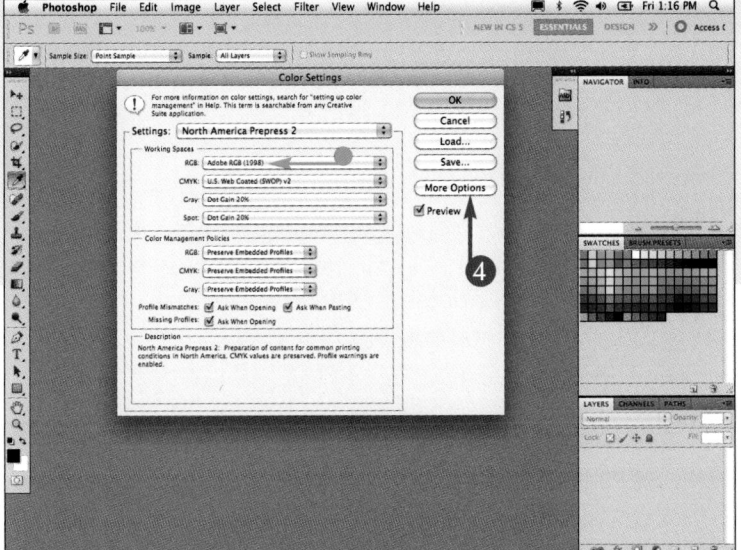

● The RGB setting changes to Adobe RGB (1998).

Note: *ProPhoto RGB is an even larger color space often preferred by professional photographers because it includes a wider range of tones and allows for fine detail editing.*

The rest of the Color Settings dialog box changes to reflect the preferred working space for images that you print.

④ Click More Options.

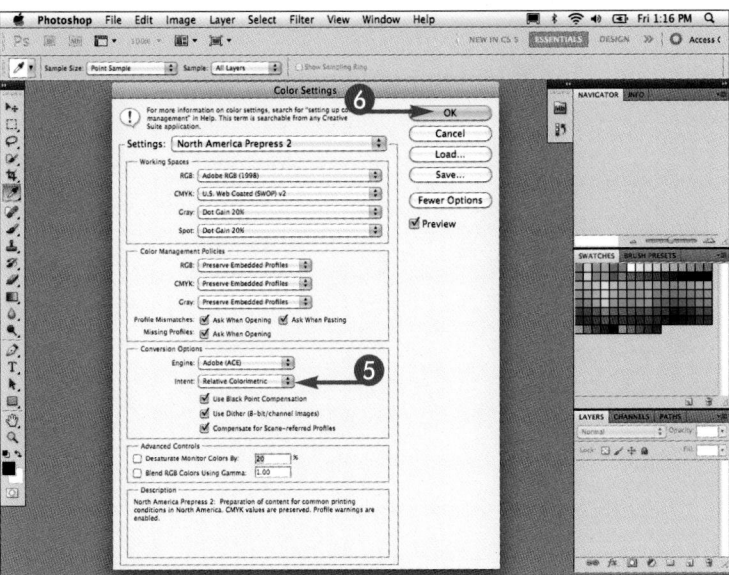

The dialog box expands.

⑤ Click here and select Relative Colorimetric for a graphic design project or Perceptual for most photographic projects.

⑥ Click OK.

Your color settings are saved until you reset your preferences.

 **TIPS**

Important!

Photoshop is all about interacting with what you see on your screen. Wallpapers and bright backgrounds will interfere with how you judge colors in your images. You should always set your desktop picture to a medium neutral gray using System Preferences on a Mac, or the Appearance and Personalization settings in the Control Panel on a PC.

Customize It!

You can save your own Color Settings preset. The name of the preset changes to Custom when you deselect any check box or make any other changes. Click Save after customizing your settings. Type a name in the Save dialog box and click Save. Your customized preset appears in the Settings menu, ready for you to choose.

Try This!

You can synchronize the color settings in other Creative Suite CS5 applications to match your saved custom Photoshop CS5 color settings. In Photoshop, click File and select Browse in Bridge. In Bridge, click Edit and select Creative Suite Color Settings. Click North America Prepress 2 and click Apply.

SET THE PREFERENCES
for the way you work

Although you can work with the default settings, changing some of the Photoshop Preferences menu options can make your computer run more efficiently or make working with your projects easier. For example, by default, Photoshop is set to use more than half of the available RAM. You can lower this setting to fit the amount of RAM installed in the computer and the number of applications you run at the same time. You can change the default colors for the guides and grid when they are similar to those in your image. Designating an additional plug-ins folder

keeps third-party items separate from those included with Photoshop. You can set a separate scratch disk, which greatly speeds up your work on large files. Each of the Photoshop-specific options under the Preferences menu opens different panes under the main Preferences dialog box. You can also change the default options for Adobe Camera RAW with the Camera RAW setting.

Read through each Preferences pane and select the settings you want to make Photoshop work for you.

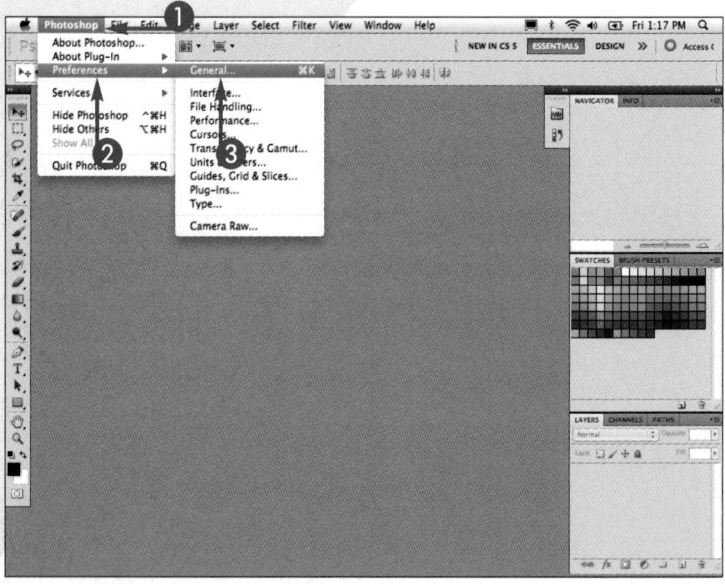

① Click Photoshop (Edit).

② Click Preferences.

③ Click General.

The General Preferences dialog box appears.

④ Click any of the arrows to change your settings.

⑤ Click to select the options you want, or deselect those you do not want.

⑥ Click Next to continue customizing Preferences.

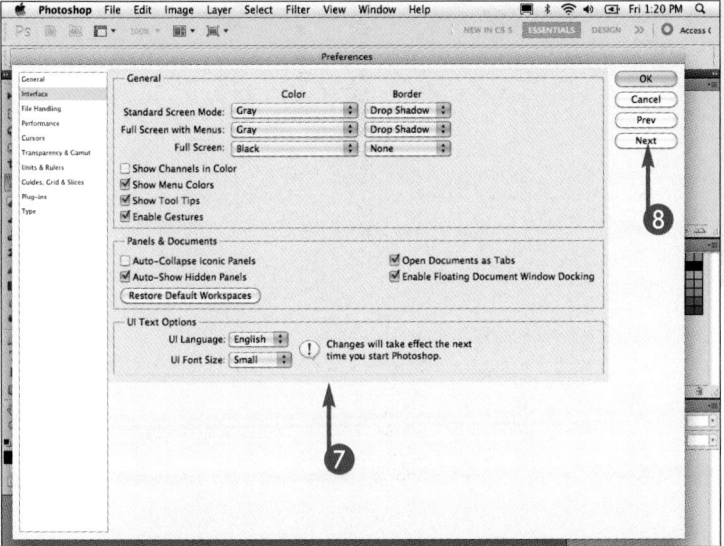

The dialog box changes to the Interface Preferences.

⑦ Click to select the interface options you want, or deselect those you do not want.

⑧ Click Next.

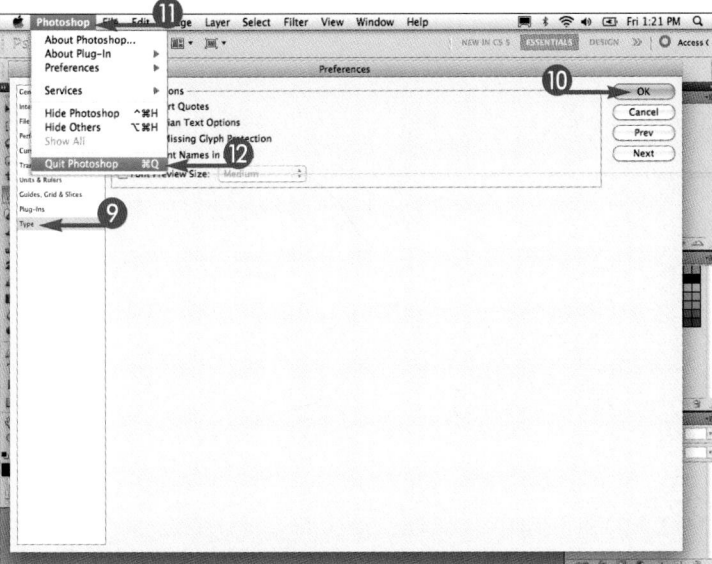

⑨ Make any other changes that you prefer in the other Preferences panes.

⑩ Click OK when you have cycled through all the Preferences panes.

⑪ Click Photoshop (File).

⑫ Click Quit Photoshop (Exit).

The next time you start the application, your own settings take effect.

TIPS

Did You Know?
You can use keyboard shortcuts to set the Preferences. Press ⌘+K (Ctrl+K). Set your options for the General Preferences. Press ⌘+2 (Ctrl+2), and so on, for each of the Preferences panes.

Try This!
You can change the default Preferences so that just pressing the appropriate letter toggles each tool. In the General Preferences pane, deselect the Use Shift Key for Tool Switch check box.

Did You Know?
You can restore the Preferences any time by pressing and holding ⌘+Option+Shift (Ctrl+Alt+Shift) as you launch the application. Click Yes in the dialog box that appears, and the Preferences are reset to the defaults.

Set up and save your own
CUSTOMIZED WORKSPACE

The workspace in Photoshop refers to the layout of the different panels and tools on your screen. Photoshop CS5 enables you to design and save the workspace to fit your needs for a particular project. You can open the panels that you use most and collapse others into buttons. You can move and resize individual panels and docks. You can move the single-column Tools panel, dock it, or change it to a two-column Tools panel. When you select Full Screen Mode With Menu Bar from the View menu, your image appears as large as possible with all the tool panels available.

When you save a new workspace in CS5, the panel locations are automatically saved and you can select whether to save the keyboard shortcut and/or menus for that workspace as well.

Photoshop CS5 includes some preconfigured workspaces, which you can use or modify to accommodate different tasks, such as one for painting, one for design, and one for photography. And when you alter any existing workspace, your changes are automatically saved.

① With an image open, click View.

② Click Screen Mode.

③ Click Full Screen Mode With Menu Bar.

The image on-screen maximizes to fill the space.

④ Click here to reduce the panel groups to buttons with names.

⑤ Click here and drag to the right to shrink the docks to buttons only.

⑥ Click here to change the width of the toolbar.

⑦ Click here and drag to move the Options bar.

⑧ Click here and drag to move the Application bar.

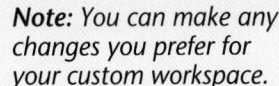

Note: *You can make any changes you prefer for your custom workspace.*

⑨ Click the double arrow to open the Workspace menu.

Note: *You can optionally click Window and click Workspace.*

⑩ Click New Workspace.

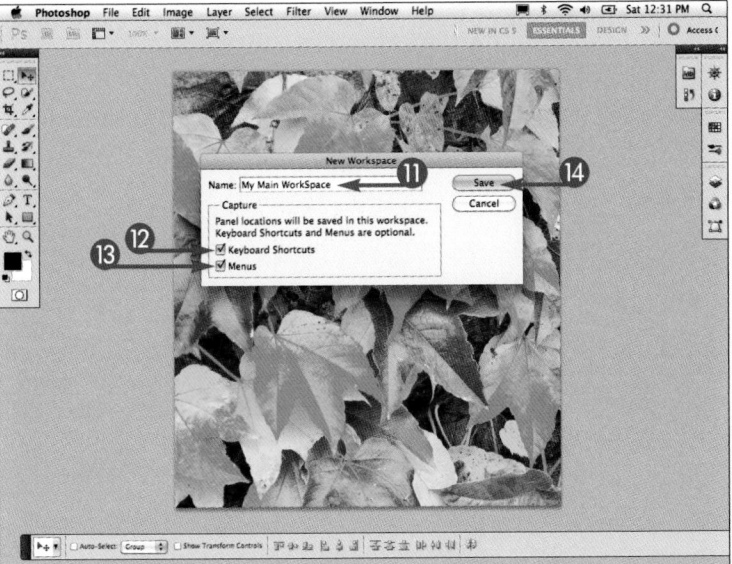

The New Workspace dialog box appears.

⑪ Type a name for your workspace.

⑫ Click to save the keyboard shortcuts with the new workspace if you changed these (☐ changes to ☑).

⑬ Click to save the menu changes with the new workspace if you changed these (☐ changes to ☑).

⑭ Click Save.

Your custom workspace is saved.

Note: *This image and others from the book are available for download from www.wiley.com/go/photoshopcs5top100. The images on the companion Web site are small low-resolution images for you to practice the steps. You will get better results and learn more when you use your own photographs.*

TIPS

Did You Know?

You can easily delete any workspaces you do not need. First click a different workspace in the Options bar to make it active. Then click the double arrow (⏩) on the Options bar and click Delete Workspace. You can also click Window, Workspace, and Delete Workspace. Click the Workspace arrow in the Delete Workspace window that appears and click Delete. Click Yes in the warning dialog box that appears. The deleted workspace no longer appears in the Workspace menu.

Important!

You can quickly revert any workspace to its original default settings. With the workspace you want to revert active, click the double arrow (⏩) on the Options bar. The name of the active workspace is shown at the top of the menu. Click Reset *workspace name* in the menu. You can also click Window, Workspace, and Reset *workspace name* to revert the workspace.

SWITCH YOUR WORKSPACES
to work more efficiently

Creating separate workspaces for different types of projects helps you work more efficiently. Photoshop makes it easy to switch between a variety of workspaces. You can use a Photography workspace to edit an image, click the Design Workspace to incorporate the photograph into a design layout, and quickly switch back to the Photography workspace to make other enhancements to the photo with different tools and panels open.

In addition to using the Window menu to change your interface, Photoshop CS5 now displays the names of all your workspaces in the Application bar. You can quickly click a workspace's name to make it active and take advantage of your custom settings. You can resize the section of the Application bar to show or hide as many workspaces at one time as your screen width allows. You can even change the order of the workspaces as they are listed on the bar.

You can also switch workspaces using the double arrow and menu on the Application bar. This menu also acts as a shortcut for resetting, deleting, and creating workspaces.

① Click the gripper bar on the application menu and drag to the left.

The workspaces section expands, revealing the other predefined workspaces.

② Click Painting.

The interface changes to show the tools and panels most needed for painting with Photoshop.

③ Click the workspace name New in CS5 and drag it to the right of the workspace name Photography.

New in CS5 now appears after the Photography workspace in the Application bar but the workspace is not selected.

④ Click the workspace name New in CS5 again to select it.

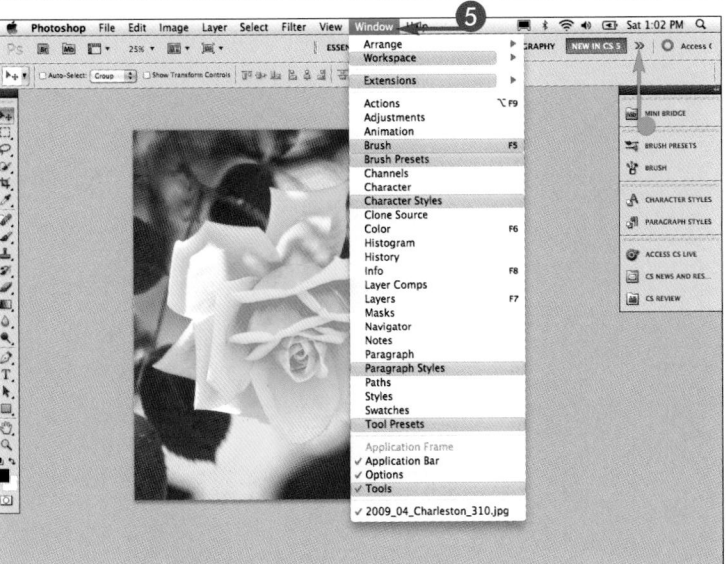

The interface changes again.

⑤ Click the Window menu.

The new or changed options for Photoshop CS5 are highlighted in blue.

● You can optionally click the double arrow to see the menu showing the existing workspaces and tools to reset, create and delete workspaces.

Note: You can click any other menu to see the new or changed options for Photoshop CS5 highlighted in blue.

TIPS

Did You Know?

If you delete one of Photoshop CS5's original workspaces, such as Essentials, Design, Painting, or Photography, you can easily restore these. Click Photoshop (Edit) on the menu bar and select Preferences. Click Interface in the left side of the Preferences pane. Then click Restore Default Workspaces under the Panels & Documents section to automatically restore all the default workspaces with all their original settings. Click OK to close the Preferences pane. Any custom workspaces you created remain in the Application bar.

Important!

Restarting Photoshop while pressing and holding ⌘+Option+ Shift (Ctrl+Alt+Shift) as you launch the application also resets all the original workspaces. However, this action also deletes all your personalized workspaces as well as any other custom settings.

Change your
WINDOW VIEWS

Photoshop CS5 enables you to open and view your images in various configurations on the screen. You can open multiple similar photographs at the same time to see which one is the best of the group. You can also have two windows of the same image open.

The default setting for Photoshop automatically opens multiple images as separate tabs in one window. You can quickly change from one image to the next by clicking the tabs, and you can close any images you do not need by clicking the X on the image tab. You can select one image and open it in a separate

window while leaving all the others as tabs in the group, or view all the images as cascading individual windows. You can also tile multiple windows so they all fit on the screen at once. You can open a second window of one image, and view an enlarged version in one window and the full photo in the other, so you can edit a particular area while still viewing the overall effect on the entire image. Comparing specific areas on similar photos is easy because you can match the areas displayed in each of the images and even match a zoomed-in location.

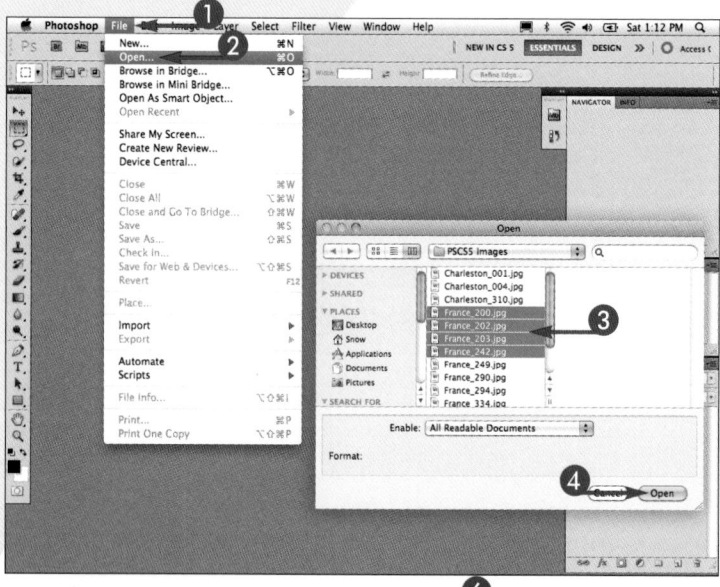

① Click File.

② Click Open.

The Open dialog box appears.

③ Shift+click multiple images to select them.

Note: Shift+click selects multiple images listed consecutively. ⌘+click (Ctrl+click) selects individual images in the list.

④ Click Open.

● The images open in the default tabbed mode.

⑤ Click any tab to view a different image.

⑥ Click Window.

⑦ Click Arrange.

⑧ Click Float All in Windows.

- The images open in separate windows cascading down the screen.

⑨ Click Window.

⑩ Click Arrange.

⑪ Click Tile.

- The images tile across the screen.

⑫ Click the Hand tool.

⑬ Click and drag in one image to move it to the bottom right corner.

⑭ Click Window.

⑮ Click Arrange.

⑯ Click Match Location.

All the windows move their contents to display the bottom right corner of each image.

TIPS

Did You Know?

If you zoom in on one image and then tile the windows, you can click Window, Arrange, Match Zoom to zoom the same amount on all the windows.

More Options!

You can drag one or more windows to a second monitor. You can then have all your tools and panels on one monitor and all your images on the other, or one version of an image on one monitor and an edited version on the other.

Try This!

Click the Arrange Documents button (▦) in the Photoshop bar and click any of the buttons to select a different tiling arrangement, or click Match Zoom, Match Location, or Match Zoom and Location to quickly change your window views.

CUSTOMIZE YOUR VIEW
of Bridge

Bridge, which ships with Photoshop CS5, acts as a power browser and central hub for all the Creative Suite 5 applications and shows all types of files and folders that are available. You can even see thumbnails of documents and files from other applications, such as Word or Acrobat files. When you double-click a thumbnail from Bridge, the other application launches. You can open Bridge from within Photoshop or as a separate application.

Bridge offers different ways to search, categorize, and view your files, options for adding information, and

automation for various repetitive tasks. By customizing and saving your own Bridge workspace, you can review and compare images more efficiently and have more fun doing so.

To launch Bridge from within Photoshop, click File and Browse in Bridge. You can also click the Bridge button in the Options bar, or press the keyboard shortcut ⌘+Option+O (Ctrl+Alt+O).

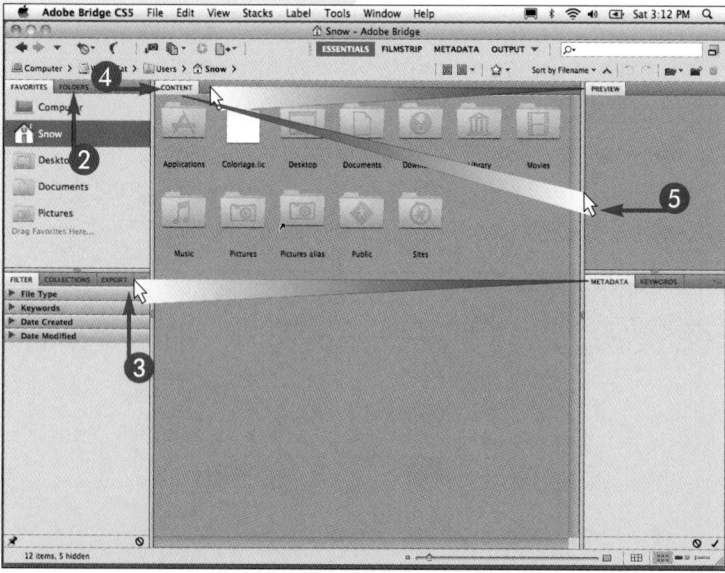

1 Launch Bridge.

Note: You can make any changes you prefer for your custom workspace.

2 Click the Folders tab to navigate to a folder of images.

3 Click and drag the Metadata and Keywords tabs to the left panel between the Folders and the Filter tab.

4 Click and drag the Preview tab to the center pane.

5 Click and drag the Content tab to the right pane.

The Content images align vertically on the right.

6 Click an image to see it in the Preview tab.

7 Click here and drag to the right.

The Preview tab enlarges and the Content tab narrows.

● You can also click the left separator bar and drag to the left to enlarge the Preview tab more.

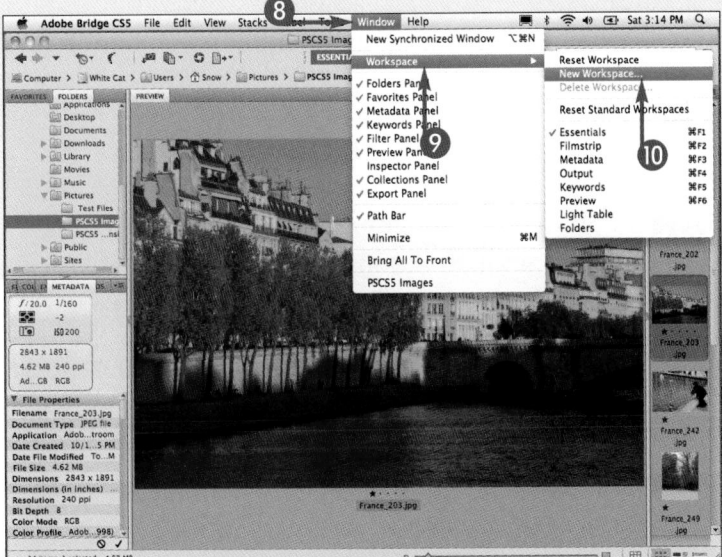

8 Click Window.

9 Click Workspace.

10 Click New Workspace.

The New Workspace dialog box appears.

11 Type a name for the workspace.

12 Make sure that both check boxes are checked.

13 Click Save.

Your custom workspace is saved and listed in the top panel.

TIPS

More Options!
You can also change the background for viewing images to a different shade by clicking Adobe Bridge CS5 (Edit) and clicking Preferences. Use the Image Backdrop slider under the General Preferences to vary the color from black to gray to white, and click OK to apply the new color.

Enlarge It!
Press Tab and the Preview window fills the screen as the other panels slide away on the sides. Press Tab again to return to your custom Bridge workspace.

Try This!
⌘+click (Ctrl+click) multiple images in the Content panel to compare them in the Preview panel. You can also stack the selected images by clicking Stacks, Group as Stack, or by pressing ⌘+G (Ctrl+G).

TAKE ADVANTAGE OF THE MINI BRIDGE
to find your files

The new Mini Bridge panel in Photoshop CS5 is a real time- and space-saving feature. You can now quickly find an image from within the Photoshop interface, without having Bridge completely take over your screen.

The Mini Bridge actually launches Bridge in the background; however, the Bridge window does not open until you click the full Bridge icon. You can set the preferences for the way the Mini Bridge displays information. Then with a click of the Mini Bridge icon

you can browse the contents of your computer, find an image, preview it in a mini preview window, and zoom in to check details, all without leaving Photoshop. You can even sort multiple images and rate them in a mini review mode window, and then filter the images you want to view in the Mini Bridge.

Finding a specific image or a group of images to work on using the Mini Bridge is the quickest way to improve your Photoshop workflow.

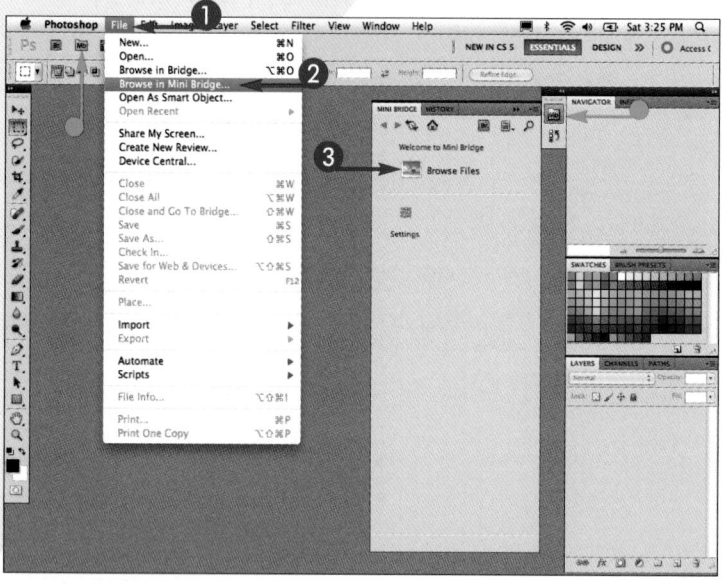

① Click File.

② Click Browse in Mini Bridge.

● You can optionally click the Mini Bridge icon in the Application bar or click the icon on the docked collapsed panels.

The Mini Bridge opens in the Home screen.

Note: To close the Mini Bridge, click its icon again.

③ Click the Browse Files icon.

The Mini Bridge opens the default layout.

④ In the Navigation pane, click a location to find your images.

⑤ In the Content pane, double-click the folder to open it.

Note: Double-click any folder to open it to the next hierarchical level.

The Content pane now displays the image thumbnails.

⑥ ⌘+click (Ctrl+click) multiple images to select them.

⑦ Click the Preview button's arrow and select Review Mode from the menu.

The screen fills with the selected images in Carousel view.

⑧ Click any of the smaller images to bring it to the front.

The image carousel rotates to that image.

⑨ Click to close the Review Mode window and return to Photoshop.

TIPS

Did You Know?

You can quickly return to Photoshop from the full Adobe Bridge CS5 window by clicking the Boomerang icon (⬅) in the Options bar of the Bridge application.

Try This!

When in Carousel view in the Mini Bridge content window, click in the front image to get a 100% preview of that section of the image.

More Options!

You can play a mini slide show inside the Mini Bridge panel or in full screen mode, and quickly return to the Photoshop interface. ⌘+click (Ctrl+click) a number of images in the content pane of the Mini Bridge. Click the Preview button's arrow (⬛) at the bottom on the Mini Bridge and click the Slideshow icon (🖥). A slide show of the selected images fills the screen. Press Esc to return to the Photoshop window.

ADD A KEYBOARD SHORTCUT
for a favorite filter

Photoshop includes keyboard shortcuts for the tools that you use most often. Many of the tools already have keyboard shortcuts assigned. Still, you may find yourself going to the menu to select an item, such as the Gaussian Blur filter, so often that a personalized keyboard shortcut becomes a huge timesaver.

You can create your own custom keyboard shortcuts or even change some Photoshop keystrokes to something that you can remember better. If the keyboard shortcut that you choose is already

assigned by Photoshop for another function, a warning appears. Although you should generally avoid keyboard shortcuts used by your operating system, you can change Photoshop's default shortcuts, or you can apply a different set of keystrokes not already assigned.

Learning and using custom keyboard shortcuts can streamline your workflow, leaving you more time for designing and photo editing.

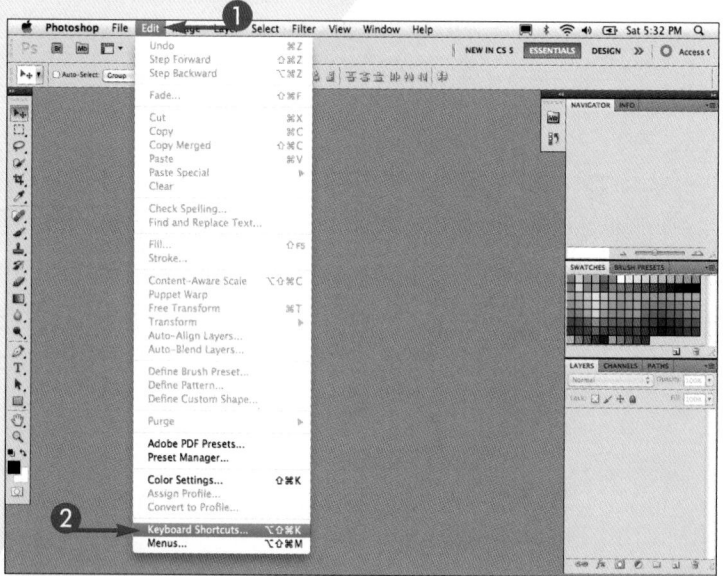

① Click Edit.

② Click Keyboard Shortcuts.

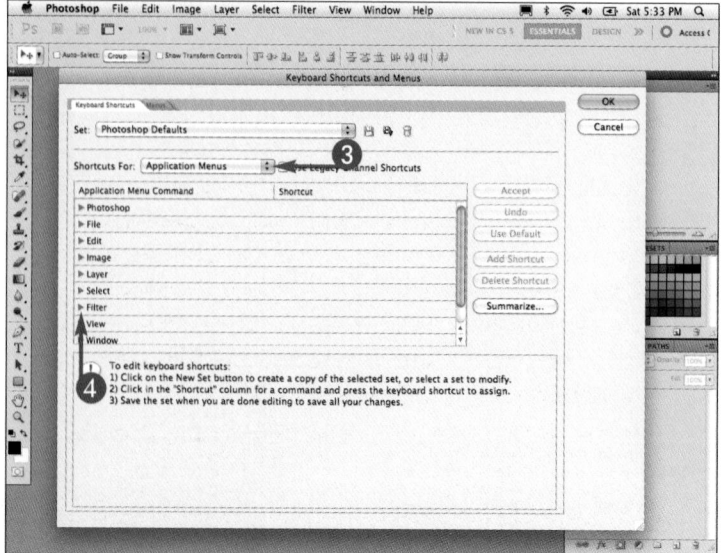

The Keyboard Shortcuts and Menus dialog box appears with the Keyboard Shortcuts tab preselected.

③ Click here and select Application Menus.

④ Click the Filter disclosure triangle.

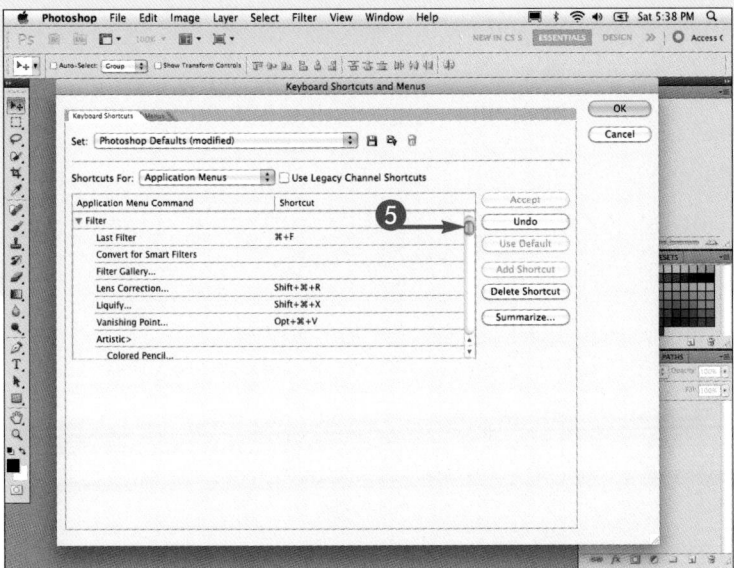

The filters are listed along with any existing keyboard shortcuts.

⑤ Scroll down to the filter for which you want to add a shortcut.

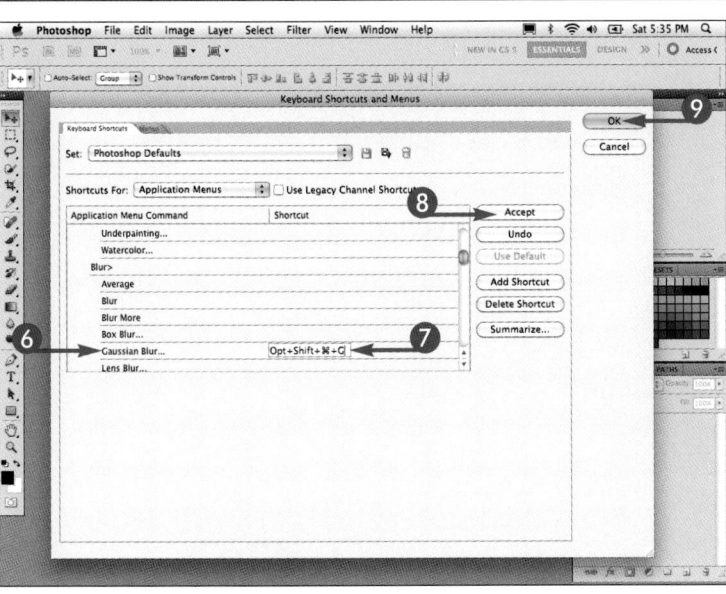

⑥ Click the filter.

An empty data field appears under the Shortcut column.

⑦ Press ⌘ (Ctrl) and type your shortcut in the data field.

Note: A shortcut must include either ⌘ (Ctrl) or an F key (function key).

⑧ Click Accept.

The Photoshop Defaults set is modified to include your shortcut.

⑨ Click OK to finish adding your custom keyboard shortcut.

TIPS

Did You Know?
You can access the Keyboard Shortcuts and Menus dialog box by using a keyboard shortcut — ⌘+Shift+Option+K (Ctrl+Shift+Alt+K).

Try This!
You can save and print a list of all keyboard shortcuts. Click Summarize in the Keyboard Shortcuts and Menus dialog box and save the file as Photoshop Defaults.htm. Open the file and print the list for reference.

More Options!
You can even save a keyboard shortcut set with a custom workspace. Click Window, Workspace, and New Workspace. In the New Workspace window, name the workspace and click Keyboard Shortcuts (☐ changes to ☑). Click Save to save the current Keyboard Shortcuts set with the workspace.

CREATE A CUSTOM ACTION
to increase your efficiency

Actions help you perform repeated steps quickly. An *action* is a series of commands that you can apply to an image with one click of the mouse. Unlike a keyboard shortcut, which can only invoke a command, an action can open a command, apply changes to an image, step through another command, apply it, and even save a file in a particular way. You can create your own actions for steps that you do over and over and add them to the Actions panel.

Using the Actions panel, you record a sequence of steps and save your new action. When you need to apply the same steps to a different image, even to an entire folder of files, you play the action, and Photoshop automatically applies the steps.

Actions can help you automate your work for repetitive tasks, leaving you more time to work on creative projects.

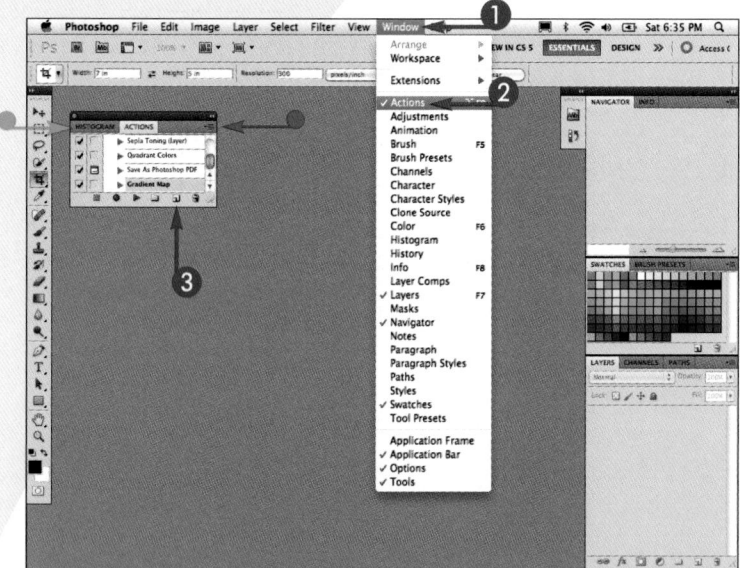

Note: As an example, the following steps show creating an action for setting up a new 7-x-5-inch document at 300 pixels/inch for a greeting card.

1 Click Window.

2 Click Actions.

● The Actions panel appears.

3 Click the Create New Action button.

● Alternatively, you can click the panel menu button and select New Action from the menu that appears.

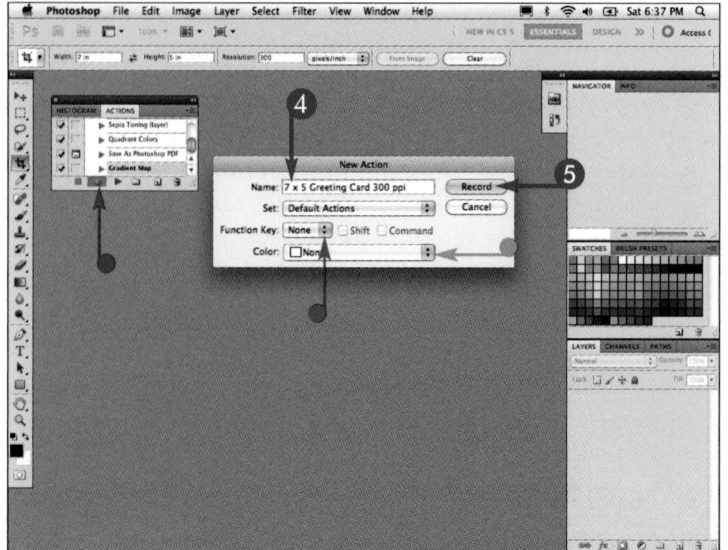

The New Action dialog box appears.

4 Type the name of your action.

● You can click here and select a function key for a keyboard shortcut.

● You can click here and select a color for the action.

5 Click Record.

● The Record button in the Actions panel turns red.

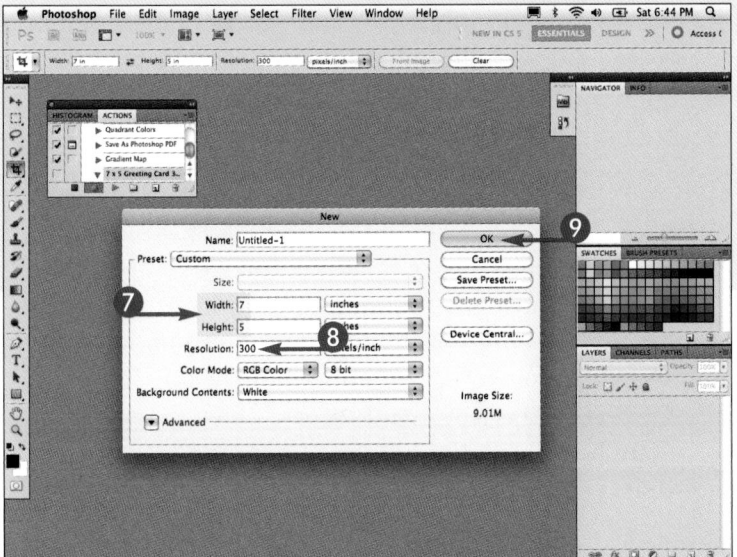

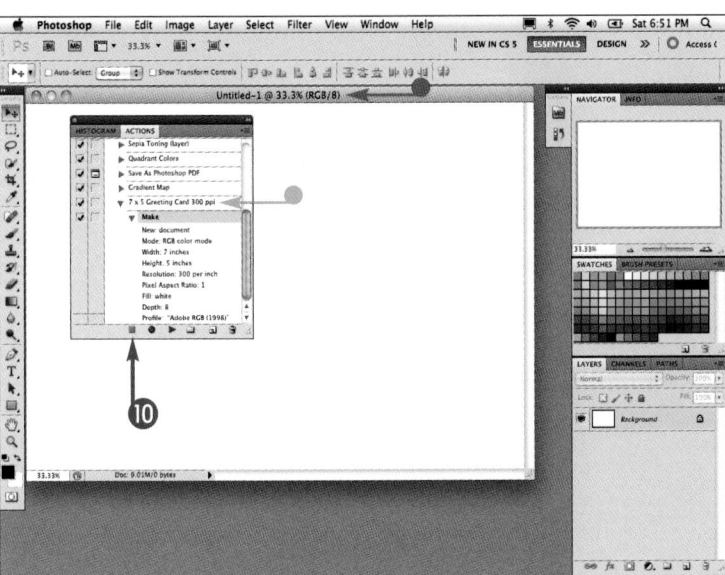

Perform the steps that you want to record as an action.

⑥ Press ⌘+N (Ctrl+N) to open a new file.

The New file dialog box appears.

⑦ Type **7** in the Width field and **5** in the Height field.

⑧ Type **300** in the Resolution field.

⑨ Click OK.

● A new untitled document appears.

⑩ Click the Stop Recording button.

● Your custom action to create a 7 × 5 greeting card is now recorded and listed in the Actions panel.

You can test your action by pressing the keyboard shortcut that you assigned.

TIPS

More Options!

You can apply an action to a folder of files by clicking File, Automate, and Batch and selecting the action and a source folder. Or you can apply an action to a group of images from Bridge by clicking Tools, Photoshop, and Batch.

Try This!

You can make the actions easier to find. Assign a color to the action in the New Action dialog box. Then select Button Mode in the Actions panel's menu. Your actions appear as color-coded buttons.

Did You Know?

Photoshop CS5 actions are saved in a folder called Actions inside the Presets folder of the Photoshop CS5 application folder.

DESIGN A CUSTOMIZED BRUSH
with your settings

Whether you retouch photographs, design brochures, or paint from scratch, you will use many different variations of the Brush tool.

The menu on the Options bar includes a variety of brushes, and you can modify the attributes of any of the existing brushes, including Photoshop CS5's new Bristle tip brushes, to suit your drawing style or your image. You can then save the modified brush as your own custom brush so that it is ready to use for your next design. You can name and save any number of custom brushes.

Many other tools also have modifiable brush options, including the Pencil tool, the Eraser tool, the Clone Stamp tool, the Pattern Stamp tool, the History Brush, the Art History Brush, the Blur tool, the Sharpen tool, the Smudge tool, the Dodge tool, the Burn tool, and the Sponge tool.

Customizing Brush tools for your projects is a timesaving technique that is also fun.

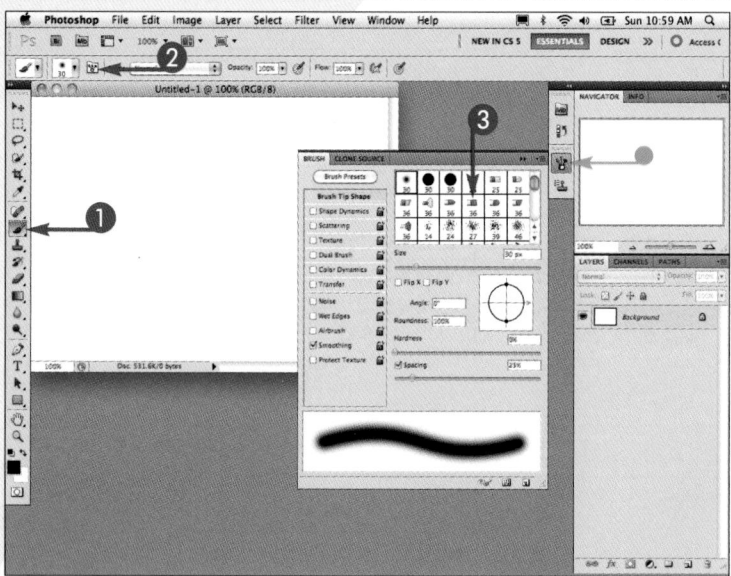

① With a new blank document open, click the Brush tool.

② Click the Brushes Panel Toggle button.

● You can also click the Brushes panel button, visible by default in the Painting workspace.

The Brushes panel opens and the controls for the brush tip shape are visible.

③ Click a Bristle tip preset brush that you want to modify into a custom brush.

④ Click and drag any of the sliders to change the size and look.

● You can optionally click here and select a different shape.

Note: The Brush Tip Shape options available with the Bristle brushes are different than those for the Standard brushes. You can change the Standard Brush Tip shapes by clicking and dragging the sides of the brush shape circle in the Brush Tip Shape pane.

● The Preview window displays the changed brushstroke.

⑤ Click and drag in the open document to test the brush effect.

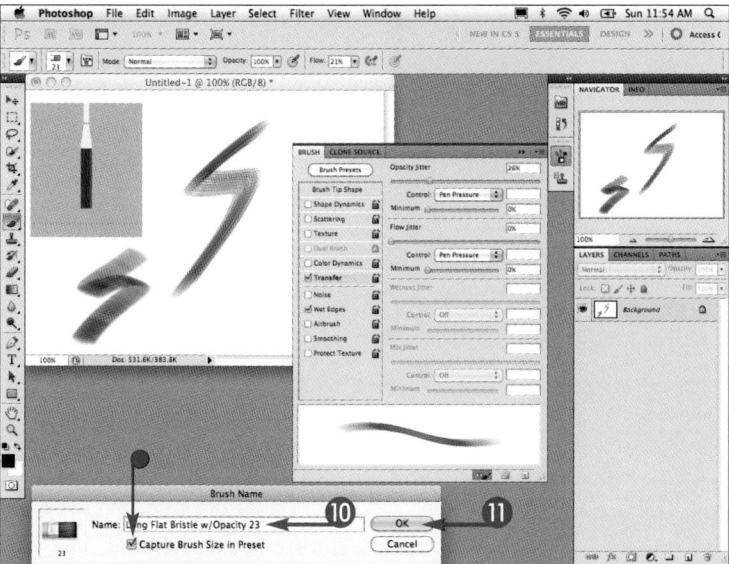

- Your customized brush stroke appears on the document.

⑥ Click the name of any of the other options in the left section of the Brush pane.

⑦ Click and drag any of the sliders to change the size and look.

Note: *To set the options for Pen Pressure, you must have a pen tablet connected (see task #14).*

⑧ Click and drag on the document to test the changed brushstroke.

⑨ Click the New Brush button at the bottom of the panel.

The Brush Name dialog box appears.

⑩ Type a name for your brush.

- You can optionally click Capture Brush Size in Preset to save the brush size (☐ changes to ☑).

⑪ Click OK.

Your customized brush is now available in the Brushes panel and stored with your Photoshop CS5 Preferences.

#10

DIFFICULTY LEVEL

TIPS

Important!

You must save your brushes as a set so they will be available the next time you open Photoshop. Click the Brush picker in the Options bar. Click the flyout arrow (▣) on menu that appears and click Save Brushes. Type a name for a customized brush set in the dialog box and click Save. Your set of brushes including your new custom brush is now saved in the Photoshop CS5 Brushes folder in the Presets folder.

More Options!

The Bristle tip brushes display an animated preview on-screen as you work. You can enlarge the window and move the Bristle Brush preview off your canvas. You can also reduce the size of the preview or click the close button on the preview to hide it. To reopen the preview, click the Bristle Brush Preview toggle (▣) on the bottom of the Brushes preset panel.

Load
OPTIONAL BRUSH SETS

Brushes are essential for working with Photoshop. When you customize a brush and create a new preset, you can use that brush with not only the Brush tool but also a number of Photoshop tools, such as the History brush, the Eraser tool, the Pencil tool, and other tools. Adding brushes gives you more options for editing photographs and many more variations for painting with Photoshop.

Photoshop CS5 installs a number of different brush sets not automatically loaded when you first open the

application. The brush sets are stored in the Presets folder. You can load any set and have the additional brushes replace the default brushes or be appended to the existing brush set using the Preset manager. Once loaded the additional brushes appear listed in the Brush picker menu, which you can view by thumbnail or by list, as well as by the default stroke thumbnail.

Adding some of the included brush sets gives your painting strokes a new dimension.

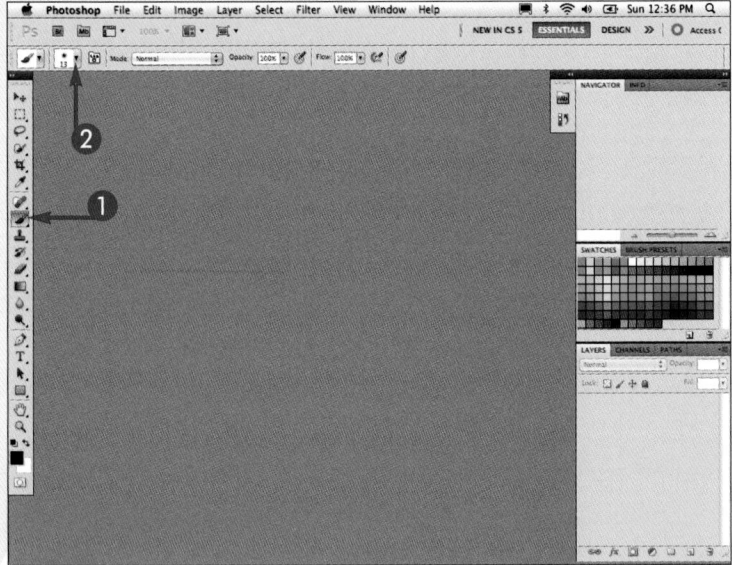

① Click the Brush tool.

② Click here to open the Brush picker.

● The Brush picker appears displaying small thumbnails of the brush tips.

③ Click the flyout arrow on the Brush picker.

The Brushes menu appears.

④ Click Large List in the menu to see the names of the brushes as well as the tip.

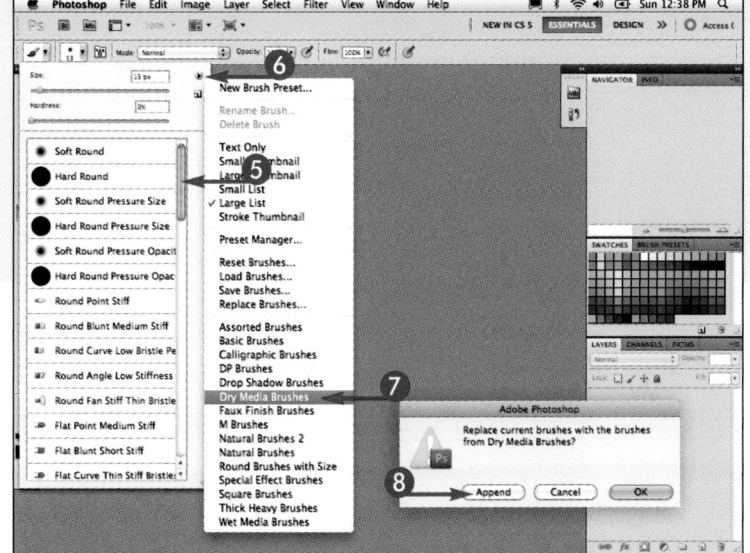

The Brush picker list changes to show the brush names.

5 Scroll down to expand the Brush picker.

6 Click the flyout arrow on the Brush picker again.

7 Click Dry Media Brushes in the bottom section of the menu.

Note: You can select any of the brush sets listed.

8 Click Append in the dialog box that appears.

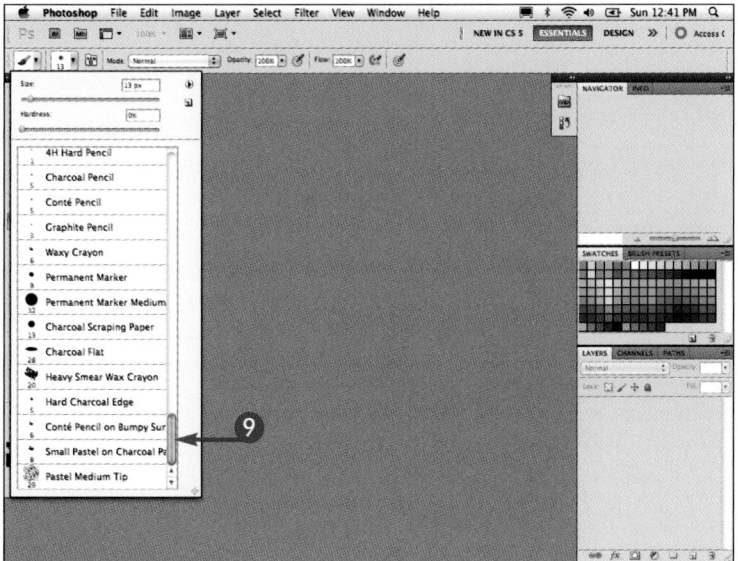

The Dry Media Brushes are added to the bottom of the Brush picker menu.

9 Scroll down the Brush picker menu to see the new added brushes.

TIPS

Try This!

You can save a copy of the Brushes folder to another location on your hard drive. Your custom brush set and any brush sets you download can then be transferred to another computer or reloaded if you have to reinstall Photoshop. By default, the Brushes folder is in Applications/Adobe Photoshop CS5/Presets/ (on Mac OS X) or C:\Program Files\Adobe\PhotoshopCS5\ Presets\ (on Windows).

Did You Know?

You can find a large number of predesigned brush sets both free and for a fee on the Web.

Try This!

You can add patterns the same way you add brush presets. Click and hold the Gradient tool on the toolbar and select the Paint Bucket tool. Click Foreground in the Options bar and select Pattern. Click the pattern icon to open the Pattern picker. Click the flyout arrow (▶) on the Pattern picker and select a different pattern at the bottom of the menu. Click Append in the dialog box that appears.

MAKE A SPECIAL GRADIENT
to suit your design

You can use the Gradient tool to blend colors to fill text with soft gradations of color, to fill backgrounds with a colored gradient, to work with layers and masks, and for making composite images. You can find more gradient color sets in the Options bar menu. You can also create your own gradient by sampling colors from areas in your image or choosing different colors altogether.

You can add intermediate colors and design a blend among multiple colors in any order that you want. You can even design gradients that fade from any color to transparent.

You can also choose a style for the gradient, such as linear, radial, angled, reflected, or diamond. You customize the gradients from the Gradient Editor. Start with an existing gradient and modify the colors, the color stops, and other variations in the dialog box. The possibilities are almost endless!

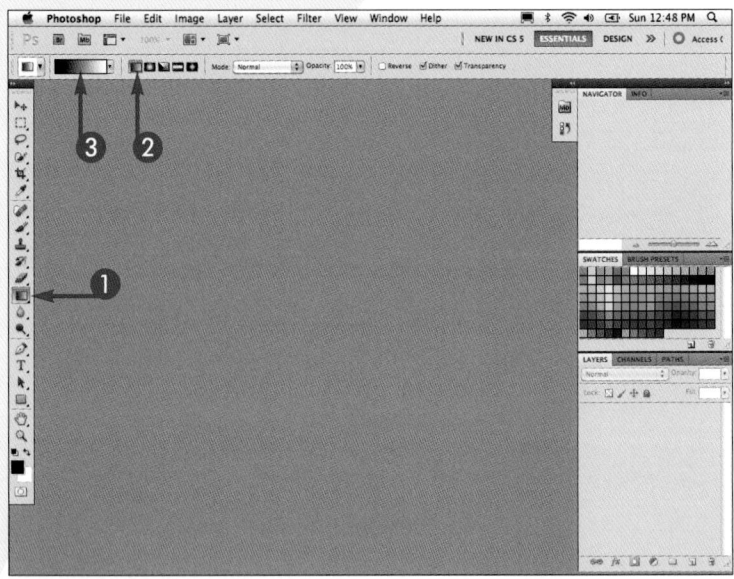

① Click the Gradient tool.

② Click a gradient type in the Options bar, a linear gradient in this example.

③ Click inside the gradient thumbnail in the Options bar.

The Gradient Editor dialog box appears.

④ Click the left color stop under the gradient bar to select it.

⑤ Click the Color thumbnail to choose a new color.

The Select stop color dialog box appears.

6 Select a color from the dialog box.

Note: *If you have an image open, you can move the cursor over the image to select a color.*

7 Click OK.

DIFFICULTY LEVEL

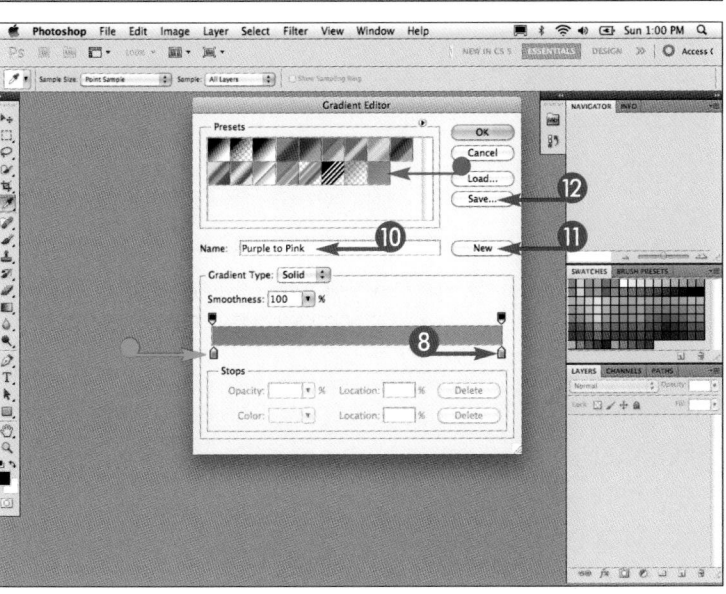

● The selected color fills the left color stop in the Gradient Editor.

8 Click the right color stop under the gradient bar to select it.

9 Repeat steps 5 and 6 to select the colors for the right color stop.

10 Type a name for your custom gradient in the Name field.

11 Click New.

● The custom gradient appears in the presets.

12 Click Save.

Your custom gradient remains in the gradient presets so you can apply it again to other projects.

TIPS

Caution!
You must save your custom gradients in a preset library to avoid losing them when you reset Photoshop's preferences. Click Save in the Gradient Editor dialog box or choose Save Gradients from the menu in the Gradient picker. Type a name for your gradient library with the suffix .grd. Click Save, and your gradients are saved in Photoshop's presets.

More Options!
Vary your custom gradient by adding color stops. Press Option (Alt) and drag the first color stop to another location or drag a new color stop over other color stops. To remove a color stop, click the color stop and drag straight down.

Chapter 1: Customize Photoshop for Your Projects

CALIBRATE AND PROFILE
your monitor for better editing

You adjust colors in Photoshop based on what you see on the screen. Because each monitor displays color differently and because a monitor's characteristics change over time, you should calibrate and profile your monitor regularly to make sure that you are viewing the colors that are actually in your files.

Calibration is the process of setting your monitor to an established color standard. Profiling is the process of creating a data file describing how your monitor reproduces color or an International Color Consortium (ICC) profile.

You need to use a hardware calibration device called a colorimeter or spectrophotometer to accurately adjust your monitor. The software-only methods included with the operating system are too subjective. Both X-Rite and DataColor make affordable devices. A colorimeter can only correct the colors on your screen. A spectrophotometer can also measure and adjust color for your monitor and other peripherals such as your printer.

Note that the following steps are those used with an X-Rite i1Pro. You can follow similar steps for an X-Rite Pantone Huey, ColorMunki, or other device.

① Install and launch the software included with the device, and plug the device into a USB port.

Note: Macintosh users should be logged in using an Admin account.

② Click the monitor image.

③ Click Easy (⊙ changes to ⊙).

④ Click the Forward button.

The Monitor Type screen appears.

⑤ Click to select your monitor type.

⑥ Click the Forward button.

⑦ Place your i1Display on a black surface or place the i1Pro in its cradle and click Calibrate.

⑧ Click the Forward button to continue.

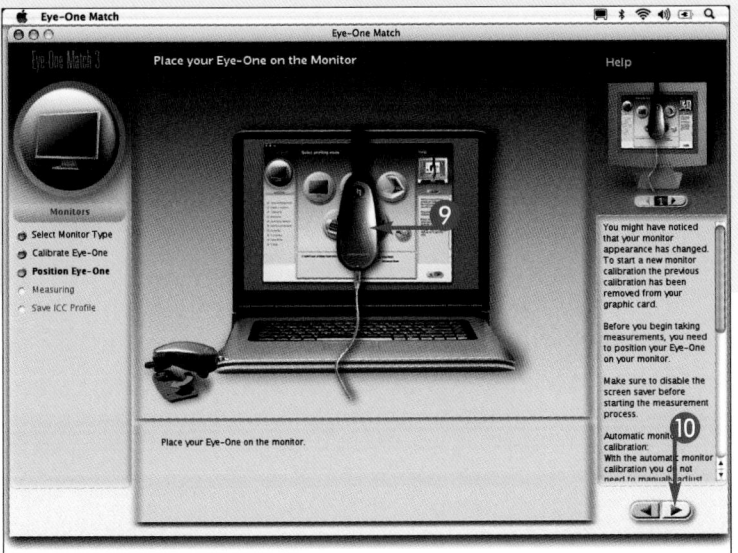

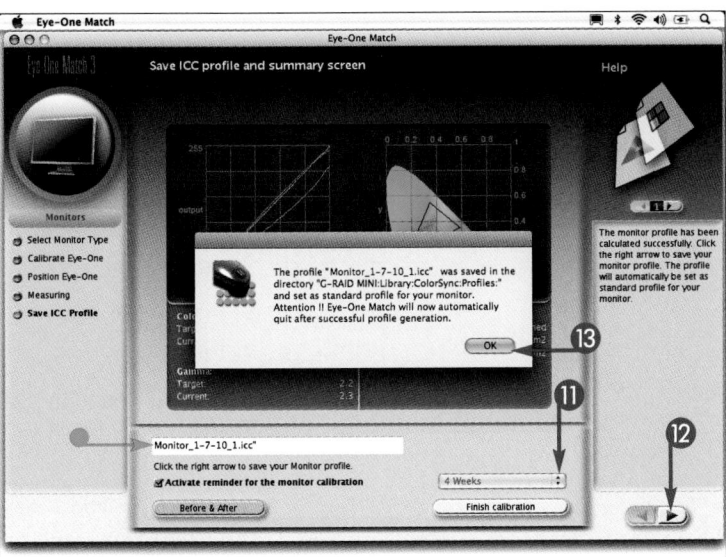

The Place Your Eye-One on the Monitor screen appears.

⑨ Place the unit on the monitor as the image shows.

⑩ Click the Forward button.

The screen goes black, and then a box appears under the colorimeter on the screen.

The box fills with white, then black, and then colors as the device automatically measures the color presentation capabilities of your monitor.

● A new screen appears, showing the name of the monitor profile created by the device.

⑪ Click here to select a reminder for the next calibration.

⑫ Click the Forward button.

A dialog box appears, telling you where the profile was saved on your computer's hard drive.

⑬ Click OK.

⑭ Quit the i1Match software application and disconnect the i1Colorimeter or Spectrophotometer.

TIPS

Did You Know?

As monitors age, they lose their color accuracy more quickly. Calibrate and profile regularly — monthly if your monitor is new or weekly if your monitor is over two years old. CRT monitors need to warm up for 30 minutes before you calibrate and create a profile.

Important!

The brightness level of LCD monitors is often set to the maximum at the factory. When you first calibrate and profile an LCD, it may appear dark by comparison; however, after calibrating and profiling, the monitor displays a more accurate representation of the colors in your images.

More Options!

X-Rite's i1Match software keeps a Help file open in a column along the right side of the screen explaining each step as you proceed. You can increase your understanding of color calibration by reading the explanations as you proceed.

Chapter 1: Customize Photoshop for Your Projects   29

Turn on the full power of Photoshop with a
PEN TABLET

Using a mouse as an input device may work for placing insertion points in text or dragging a rectangular selection in Photoshop, but using a Brush tool or selecting specific areas with a mouse is similar to writing your name with a bar of soap — clunky and inaccurate. You can edit images with greater comfort and control using a pressure-sensitive tablet and pen, such as the Wacom Intuos or Cintiq. More than 20 Photoshop tools, such as the Brushes, the Eraser, the Quick Selection tool, the Clone Stamp, the Dodge and Burn tools, and other tools can be fully customized only

when a tablet is connected to the computer. You can then change brush size, roundness, flow, or opacity by applying more or less pressure with the pen.

Instead of scooting the mouse around, you use the pen to place the cursor exactly where you want, and make precise selections or paint digitally as with a traditional paintbrush on paper.

The key to using a tablet and pen and turning on the full power of Photoshop is to start by setting the Tablet Preferences located in the System Preferences or Control Panel.

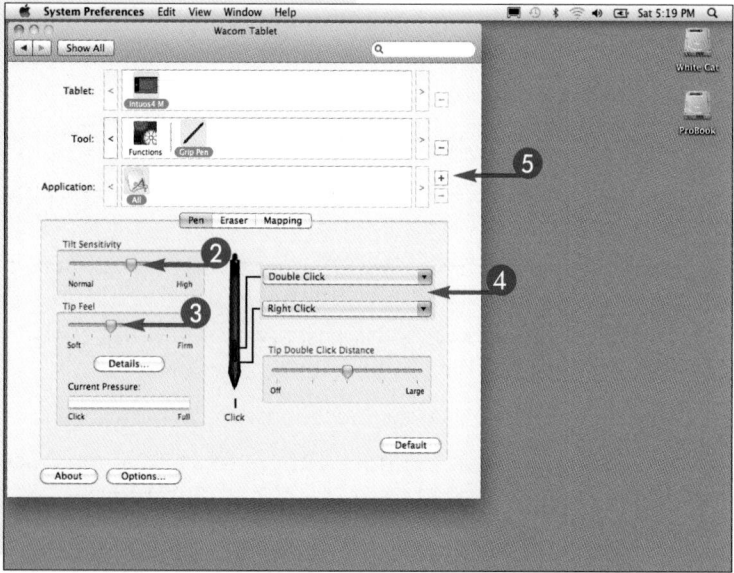

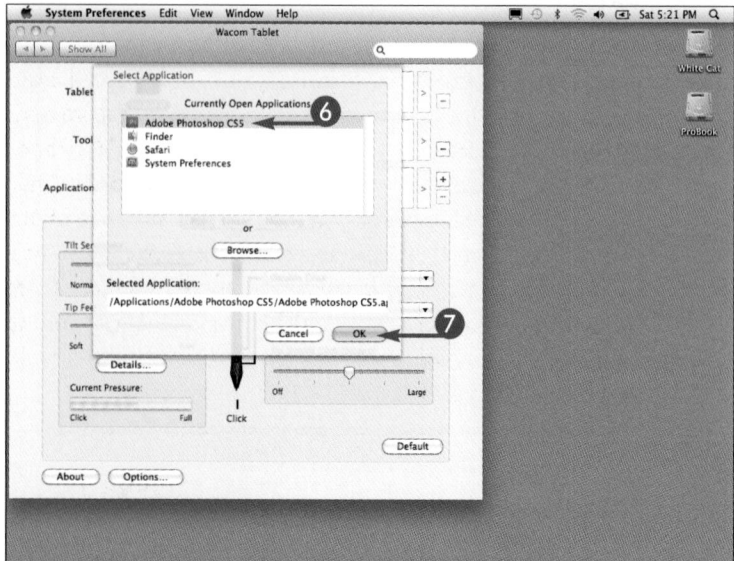

① With a Wacom tablet plugged into a USB port and the Wacom driver installed, open the Tablet Preferences from System Preferences (from Control Panel on a PC).

The Tablet Preferences open with the Pen tab selected.

② Click and drag the Tilt Sensitivity slider to the right for greater tilt response.

③ Click and drag the Tip Feel slider for a softer or firmer touch.

④ Click here to select different rocker switch settings.

⑤ Click the plus sign in the Application section.

The Select Application window drops down.

⑥ Click Adobe Photoshop CS5.

⑦ Click OK.

Note: *If Photoshop is not running, click Browse and navigate to the Photoshop CS5 application.*

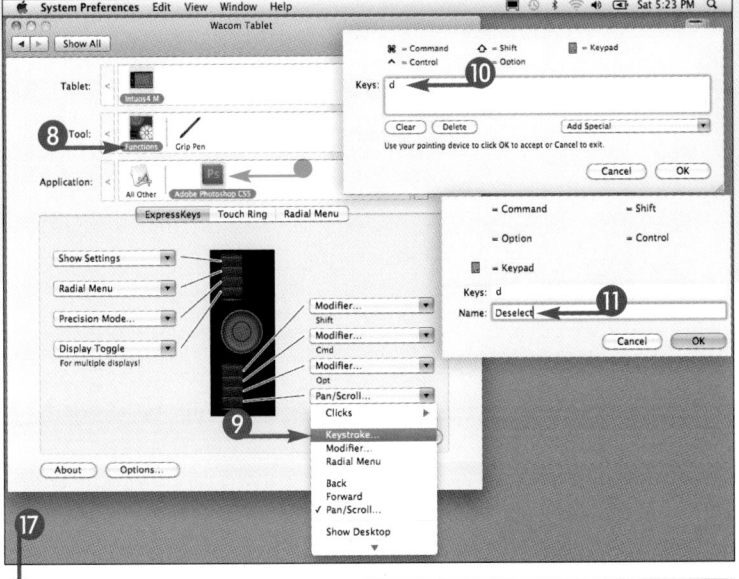

● Photoshop CS5 is listed in the Application section.

⑧ Click the Functions tool to customize the tablet keys.

Note: *Make sure that Photoshop CS5 is still highlighted in the Application section.*

The Functions tools appear with the ExpressKeys tab selected.

⑨ Click any ExpressKey arrow to change the setting to Keystroke.

⑩ Type a keystroke, such as D for Deselect, and click OK.

⑪ Type a name for the Keystroke and click OK.

⑫ Repeat steps 9 to 11 for any other ExpressKey you want to change.

The ExpressKeys display the names you typed.

⑬ Click the Touch Ring tab.

The Touch Ring Preferences appear.

⑭ Click and drag the Speed slider to change the scrolling speed.

⑮ Click any of the Functions arrows to select different settings.

⑯ Repeat steps 10 and 11 to set any other Photoshop-specific functions.

⑰ Click the Close button.

Your custom settings are saved in the Wacom Preferences or Wacom Control panel.

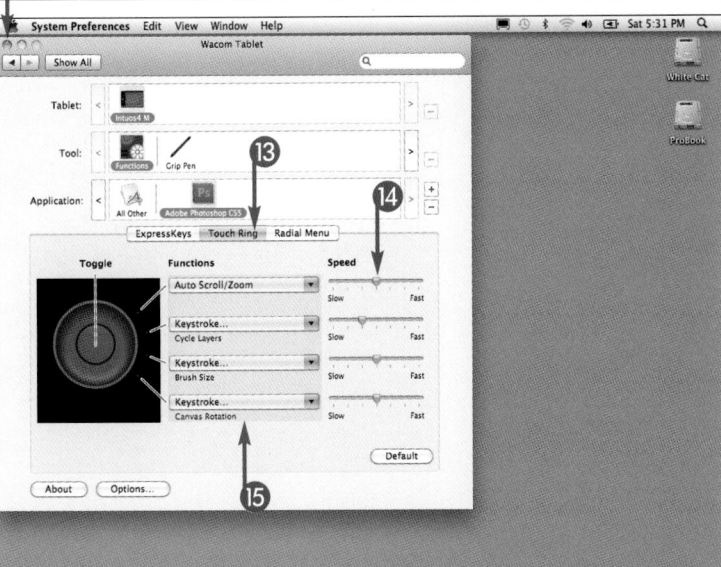

TIPS

Try This!

Set one ExpressKey for the Radial menu. Click the Radial Menu tab in the Wacom Tablet Preferences (Control Panel) and click one section of the Radial menu. Click the Function arrow and set your custom settings as in the task steps. Now when you click the ExpressKey, the Radial menu appears on-screen so you can click to launch an application, run an action, or use the keystroke depending on your custom settings.

Did You Know?

Many Photoshop tools are specifically designed for use with a pressure-sensitive tablet and pen. For example, using a mouse, you can only select Off or Fade for Brush opacity. With a tablet attached to the computer, you can also select Pen Pressure, Pen Tilt, and Stylus Wheel, giving you more natural and responsive control when painting or editing photos.

Important!

There are three basic types of Wacom pen tablets: the Bamboo, the Intuos, and the Cintiq, and each comes in multiple sizes. The Preferences dialog box varies slightly depending on the type of Wacom tablet you have connected.

Chapter 2

Work with Layers, Selections, and Masks

Layers, selections, and masks are the key to using Photoshop for any photographic or design projects. You may simply duplicate a layer as a safety step or build a complex multilayered image combining layers and layer effects with selections and masks.

A *layer* is similar to a transparency sheet with or without an image on it. You can edit, transform, or add filters to a layer independently from other layers. You can make one layer alter the look of a layer above or below it. You can flatten all the layers to finalize an image or save a file with the layers for future editing. You can also drag a layer from one document to another.

Selections enable you to isolate areas in your image and apply different effects or filters without affecting the rest of the image. You can even select areas on one layer and create a new layer with that selection. You can make selections and refine them with many Photoshop tools depending on the type of area that you need to isolate or remove. You can copy, move, paste, and save selections.

A *mask* is a selection shown as a grayscale image: The white areas are selected; the black areas are not. You can use masks to block out areas of an image or to prevent edits. You can create bitmap layer masks with painting tools or resolution-independent vector masks with a shape or type tool.

Top 100

NAME AND COLOR-CODE LAYERS
to organize the Layers panel

Layers are one of Photoshop's most powerful features and essential to editing any image. You can name individual layers to help you remember which one applied a specific adjustment to an image. You can also color-code your layers to help you visually organize the Layers panel. You can view all the layers by scrolling, or you can expand the Layers panel to view all the layers at once by clicking and dragging the Layers panel tab to separate it from the other panels on the screen. You can also close any panel

tab groups you are not using so the Layers panel expands automatically to fill the space.

Although the tasks in this chapter add only a few layers to each image, you will accumulate many more layers in the Layers panel as you work, depending on the complexity of the project. Whether you work alone or with a group of designers and share projects, naming layers and color-coding them helps you maintain an organized Layers panel and streamlines your workflow and the entire editing process.

Close Layer Tabs

① Click the panel menu button on any unused tab group.

② Click Close Tab Group.

The tabbed group disappears and the other tabbed groups expand to fill the space.

Note: You can optionally repeat steps 1 and 2 for other unused groups.

Note: You can also click and drag a panel out of a group to maintain it on the screen before closing the other tabs in the tabbed group.

Rename Layers

① Double-click the name of a layer.

② Type a new name in the box.

③ Repeat for any other layers to give each layer a distinctive name.

Color Code Layers

DIFFICULTY LEVEL

1. Start by clicking one layer, such as a photo layer, to select it.

2. Click the panel menu button on the Layers tab.

3. Click Layer Properties.

   The Layer Properties dialog box appears.

4. Click here and select a different color.

5. Click OK to apply the color to the layer.

- The layer's Eye icon box changes color.

6. Repeat steps 1 to 5 to color other layers.

Try This!

You can group multiple layers into one layer group by selecting the layers and then clicking the New Group button (▢) on the bottom of the Layers panel, or by clicking Layer and selecting Group Layers from the main menu. Layer groups can be opened for editing purposes and then collapsed to display a single folder. You can also move layers in a group all at once. And in CS5, layer groups can be nested more than five levels deep.

More Options!

You can merge any layers that do not need to remain separately editable. Make sure the two layers are one above the other in the Layers panel by clicking and dragging them if necessary. Click the top layer to select it. Click the Layers panel menu button (▾≡) and select Merge Down, or press ⌘+E (Ctrl+E). You can also merge layers by ⌘+clicking (Ctrl+clicking) two or more layers and then clicking Layers and Merge Selected.

DUPLICATE AND CHANGE
the Background layer for more options

The Background layer is generally the bottommost image in the Layers panel — and the only layer in the file when you first open a new photograph. You can duplicate the Background layer and use it to edit the photo or simply work on the duplicated layer to protect the original. Layers are the key to *nondestructive image editing* — that is, working on your images without damaging existing pixels.

Although it does increase the file size, working on a duplicated layer works well for simple changes and can be used as a safety step in many workflows. With a

duplicate Background layer, you can quickly compare your modified image with the original by clicking the Eye icon in the leftmost box next to the layer thumbnail in the Layers panel, to toggle the duplicated layer on and off to see the changes you made.

You can add layers above the original Background layer to edit the image. You can also convert the original Background layer to a regular unlocked layer so you can apply special layer effects directly to this layer, change its fill or opacity settings, or move it to another position in the Layers panel.

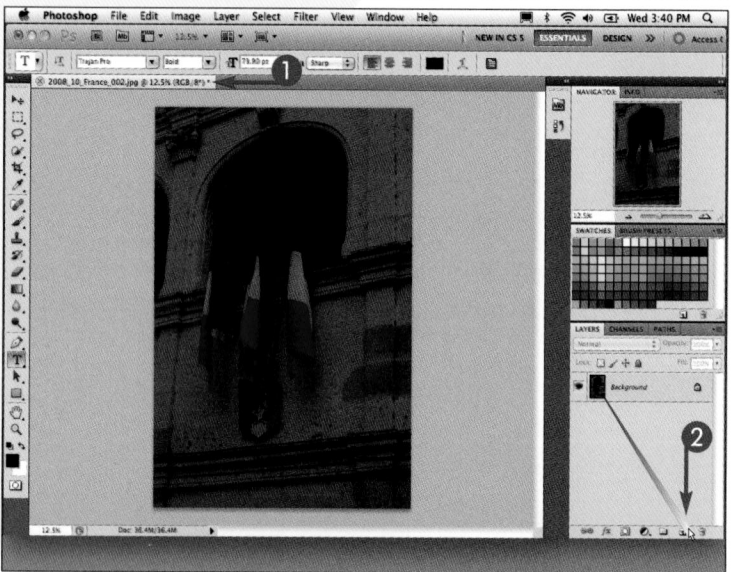

① Open an image in Photoshop.

Note: In this example, the exposure in an underexposed image is adjusted with a duplicate layer. You can accomplish the same effect in multiple ways in Photoshop. This task helps you understand layers.

② Click and drag the Background layer thumbnail over the New Layer button and release the mouse button.

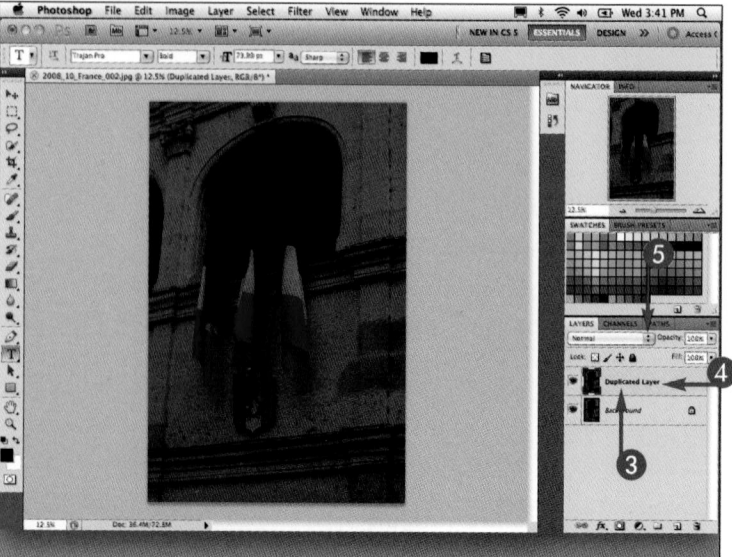

Photoshop places a duplicated Background layer above the original.

③ Double-click the Background copy's name in the Layers panel to highlight it.

④ Type a different name for the copy as in the previous task.

⑤ Click here and change the blend mode to Screen.

36

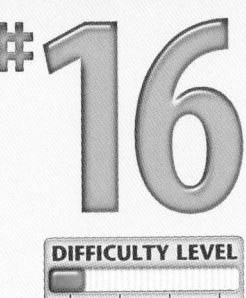

The photo appears lighter.

⑥ Click and drag the copied layer over the New Layer button and release the mouse button.

⑦ Repeat step 6 until the photo appears slightly light.

⑧ Click Opacity and drag to the left to lower the opacity of the top layer until the photo appears properly exposed.

TIPS

Did You Know?
The selected layer is called the *active layer*. You can select multiple layers by pressing ⌘ (Ctrl) and clicking them. You can then move them together to another open document or add effects to them all at the same time.

Try This!
You can duplicate the Background layer or any other layer with a keyboard shortcut. Click the layer to be duplicated in the Layers panel to select it and make it the active layer. Press ⌘+J (Ctrl+J).

More Options!
To move the Background layer, you must unlock it by double-clicking its name, typing a new name in the dialog box that appears, and clicking OK.

Adjust a photo with an
ADJUSTMENT LAYER

You can make a variety of adjustments to an image using the Adjustments option on the Image menu. However, each time you change the pixels in an image, you lose some data. If you combine adjustments, you lose even more pixel information. By applying an adjustment layer instead, you can make color and tonal changes to your image in a nondestructive way, without changing any pixel values.

With adjustment layers, you can edit the adjustment at a later time. You can reduce or vary the effect of

the adjustment by using the Opacity or Fill sliders. You can also combine various adjustment layers.

You can access the adjustment layers from either the Layer menu in the Layers panel, or the Adjustments panel, which provides more options. With the Adjustments panel open, you can quickly add adjustment layers and access the adjustment tools without opening menus or dialog boxes to block your view of the image. Using the options in the Adjustments panel, you can make the adjustment affect all the layers below, or just the selected layer.

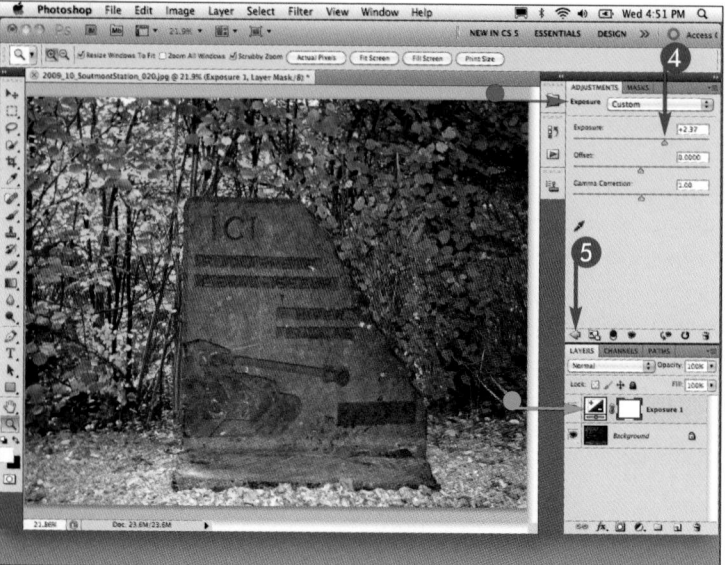

Note: *Make sure to start with the Photography workspace to see the Adjustments panel. See task #4 for more about workspaces.*

1 Open an underexposed image to adjust in Photoshop.

Note: *In this example, an underexposed image is edited using an adjustment layer.*

2 Click the Histogram panel menu button and select Close Tab Group as in task #15 to create more space for the Layers panel if necessary.

3 Click one of the adjustment layer buttons such as Exposure.

● An adjustment layer appears above the Background layer in the Layers panel.

● The Exposure adjustment options appear.

4 Click and drag the sliders to adjust the photo.

The adjustment layer's changes are applied to the image.

5 Click the Return to Adjustment List arrow.

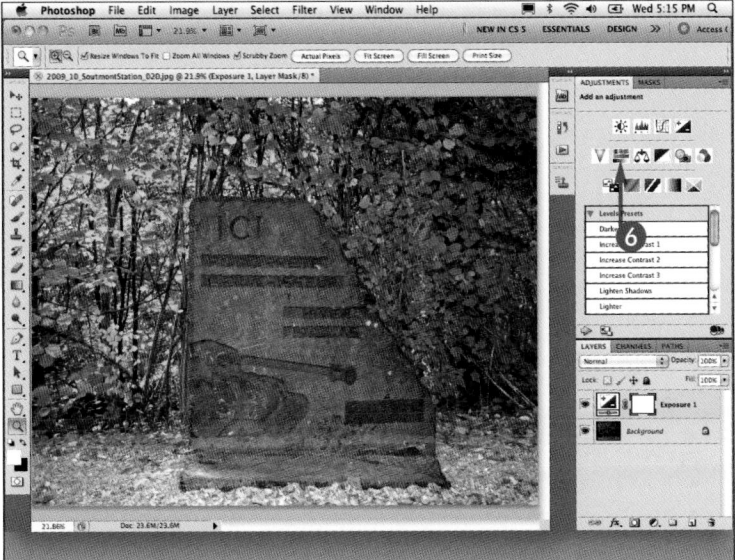

The Adjustments panel returns to the adjustment layer list.

6 Click another adjustment such as Hue/Saturation.

● Another adjustment layer appears in the Layers panel and the Hue/Saturation adjustment options appear in the Adjustments pane.

7 Click and drag the sliders to change the values.

8 Click the Eye icon to toggle the visibility of the adjustment layer on and off.

9 Click the View Previous State button to temporarily view the adjustment before the slider changes you made.

10 Click the Reset button to reset the adjustment layer to the default settings.

11 Click the trash button to delete the adjustment layer.

TIPS

More Options!

All adjustment layers include a layer mask, represented by a white thumbnail in the Layers panel. You can click the layer mask thumbnail and paint with black in the image to limit where the adjustment affects the underlying photo. If you accidentally reveal too much of the underlying image, you can change the foreground color to white and paint in the mask or use the eraser tool to reapply more of the adjustment.

Did You Know?

The Hue/Saturation and the Black & White adjustment layers include an option for clicking and dragging directly on specific areas in the image to make the changes. Click the On-Image Adjustment tool ([⟲]) to select it. Click and drag on an area in the photo to modify the hue/saturation. Click [⟲] again to return the tool to the Adjustment panel.

BLEND TWO PHOTOS TOGETHER
with an automatic layer mask

Layer masks open a world of imaging possibilities that you just cannot create with traditional tools. Using a layer mask to hide parts of an image, you can easily blend one photograph into another and create designs that are sure to grab a viewer's attention. For example, you can blend a photograph of a wedding couple into a photo of the bride's bouquet or blend a photo of a potato with a photo of a person lying on a couch.

Generally, to blend a photo on one layer into the photo on the layer below, you add a layer mask to

the top layer and paint with black on the layer mask to blend the images. To hide some of the area you just revealed, simply reverse the colors and paint with white.

You can also have Photoshop create the layer mask for you automatically. By copying one photo to the clipboard and creating a selection on the other photo, you can use Photoshop's Paste Into command. You can then use the Brush tool to add or remove areas if necessary. You can also adjust the way the images blend using the opacity slider on the Layers panel.

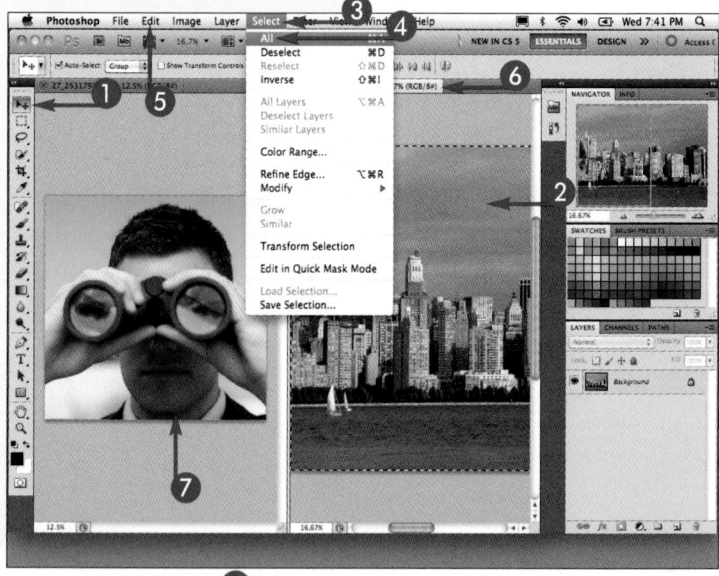

1. With the two photographs you want to blend open, click the Move tool.

2. Click the photo that will be blended into the other to target it.

3. Click Select.

4. Click All.

5. Click Edit and click Copy.

6. Click the close button on this photo.

7. Click the main photo to target it.

8. Click the Quick Selection tool or any other selection tool.

9. Click and drag on the areas to select them.

   Note: You can adjust any selection with the current tool by pressing ⌘+Option (Ctrl+Alt) as you click and drag to remove from a selection and pressing Shift as you click and drag to add to a selection.

10. Click Edit.

11. Click Paste Special.

12. Click Paste Into.

18

- The first photo appears in the active selection.

⑬ Click the Move tool.

⑭ Click and drag in the area to reposition it.

Note: You can optionally resize the photo in the selection to fit better by clicking Edit and selecting Free Transform. Press and hold Shift as you move the corner handles of the bounding box.

⑮ Click Opacity and drag to the left to reduce the Layer Opacity to blend the images more naturally.

TIPS

Try This!

You can make two images blend together with a smooth transition by using the Gradient tool () to apply a black-to-white gradient on the layer mask.

Customize It!

When you use a pen tablet to paint on a layer mask, you can easily control how much of the image you reveal with each brush stroke by setting the brush opacity to respond to pen pressure. Click the Brushes thumbnail to open the Brushes Presets. Click Shape Dynamics and set Size Jitter Control to Pen Pressure.

Did You Know?

You can add a layer mask to a layer by clicking the Layer Mask button (⬛) in the Layers panel or by clicking the Pixel Mask button (⬛) in the Masks panel. ⌘+click (Ctrl+click) a mask button to add a white layer mask that reveals all on that layer. Option+click (Alt+click) a mask button to add a black layer mask that conceals everything on that layer.

Add a design with a
CUSTOM SHAPE LAYER

Custom shapes are resolution-independent vector shapes, meaning that they maintain crisp edges when resized or saved in a PDF file. You can select any of Photoshop CS5's predesigned custom shapes or create your own shape with the Pen tools. You can also load custom shapes you purchase from third-party vendors. You can add shapes to any image as a design element or to alter the shape of a photo.

Shapes are applied as separate layers, and each shape layer has two parts: the fill layer and a linked

vector mask. The mask is the shape's outline. You can choose the fill layer's color in the Options bar before you draw the shape, or you can click in the fill box for the shape layer in the Layers panel and select a different color for the shape. You can also set the fill color to a zero opacity fill.

You can add special effects such as a drop shadow or a stroke to a shape layer by clicking the Layer Style button (*fx*) at the bottom of the Layers panel.

1 Press ⌘+J (Ctrl+J) to duplicate the Background layer of an image.

2 Click the Shape tool.

3 Click the Custom Shape tool in the Options bar.

4 Click here and double-click a shape in the menu.

5 Click here.

6 Double-click a style button in the menu.

Note: *You can optionally click the Color panel menu to close the tab group.*

7 Click and drag in your image to draw the shape.

8 ⌘+click (Ctrl+click) the shape thumbnail.

The shape changes to a selection.

9 Click the layer thumbnail and drag it to the trash.

The selection remains on the image.

10 Press D to reset the foreground and background colors.

11 Press X to make the foreground color white.

 # 19

⑫ Press ⌘+J (Ctrl+J) to duplicate the selection onto its own layer.

⑬ Click Layer 0 (the duplicated layer) to select it.

⑭ Click the Adjustment Layer button in the Layers panel.

⑮ Click Gradient.

The base image is covered with a white-to-transparent gradient fill.

⑯ Click OK in the Gradient Fill dialog box or change the attributes.

The shape highlights the subject of the photo.

TIPS

More Options!

You can access more custom shapes than the default set by clicking the Custom Shape button (🖼) in the Options bar and clicking the Shape arrow to open the menu. When you click the arrow on that menu, you can select one of the shape groups at the bottom of the menu or select All to see all the installed shapes at once. Then double-click a shape thumbnail to select it.

Try This!

Create a gradient fill with a color from your image. Click the Foreground Color box to open the Color Picker. Move the cursor outside of the Color Picker dialog box and click a color from your image. Click OK to close the dialog box.

ACCENTUATE A SKY
with a gradient fill layer

You can give a scenic photo a more dramatic look or simply increase the colors in a sky with a gradient fill adjustment layer. The colors you see are often better than what your camera captures, particularly when you photograph a sunset or a sunrise. You can easily increase the intensity of the sky with a gradient fill. You can enhance the existing colors by using a black foreground color, using a more intense version of the same color, or even selecting another color to create

a stylized image. You can adjust how much of the photo to cover with added color. Because you are using a fill layer, you can go back and increase or decrease the amount of color after you apply the gradient fill layer. You can even change the color that you applied to get a different effect or to create a more dramatic look. This technique is most effective on a photo with a large sky area and an open horizon.

① Open an image that has a large area of sky.

② Click the Default Colors icon to set the foreground to black.

Note: *Optionally, click to select a color to use a gradient for a creative effect.*

③ Click the New Fill or Adjustment Layer button.

④ Click Gradient.

The Gradient Fill dialog box appears, and a foreground-to-transparent gradient is applied to the image.

⑤ Make sure that the angle is set to 90 degrees.

6 Click Reverse
(☐ changes to ☑).

The gradient reverses
to black or the selected
color at the top,
changing to transparent
at the bottom of the
image.

7 Position the cursor over
the image.

8 Drag upward in the
image until the gradient
covers only the sky.

9 Click OK.

10 Click here and click Overlay.

11 Double-click the layer thumbnail
for the gradient fill.

The Gradient Fill dialog box
reappears.

12 Position the cursor over the
image.

13 Drag downward in the image to
increase the darkened sky or drag
upward to lessen the effect.

Each time that you drag in the
image with the Gradient Fill layer
selected, the look of the sky
changes.

TIPS

Did You Know?

Multiple layers increase the file size of
your image. Because Photoshop requires
more memory to work on larger files, you
should merge layers that will not be
changed later. Pressing ⌘+E (Ctrl+E)
merges a selected layer with the layer
below. Pressing ⌘+Shift+E (Ctrl+Shift+E)
merges all the visible layers. Click Layer
and then Flatten Image to flatten all the
layers into a new Background image.

Try This!

You can apply a gradient
fill layer on a photo
showing a large body of
water such as a lake or
the ocean. Experiment
with different foreground
colors for the gradient fill
for both dramatic and
creative effects.

Make a selection with the
QUICK SELECTION TOOL

The Quick Selection tool in Photoshop CS5 enables you to easily select broad areas of an image by simply painting over them. You can use the Quick Selection tool to remove a background and isolate the main subject.

You can brush over different parts of a photo, varying the brush size as you work, or just click areas for a more limited selection. Once you have made your first selection, the tool automatically changes to the Add to Selection tool, so you can easily add areas without pressing any additional keys. You can subtract from the selection by pressing and holding Option (Alt) as

you paint, or using the Subtract from Selection tool in the Options bar.

This task shows the basic steps for selecting a subject and putting it on a separate layer. You can also select the background on a duplicated layer and press Delete (Backspace) to remove the background from the image, leaving just the subject on the layer. With any active selection you can click Layer in the menu and click Inverse to invert the selection.

For most selections, you will need to use the tools in the following two tasks to refine the selection.

1 Click the Quick Selection tool.

2 Click here to open the Brush picker.

3 Click and drag the Size slider to make the brush tip small.

● If you have a pen tablet attached, you can click here to set the brush size with pen pressure.

4 Press ⌘+spacebar (Ctrl+spacebar) and click to zoom in or click and drag in the image to dynamically zoom in.

Note: Although on a Mac the Spotlight feature momentarily opens with the same keystrokes, using ⌘+spacebar in Photoshop CS5 still zooms in.

5 Click and drag inside the part of the image you want to select.

6 Click and drag in another area to be selected.

● The tool changes to the Add to Selection option.

⑦ Continue changing the brush size and clicking and dragging in the image to select more areas.

⑧ Press and hold Option (Alt).

● The tool temporarily changes to the Subtract from Selection tool.

⑨ Click in areas that you want to remove from the selection.

⑩ Press and hold the spacebar and click in the image to move to a different area.

⑪ Click any other areas to remove them from the selection.

⑫ Press ⌘+J (Ctrl+J) to put the selection on its own layer.

● The selected area appears on a new layer above the Background layer.

TIPS

Enhance It!

You can click the Auto-Enhance option in the Options bar (☐ changes to ☑) to reduce the roughness of the selection boundary and extend the selection toward the edges it detects. Depending on the speed of your computer, adding the Auto-Enhance option may slow the selection process.

Keyboard Shortcuts!

To quickly change the brush size as you work, you can use the keyboard. Press the left bracket key to decrease the brush size or the right bracket key to increase the brush size.

More Options!

To quickly zoom in and out of the photo to make it easier to select the subject, press ⌘+spacebar (Ctrl+spacebar) to zoom in and Option+spacebar (Alt+spacebar) to zoom out as you select different areas.

USE REFINE EDGE
to improve any selection

The Refine Edge floating panel is accessible in the Options bar whenever any selection tool is selected. Using Refine Edge, you can clean up selections, soften or feather the edge outlines, and remove edge artifacts or jaggies. The panel offers various previewing options, showing the selection on a white or black background, against a red overlay, or on an empty layer to help you see the edges of the areas you are selecting and the changes you are making. You can use the Refine Edge panel with any active selection, regardless of the tool used to create the selection. The Refine Edge tool is particularly useful when selecting very irregular edges, such as the fur on a bear or a dog. Whenever there is a selection in the image, the Refine Edge button appears in the Options bar.

With the subject selected as in the previous task, you can use the tool to fine-tune the details in the edges of your image to get the best selection possible.

① Open another image and repeat steps 1 to 11 in the previous task to make a selection.

● The foreground subject is selected.

Note: *Depending on the image, you might click on the background and then invert the selection to show the subject matter in the selection marquee.*

② Click the Refine Edge button in the Options bar.

The subject appears against a solid background.

③ Click the Zoom tool and click in the image to enlarge certain areas.

Note: *Click the Hand tool (✋) and click and drag to move around the image.*

④ Click and drag the Radius slider to refine the edge selection.

⑤ Click and drag the Contrast slider to remove edge artifacts and to sharpen edges.

⑥ Click here to select another view mode from the menu that appears.

7 Click and drag the Smooth slider to create a smoother selection outline.

8 Click and drag the Feather slider to create a softer-edged transition.

9 Click and drag the Shift Edge slider to adjust the selection edges.

10 Click Decontaminate Colors (☐ changes to ☑).

11 Click and drag the Amount slider to replace the color fringes with the color of the subject.

12 Repeat steps 4 to 11 to make the best selection possible.

13 Click here to have the selected area appear as a selection or a mask on the current layer or placed on a new layer.

14 Click OK to save the selection.

● Your refined selection appears on the image as a New Layer or as a New Layer with Layer Mask.

Try This!

You can use a keyboard shortcut to quickly change the preview mode when using the Refine Edge panel. Press F to cycle through each preview mode. Press X to temporarily view the original image.

Did You Know?

Moving the Radius slider improves the edge of the selection and helps in areas with more detail. Increasing the Contrast amount sharpens the edges of the selection. The Smooth slider removes jagged edges of a selection, and the Feather slider adds a uniform blur to the selection edge.

Important!

Clicking the Decontaminate Colors option in step 10 requires the selection to be placed on a new layer or document because it changes the colors of pixels.

PAINT A QUICK MASK
to make a detailed selection

You can select a rectangular or oval area with the marquee tools or select free-form or geometric areas with the lasso tools, or make other selections with the Quick Selection tool. You can also use the Brush tool in the Quick Mask mode to make a detailed selection or use the Brush tool in Quick Mask mode to adjust any previously selected area.

The Quick Mask mode is an editing mode in which protected areas are covered with a translucent colored mask. You paint directly on the areas you want to select, adjusting the brush size as you work

to make the selection more precise. The quick mask covers the area with a translucent red so you can see what you are selecting. You can also specify a different masking color if the area you are selecting has a lot of red in it.

Using this masking technique, you are actually masking the areas you paint, so you must invert the selection before making any adjustments. The areas you painted over are then selected, and the remainder of the image is now masked.

① Click the Zoom tool and click and drag to enlarge the area you want to select.

② Click the Default Colors icon to set the foreground color to black and the background to white.

③ Click the Quick Mask Mode button.

④ Click the Brush tool.

⑤ Click here to open the Brush picker.

⑥ Select a hard-edged brush.

⑦ Click and drag the Size slider to adjust the size.

⑧ Paint over the areas you want to select.

● The painted areas are covered with a red translucent mask.

Note: Click the left bracket key to reduce the brush size as you work in detailed areas.

9 Click the Switch Colors icon to reverse the foreground and background colors and make white the foreground color.

10 Paint over any areas that you do not want selected.

11 Click the Switch Colors icon to make black the foreground color.

12 Continue painting until the whole area is covered in red.

13 Click the Quick Mask Mode button to turn off the Quick Mask mode.

● Dashed lines indicate the areas that were covered with the red overlay and are not selected.

Note: You can optionally press Option+spacebar (Alt+spacebar) to zoom back out to see the edges of the image.

14 Click Select.

15 Click Inverse.

The selection now includes only the area you painted in the Quick Mask mode.

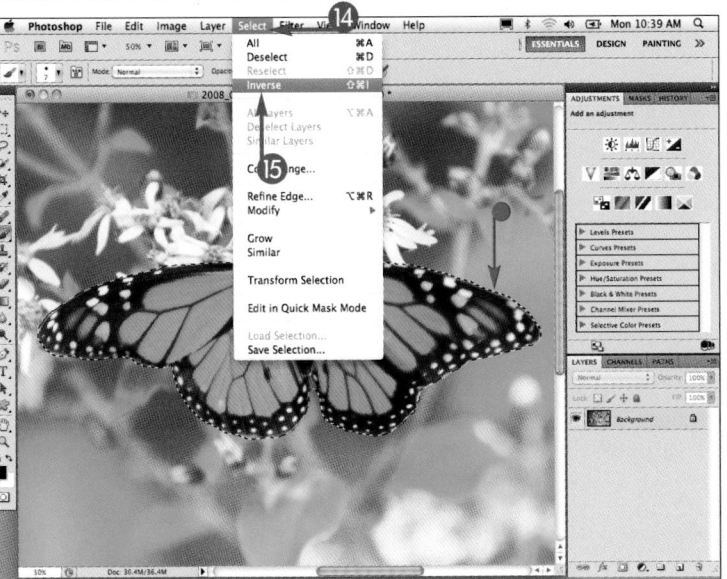

TIPS

Caution!

Remember that you are creating a mask, which actually selects the inverse of the area you are painting over. You must invert the selection by clicking Select and selecting Inverse before you make adjustments to the selected area.

Important!

You may need to feather a selection before you make adjustments. After you invert the selection, click Select and click Refine Edge to adjust the selection using the Refine Edge panel as in the previous task.

More Options!

If the image you are painting on is very red, change the masking color. Double-click the Quick Mask Mode button (🔲) and click the color box in the Quick Mask Options dialog box to pick a new color. You can also reduce the default mask opacity of 50% if necessary to see the selected area below the mask more clearly.

ADD LAYERS
as Smart Objects for flexible changes

A *Smart Object* layer is a special type of layer used for non-destructive editing. This type of layer gives you creative flexibility because the original pixel data of the image, or vector data in some cases, is preserved. You can edit a Smart Object layer and then change the adjustment you applied without altering the image quality.

For example, when you transform or scale a regular image layer to reduce the size, some pixels are removed. If you then transform the layer back again, you lose image quality because your previous changes permanently altered the actual pixels.

However, if you open the same photograph as a Smart Object layer, or convert the layer to a Smart Object layer, you can scale the layer without any image data loss.

You can open a document as a Smart Object, convert one or more layers in Photoshop to Smart Object layers, or move a Smart Object layer into another document, maintaining its quality as a Smart Object. You can also place an Illustrator or other vector file into a document as a Smart Object and maintain the vector's sharp edges or forms even when resizing.

Open an Image as a Smart Object

1 Click File.

2 Click Open As Smart Object.

The Open dialog box appears.

3 Navigate to and click a file to open.

4 Click Open.

The file opens as a Smart Object.

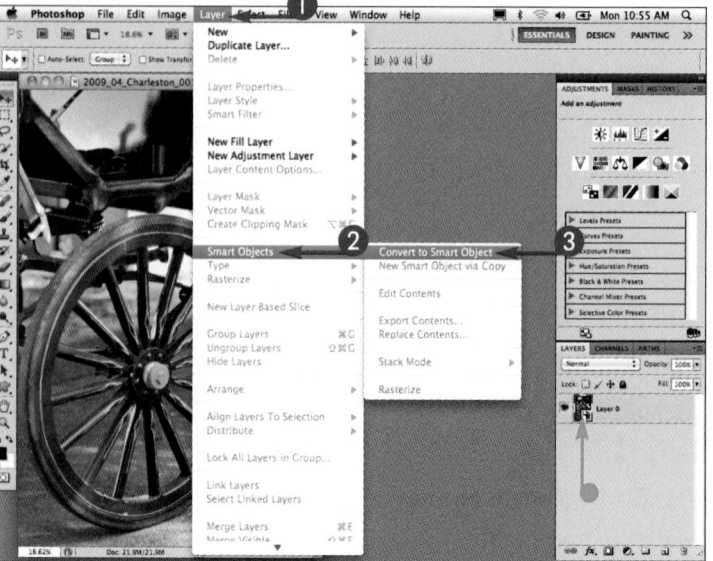

Convert an Open Image Layer to a Smart Object Layer

1 With an image already open, click Layer.

2 Click Smart Objects.

3 Click Convert to Smart Object.

● The layer is changed to a Smart Object layer and appears in the Layers panel with the Smart Object button. The layer is also renamed to Layer 0.

Note: You can also click the Layers panel menu button ( ) and select Convert to Smart Object.

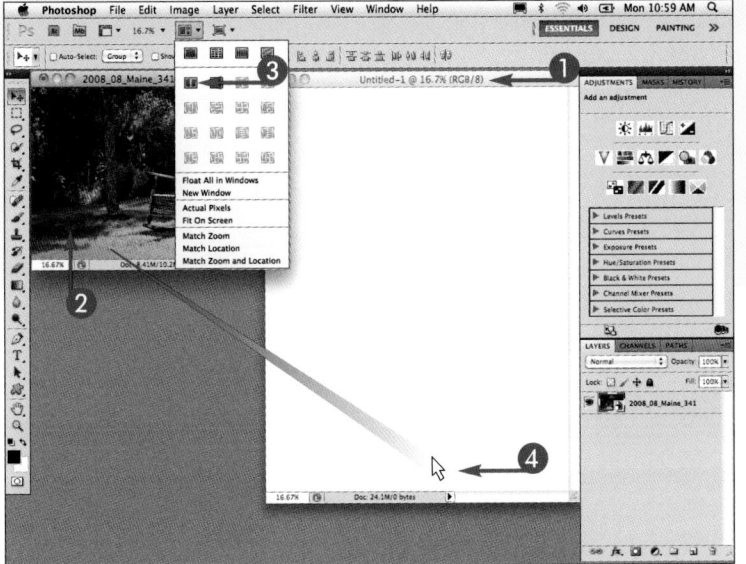

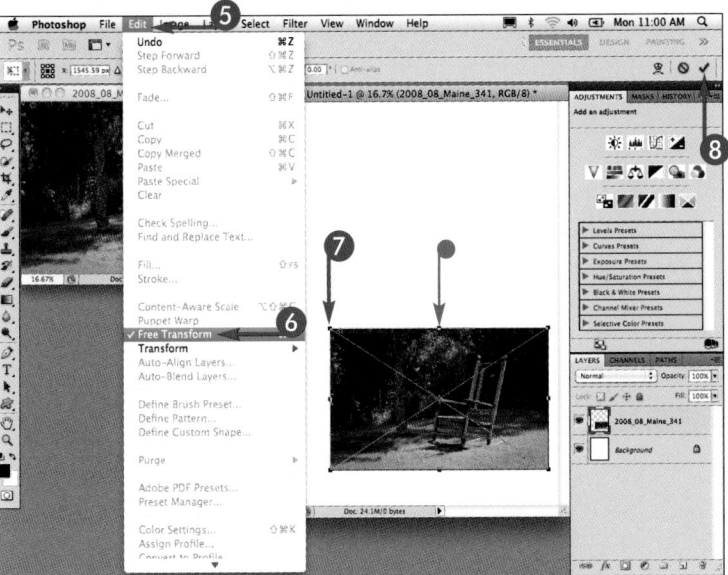

Open an Image as a
Smart Object and Copy
It to Another Document

 # 24

DIFFICULTY LEVEL

1 Open a new blank document.

2 Open an image as a Smart Object as in the first section of this task.

3 Click the Arrange Documents button and click the 2 Up button so that you can view both images on-screen.

Note: You can also click Window and then Float All in Windows. Then click Window and Tile.

4 Click and drag the Smart Object layer from the first document to the blank document.

The Smart Object layer appears in the other document.

5 Click Edit.

6 Click Free Transform.

● Handles and a bounding box appear on the Smart Object layer.

7 Shift+click and drag an anchor point to reduce the photo size.

8 Click the Commit button to apply the transformation.

The image on the layer is scaled down, but can be resized back up to its original size without any data loss.

TIPS

More Options!

You can edit the contents of any Smart Object layer. Click Layer, Smart Objects, and Edit Contents. Click OK in the warning dialog box that appears. Edit the original file and press ⌘+S (Ctrl+S). The Smart Object image is updated.

Try This!

You can create duplicates of a Smart Object layer in a document and link them. When you replace the contents of one Smart Object layer, all the duplicates are automatically updated at the same time.

Did You Know?

You can open a RAW file (such as a DNG, CR2, or NEF file) as a Smart Object by Shift+clicking the Open Image button in Camera Raw. You can then return to Camera Raw even after making edits to the image to make more changes without any data loss.

APPLY FILTERS AS SMART FILTERS

for dynamic adjustments

Filters in Photoshop are used to add blur, reduce noise, sharpen, or style an image. When you apply a regular filter you permanently alter the pixels. By applying a Smart Filter instead, you can edit and change the settings of the filter at any time, even after the document has been saved and reopened. Any filter applied to a Smart Object layer becomes a *Smart Filter*.

You can apply a Smart Filter to the entire Smart Object layer or to a selection on a Smart Object layer. You can remove or hide Smart Filters at any time.

You can add multiple Smart Filters one on top of another and then change the order of the Smart Filters to change the resulting effect. You can also add a mask to a Smart Filter. You can then paint on the mask with black to hide or white to reveal different areas of the filter and create detailed edits on specific areas, all without altering the image data.

Most Photoshop filters, with the exception of Liquify and Vanishing Point, can be applied as Smart Filters.

1 Open or convert an image as a Smart Object as shown in the previous task.

2 Click Filter.

3 Click a filter such as Radial Blur.

4 Click and drag the sliders and adjust any options in the dialog box that appears.

5 Click OK.

● The Smart Filter appears below the Smart Object layer in the Layers panel.

● A layer mask is automatically applied to the Smart Filter.

6 Click the Brush tool.

7 Click here to open the Brush picker.

⑧ Click the first soft-edge brush in the Brush picker.

⑨ Click and drag the Size slider to adjust the size.

⑩ Click the Smart Filter layer mask thumbnail to select it.

⑪ Click Default Colors icon to restore the default black and white foreground and background, making sure black is the foreground color.

⑫ Click in the image to paint with black to remove the filter from specific areas.

● The painted areas appear black in the layer mask, and the filters are removed from those areas in the photo.

⑬ Double-click the filter name to reopen the dialog box and adjust the filter's settings.

⑭ Click OK.

Try This!

Click the triangle (▾) by the Smart Object layer to reveal the Smart Filters or any layer effects applied to the layer. Double-click the Edit Blending Options button (⬌) next to the Smart Filter. A blending mode dialog box appears. Click Mode to select a different blending mode. Click Opacity to drag the slider to a different percentage.

More Options!

To change the effect when using multiple Smart Filters, click and drag one Smart Filter above or below another one in the Layers panel. To delete an individual Smart Filter, click its name and drag it to the Layers panel trash (🗑). To delete all the Smart Filters on a layer at once, click and drag the text *Smart Filters* on the Smart Object layer to the trash.

Did You Know?

You can copy a Smart Filter or a group of Smart Filters to another Smart Object layer in the Layers panel by pressing Option (Alt) and dragging the Smart Filter. However, you cannot drag a Smart Filter onto a regular layer.

AUTOMATICALLY BLEND
multiple images to get the best color

You can easily combine two or more separate photographs of the same subject and let Photoshop CS5 blend these to achieve a better image. You can combine images that do not have identical alignments and Photoshop can automatically align them. You can combine images photographed with different exposures, making some too light and others too dark, and Photoshop CS5 blends these to achieve better color and tone.

The Auto-Align Layers command aligns layers based on similar content in different layers, such as corners and edges, and automatically generates the required masks.

The Auto-Blend Layers command helps you create composites of a scene from multiple images with over- or underexposed areas or even content differences. Auto-Blend Layers creates masks to each layer and to hide or show different areas from each image to create a better and seamless composite image.

Using the Auto-Align and Auto-Blend Layers commands as in the following technique is an automated, easy-to-use technique and is not the same as creating an HDR (High Dynamic Range) image.

① Open multiple images to combine.

② Click the Arrange Documents button and select a window layout so you can see all the images.

Note: Only two images are shown in this task; however, you can use multiple images.

③ Shift+click and drag each image onto one image to make multiple layers on one document.

④ Close all the other open images.

⑤ Shift+click all the layers in the Layers panel.

⑥ Click Edit.

⑦ Click Auto-Align Layers.

⑧ Click an alignment option in the dialog box that appears.

⑨ Click OK.

Photoshop automatically aligns the layers based on the content.

⑩ Shift+click all the layers in the Layers panel.

⑪ Click Edit.

⑫ Click Auto-Blend layers.

DIFFICULTY LEVEL

⑬ Click Stack Images in the dialog box (○ changes to ◉).

⑭ Click Seamless Tones and Colors in the dialog box (☐ changes to ☑).

⑮ Click OK.

Photoshop automatically blends the layers.

⑯ Click the Crop tool.

⑰ Click and drag in the image to select the finished composite.

⑱ Click the Commit button to apply the crop.

Note: You can optionally click Layer and click Flatten Image to combine all the layers into one composite image.

TIPS

Did You Know?

The Auto-Align command automatically changes the locked Background layer into a regular layer and changes the name to Layer 0.

More Options!

After applying the Auto-Align command, you can click Edit and Free Transform and then use the anchor points to fine-tune the alignment or even to make tonal adjustments by changing exposure differences between layers.

Try This!

⌘+click (Ctrl+click) directly on one of the layer masks in the Layers panel to see what areas were added or removed from one layer.

Chapter 3

Straighten, Crop, and Resize

A well-balanced image, free from odd-looking distortions, can mean the difference between a snapshot and a good photograph. The overall layout of the image, how it is cropped, and where the main subject is placed in relation to the background are essential visual elements in any image. Your digital photo may have buildings that appear top heavy or out of perspective. A crooked horizon or unbalanced subject matter can make even a great image look like the work of a beginner. Your digital photos almost always need to be resized to fit your projects. Even the best photographers have images that require some cropping or resizing. You can follow similar guidelines in both design projects and photographs.

With Photoshop CS5, you can use a variety of straightening and cropping tools to improve the

composition of an image. You can also straighten and crop several crookedly scanned photos in one step. You can even make multiple photos from one original image or create a panorama from several separate images. Using Photoshop and Camera Raw, you can fix various types of camera lens distortions and correct the perspective on buildings; the software does most of the work for you.

Photoshop CS5 makes all such previously time-consuming or difficult tasks quick and easy. Tools and resampling algorithms help you straighten, crop, adjust, and resize images, saving hours of tedious work to make all your images look better.

CROP YOUR IMAGES
to improve composition

#27

Designers and photographers use various techniques to balance an image and focus the viewer's attention. They often use a Rule of Thirds principle and change the placement of the horizon to the upper or lower third of the image or place the main subject at the intersection of the thirds. They may just offset the main subject to guide the viewer into the image. Perfectly composing a photograph in the camera's viewfinder is not always possible; however, you can recompose and improve many photos by cropping them in Photoshop.

Using the Crop tool, you can easily strengthen the composition of your images by changing the relative position of the main subject or the strongest lines. Photoshop CS5 includes a new Rule of Thirds crop guide overlay, which is applied by default once you use the Crop tool on the image. You can use a Grid instead, or select None to compose your crop visually any way you want.

DIFFICULTY LEVEL

Optionally, you can crop by specifying dimensions in the Options bar, using one of the preset sizes, or by creating and saving your own preset.

① With the image you want to crop opened, click the Crop tool.

● The options in the Options bar show the Crop tool size selections.

② Click and drag across the entire image.

● The options in the Options bar change and the Rule of Thirds guide overlays the image.

③ Click and drag the side anchors to reposition the crop on the image.

④ Click and drag anywhere inside the crop lines to change the overall area to be cropped.

⑤ Click the Commit button to apply the crop.

Easily level a
CROOKED HORIZON

You may have a perfect photograph for your design, but the photo was shot at a crooked angle. You can easily fix that photograph in Photoshop without doing any math to adjust the angle of the horizon line.

Photoshop includes a Ruler tool, found in the Tools panel under the Eyedropper tool. This tool is intended to help you position elements precisely in a design layout and can calculate distances between two points in the unit of measure that you have set in Preferences. When you click and drag the Ruler tool across your image, a nonprinting line is drawn, and

the Options bar displays all the numeric information relating to the line and angle.

With Photoshop CS5, you can easily straighten a crooked horizon by clicking and dragging with the Ruler tool along a line that should be horizontal and parallel to the horizon, and then clicking the Straighten button on the Options bar. Photoshop automatically levels the crooked photograph, and crops the image as needed to remove any angled edges.

1 In an image with a crooked horizon line, click and hold the Eyedropper tool to reveal the Ruler tool.

2 Click the Ruler tool.

3 Click and drag from one side of the image to the other, along what should be a horizontal line.

The Ruler tool draws a line across the image.

Note: You can click and drag along a building or any line that should be horizontal.

4 Click the Straighten button in the Options bar.

The image is rotated and cropped to fit with a level horizon.

Expand the canvas with a
REVERSE CROP

When you think of cropping, you generally think of reducing the physical size of an image by cutting away areas around the borders. In Photoshop, you can also use the Crop tool to expand your canvas, give your photo or image a wider border, or quickly create a new colored background for a photo.

Expanding the canvas with the Crop tool is quick and you can see exactly how your image appears on the enlarged canvas. In addition, using the reverse-crop method, you can create an uneven border, larger on

one side than the other for a page layout or a note card, or larger on the bottom than on the top as in a gallery print.

You can use this technique to enlarge your canvas visually or use precise dimensions for your final image. By specifying the width and height for your finished design in the boxes in the Options bar, you can click and drag out the crop marquee in the image and maintain the exact dimensions you typed.

① With an image opened, click Window and select Application Frame.

The workspace window positions change.

② Click the Default Colors icon to reset the foreground to black and the background to white.

③ Click the Zoom tool.

④ Click the Zoom Out box in the Options bar.

⑤ Click in the image several times to zoom out, adding some space around the image.

The image view becomes smaller on a gray background area.

⑥ Click the Crop tool.

⑦ Click and drag across the entire image.

● The crop marquee appears on the image.

⑧ Click and drag the corner anchor points of the crop marquee to extend the crop area.

⑨ Click and drag the expanded area around your photo to fit your design.

⑩ Click the Commit button in the Options bar to commit the crop.

DIFFICULTY LEVEL

● The canvas is enlarged and filled with the background color.

⑪ Click the Type tool and type over the white of the background area.

A Trip Through France

TIPS

Try This!
Click the Background Color box in the Tools panel to open the Color Picker. Click another color to select it as the foreground color, and then follow the steps above to enlarge the canvas using the reverse-crop method. The extended canvas area fills with the selected color instead of white.

Did You Know?
On a Mac, the Application frame groups all the workspace elements into one window. You can move or resize the Application frame or any of its elements, and all the parts correspond, avoiding any overlapping panels and tools.

Change It!
Click the Crop tool (🔲) and type the width and height for your finished design in the boxes in the Options bar. When you click and drag out the crop marquee in the image, it maintains the exact dimensions you typed.

STRAIGHTEN CROOKED SCANS
quickly

When you are not bogged down with repetitive tasks, you can be more productive and creative. Photoshop has many features to help both your productivity and your creativity, such as automated image processing.

Scanning images one at a time is one of those projects that can be very time-consuming. You have to scan one image, crop it, and save it — and then lift the scanner top, reposition another image on the scanner bed, and start over.

Using a flatbed scanner with a large scanning area, you can scan multiple images at one time and let

Photoshop separate these into multiple files. Photoshop's Automate command for cropping and straightening photos even saves time when scanning just one photo. You can place a photo on the scanner bed without lining it up perfectly because Photoshop's Crop and Straighten Photos command can crop and straighten that one scan.

The Crop and Straighten Photos command works best when the images have clearly defined edges and there is at least 1/8 inch between each image. The command may work more quickly if all the images have similar tones.

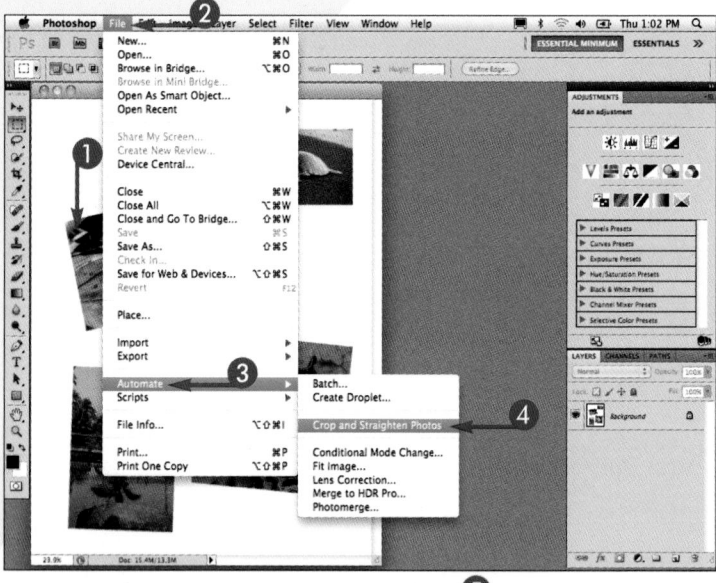

1. In Photoshop, open a file that has multiple scans.
2. Click File.
3. Click Automate.
4. Click Crop and Straighten Photos.

● Photoshop automatically crops and separates the images onto separate windows as tabs.

5. Click Window.
6. Click Arrange.
7. Click Float All in Windows.

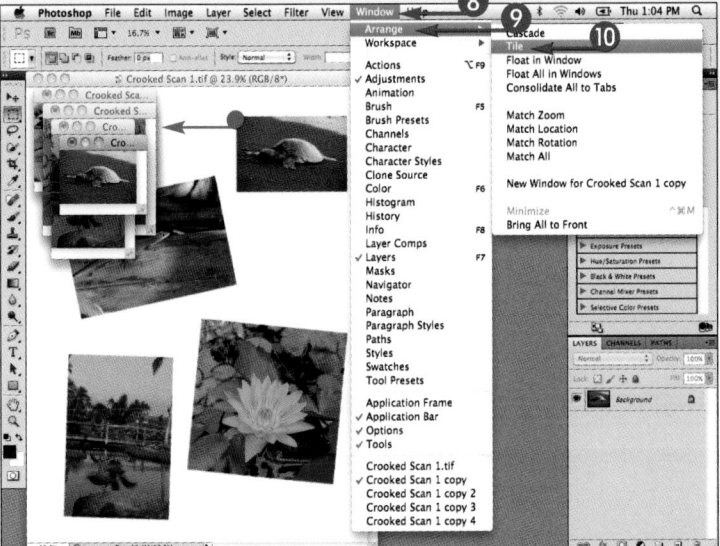

● Photoshop places all the separate images in windows cascading on the screen.

⑧ Click Window.

⑨ Click Arrange.

⑩ Click Tile.

● Photoshop arranges the original scan and all the separate images on the screen.

Note: The Crop and Straighten Photos command does not automatically save the separate image files.

TIPS

Important!

Photoshop does not replace the original scan with the separated photos, and it does not automatically save the separate images. Instead, Photoshop renames each separated file using the same name as the original scan and labels it "copy," "copy 2," and so on. Be sure to click File and Save As to rename and save each file.

More Options!

You can scan multiple images at once and decide to keep only one of them. Make a selection border around that one image, including some background. Press and hold Option (Alt) as you select File, Automate, and then Crop and Straighten Photos. Photoshop crops and straightens that one photo and puts it in a separate file.

CROP CREATIVELY
for a diptych, triptych, or quadriptych

Artwork comprised of two or more photographs, drawings, or paintings normally involves changing width and height, resolution, cropping, and mathematic calculations. With Photoshop, you can easily create such art pieces without any math. The images can be of different sizes and even have different aspect ratios.

Select images whose colors and tone or subject matter are complementary. After adjusting the rotation and size of each image individually, crop to adjust the dimensions of each image to match one another. Photoshop calculates the changes for you. Create one document with the different images on layers and move each layer to position it on the final art piece. You can place the images two up, three up, or four up both horizontally or vertically. You can add white space between the images, and you can add more canvas all around the artwork as a whole.

The following task uses four images to create a quadriptych. You can also create diptychs and triptychs by moving one image layer to one side or the other.

Start by opening four images you have previously straightened and cropped as in tasks #27 and #28, and use the Arrange Documents button to tile them across the screen.

1 Click the Crop tool.

2 Click the image with the desired size to select it.

3 Click the Front Image button.

● The Options bar shows the width, height, and resolution of the selected image.

4 Click the next image to select it.

5 Click and drag across the image with the Crop tool.

6 Press Return (Enter) to apply the crop.

7 Repeat steps 4 to 6 for each additional image to adjust the dimensions.

Note: Decide on one image to be the bottom image in the layers.

8 Click the Move tool.

9 Shift+click and drag one image onto another image.

10 Close the file for the image you just dragged.

11 Repeat step 9 for any additional images.

12 Click Window and select Application Frame as in step 1 of task #29 and zoom out if necessary.

One open file with multiple layers remains on the screen.

⑬ Double-click the Background layer in the Layers panel and click OK in the dialog box.

● The Background layer changes to Layer 0.

⑭ Shift+click the top two layers in the Layers panel to select them.

⑮ Shift+click and drag to the right on the image until the outline of the two top images snaps to the edge of the underlying image.

Note: You can no longer see the two top image layers on the screen.

⑯ Shift+click the two middle layers in the Layers panel to select them both.

⑰ Repeat step 15, dragging down on the image until the two middle images snap to the bottom edge of the visible image.

⑱ Press ⌘+minus sign (Ctrl+minus sign) to zoom out.

⑲ Click Image.

⑳ Click Reveal All.

● The window displays all four images in a quadrant.

DIFFICULTY LEVEL

TIPS

More Options!

To add white space around the images, expand the canvas with a reverse crop as in task #29. Then click each layer and use the arrow keys to move the layers individually. To see a white background, open the Transparency settings of Photoshop Preferences and change the Grid Size to None.

Important!

When you use the Crop tool (⬚) and the Front Image button, the crop dimensions for any subsequent image are automatically set to match those of the first image. You must click the Clear button to clear all previous settings to reuse the Crop tool with different dimensions.

Did You Know?

When the two images meet as you click and drag one image to the edge of another (in steps 15 and 17) the black arrow of the Move tool changes to a white arrow.

CHANGE YOUR PERSPECTIVE
with the Crop tool

When you photograph an object from an angle rather than from a straight-on view, the object appears out of perspective, displaying *keystone distortion*. The top edges of a tall building, for example, photographed from ground level, appear closer to each other at the top than they do at the bottom. If you photograph a window and cannot get directly in front of it to take the shot, the window appears more like a trapezoid. Depending on the photograph, you can correct this type of distortion with a number of Photoshop's tools.

The Crop tool in Photoshop CS5 has a special option that enables you to transform the perspective in an image and quickly adjust the keystone distortion. Your image must have an object that was rectangular in the original scene for the Crop tool's perspective function to work properly. You first adjust the cropping marquee to match the rectangular object's edges and then extend the marquee to fit your image. When you click the Commit button, Photoshop crops the image as large as possible while maintaining the angles of the rectangular object.

1 Open a photo containing a distorted rectangular object.

2 Click the Crop tool.

Note: If there are any dimensions in the fields in the Crop tool Options bar, click the Clear button in the Options bar to remove them.

3 Click and drag a cropping marquee anywhere inside the image.

The selected area is light, and the area that you want to crop away is dimmed.

Note: To zoom in with the crop marquee showing, press ⌘+spacebar (Ctrl+spacebar) and click and drag in the image. Press Option+spacebar (Alt+spacebar) and click and drag in the image to zoom out.

Note: Although on a Mac the Spotlight feature momentarily opens with the same keystrokes, using ⌘+spacebar in Photoshop CS5 still zooms in.

4 Click Perspective (☐ changes to ☑).

5 Click and drag each corner anchor of the cropping marquee and align it with a corner of a rectangular object that appears at a perspective angle.

● You can optionally click Shield in the Options bar to see the image clearly (☑ changes to ☐).

6 Click and drag out each of the center anchor points to fit the edges of the entire image.

7 Click the Commit button in the Options bar to commit the crop.

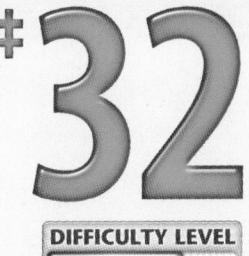

#32

DIFFICULTY LEVEL

Photoshop realigns the image and changes the perspective.

TIPS

Attention!

The Crop tool () may not fix the perspective distortion if it is applied to an image that has already been cropped for size. Also, if the perspective is not adjusted, you may not have placed the corner handles precisely. Click the Cancel button () in the Options bar and try adjusting the cropping marquee.

Keyboard Shortcuts!

Press C to access the Crop tool. Press Return (Enter) to commit the perspective crop or Esc to cancel it, or Control+click (right-click) in the image and select Crop or Cancel from the menu.

Change It!

Click Opacity in the Options bar and drag to change the darkness of the shield on cropped areas, or click in the Color box and select a different color for the shield. You can also turn the shield off by clicking the check box to deselect it.

Correct geometric distortion with the
LENS CORRECTION FILTER

Depending on the focal length of a camera lens or the f-stop used, a photograph may show common lens flaws such as barrel and pincushion distortion. *Barrel distortion* causes straight lines to bow out toward the edges of the image. *Pincushion distortion* displays the opposite effect, where straight lines bend inward. If the camera tilts up or down or at any angle, the perspective also appears distorted. The Lens Correction filter in Photoshop CS5 can help you correct these and other lens defects.

The Lens Correction filter in Photoshop CS5 includes an automatic correction based on specific lens profiles.

If your lens and camera are listed in the profiles, you can automatically correct geometric distortion as well as remove a *vignette*, the appearance of darker corners or edges in the image, and any chromatic edge discolorations, called *chromatic aberration*.

You can also choose to correct the distortions manually using the tools in the Lens Correction dialog box. You can line up the perspective of the buildings with a vertical plane and even turn on the filter's image grid to make your adjustments more accurately.

Use the Automatic Correction

1 Open an image as a Smart Object, or open a file and convert it to a smart object layer.

   Note: Opening as a Smart Object enables you to make changes nondestructively and edit the changes after they are applied. See task #24 for information about Smart Objects.

2 Click Filter.

3 Click Lens Correction.

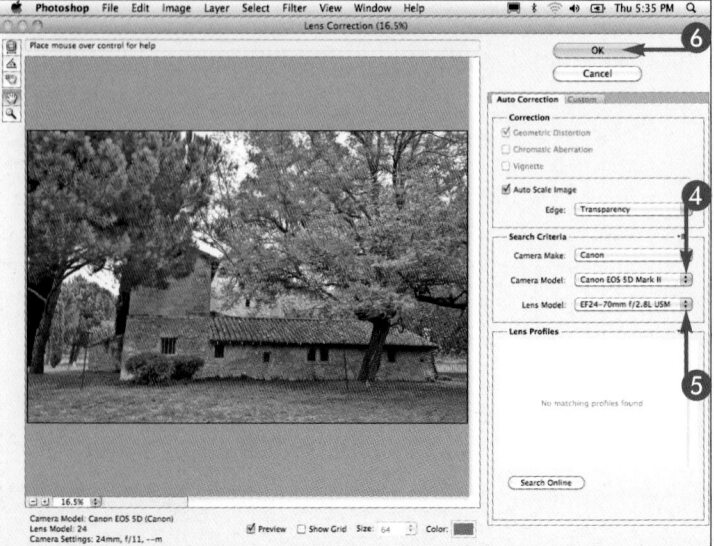

The Lens Correction dialog box appears with a large preview of the image.

4 Click here and select a camera model from the menu.

5 Click here and select the lens model from the menu.

6 If the correction is satisfactory, click OK to commit the changes.

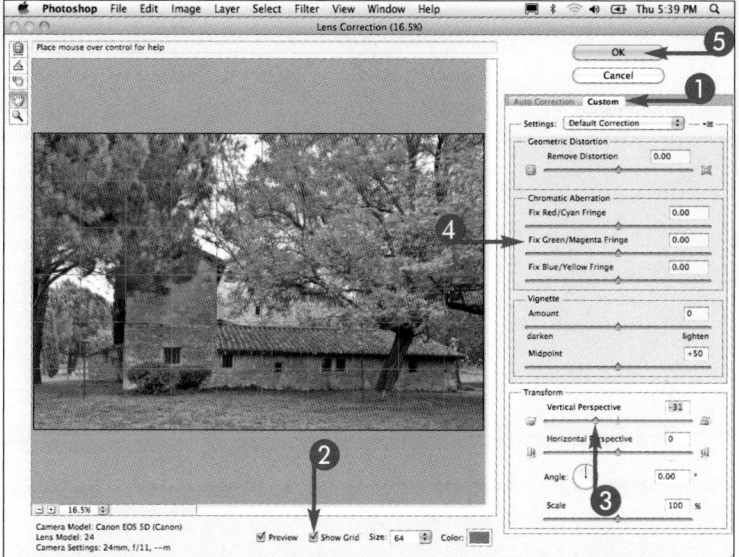

Use the Custom Correction

1 Click the Custom tab.

2 Click Show Grid (☐ changes to ☑).

3 Click and drag the Vertical Perspective slider to align the building with the grid.

Note: The type of distortion in the image determines which sliders to adjust.

4 Click and drag any of the other sliders to adjust the image.

5 Click OK to commit the changes and reopen the photo in Photoshop.

The image reopens in Photoshop with a changed perspective plane.

● You can optionally click the Crop tool and crop the image to fit if necessary.

TIPS

Try This!

In the Lens Correction dialog box, click the Auto Scale Image check box (☐ changes to ☑) and select Edge Extension from the menu. Photoshop automatically tries to fill the empty corrected areas with areas similar to the edges of the photo.

Did You Know?

If your camera or lens model is not listed, you can click the Lens Profiles panel menu button (▾☰) and select Browse Adobe Lens Profile Creator Online. You can then search online for profiles created and uploaded by other photographers, and even try them in an online preview mode before you save the profile locally to your computer.

More Options!

You can also download the Adobe Lens Profile Creator tool from http://labs.adobe.com to generate your own custom camera and lens profiles. You can save the profiles to a folder for use with Photoshop and Camera Raw, as well as Adobe Lightroom. You can also send the profiles to Adobe to share with other photographers.

Use Photomerge to
ASSEMBLE A PANORAMA

You can combine multiple photographs into one continuous image to create a panorama. For example, you can take two or more overlapping photographs of a scenic horizon, or even a number of scans of parts of a large document, and then assemble them in Photoshop with the Photomerge command. You can combine photos that are tiled horizontally as well as vertically.

The Photomerge command in Photoshop CS5 can automatically position and blend each layer using individual layer masks. You can also choose to blend the images manually using Interactive Layout.

To make any Photomerge project as successful as possible, photos or scans intended for merging should have an overlap of 25 to 40 percent. You should also maintain the same exposure for each photograph or keep the same scanning settings for each scan. If you are shooting the photos, use a tripod to keep the camera level so the photos line up correctly. By shooting in the Portrait mode or vertically, and shooting more images, you have a larger area to crop from for your final image, giving you a taller and more realistic result.

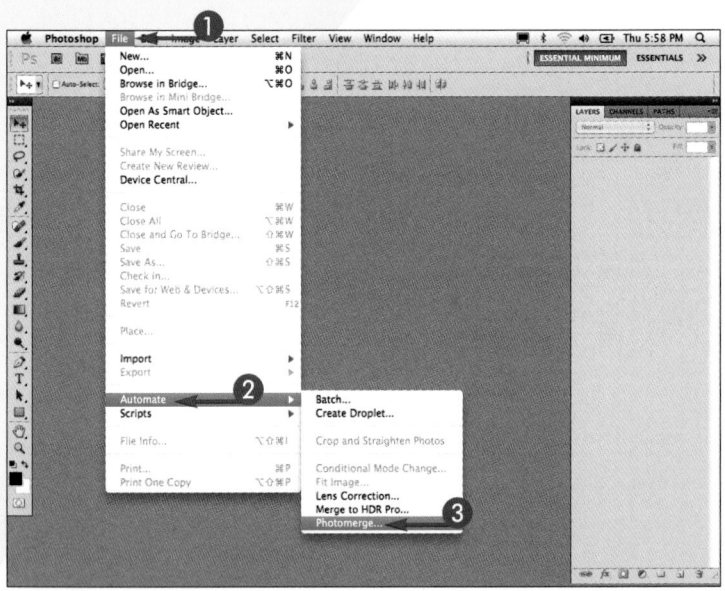

① In Photoshop, click File.

② Click Automate.

③ Click Photomerge.

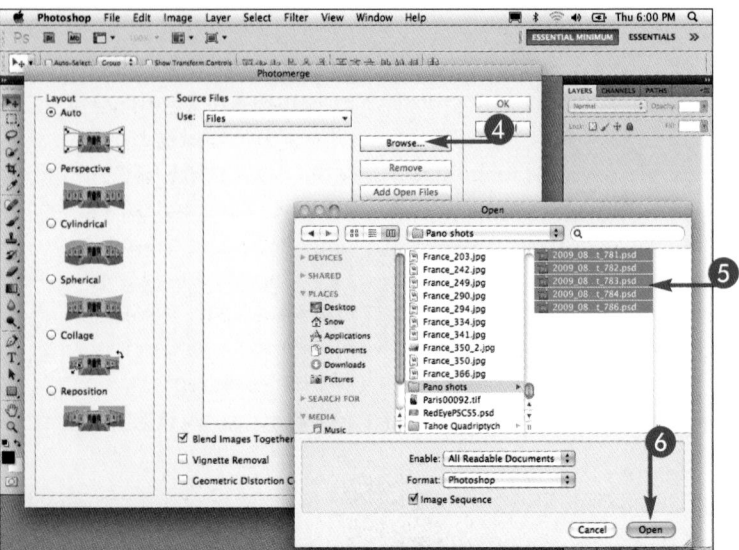

The Photomerge dialog box appears.

④ Click Browse.

The Open dialog box appears.

⑤ Navigate to and ⌘+click (Ctrl+click) the images to select them.

⑥ Click Open.

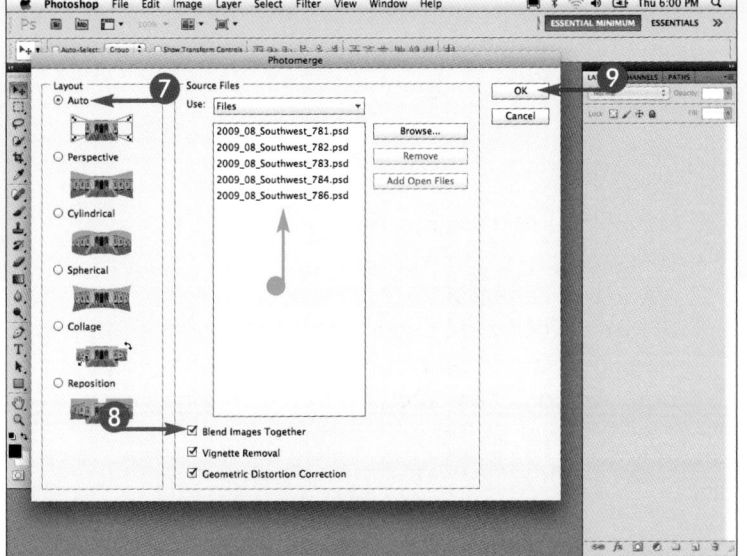

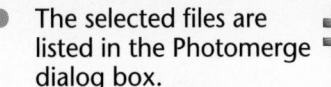

● The selected files are listed in the Photomerge dialog box.

⑦ Click Auto to select the automatic layout (○ changes to ●).

Note: *If you shot a series of images that cover 360 degrees, use the Spherical alignment option.*

⑧ Make sure that Blend Images Together is selected.

Note: *Depending on the images, you can also select Vignette Removal and Geometric Distortion Correction.*

⑨ Click OK.

Photoshop aligns the images based on content and blends them into a single image.

Note: *The new image is a multilayered file.*

⑩ Click the Crop tool.

⑪ Click and drag across the blended image to make your final panorama.

⑫ Adjust the corner anchors to fit your image.

⑬ Click the Commit button in the Options bar.

The panorama is cropped to the selected edges.

TIPS

Did You Know?

Perspective (see step 7) uses one image as a reference and adjusts the perspective of the others by overlapping the content of the reference image. Cylindrical reduces the bowed shape that can occur in some merged photos, and Spherical has the opposite effect. Collage and Reposition help Photoshop align uneven images.

More Options!

Select Vignette Removal if your images have darkened edges caused by a particular lens or if the lens was improperly shaded. Select Geometric Distortion Correction to compensate for barrel or other lens distortions.

Change It!

You can add more files to be included in the merge by clicking the Browse button again in the Photomerge dialog box, and navigating to the new source files to be added. You can always remove a file from the list by selecting the file and clicking Remove.

RESIZE YOUR IMAGE
with minimal visible loss

You often need a different size image than the original. You can resize images using the Image Size dialog box.

By deselecting the Resample Image check box in the dialog box, you can adjust the width, height, or resolution without affecting image quality or pixel dimensions. However, to change the overall size of an image, you must check the Resample Image box, and Photoshop resamples by adding or removing pixels to adjust for the changes.

Photoshop's *interpolation algorithm* — the way that it assigns values to added pixels and smoothes transitions between juxtaposing pixels — works well to preserve the quality and detail as long as the size changes are not extreme. Third-party plug-ins such as Alien Skin's Blow Up, OnOne's Genuine Fractals, and AKVIS Magnifier are sometimes better for enlarging greater than 150 to 200 percent, depending on the image.

The generally recommended resampling method for reducing image size is Bicubic Sharper, and Bicubic Smoother is intended for enlarging. However, depending on the image, many photographers find that the Bicubic Sharper resampling method actually works best both for enlarging and reducing photos.

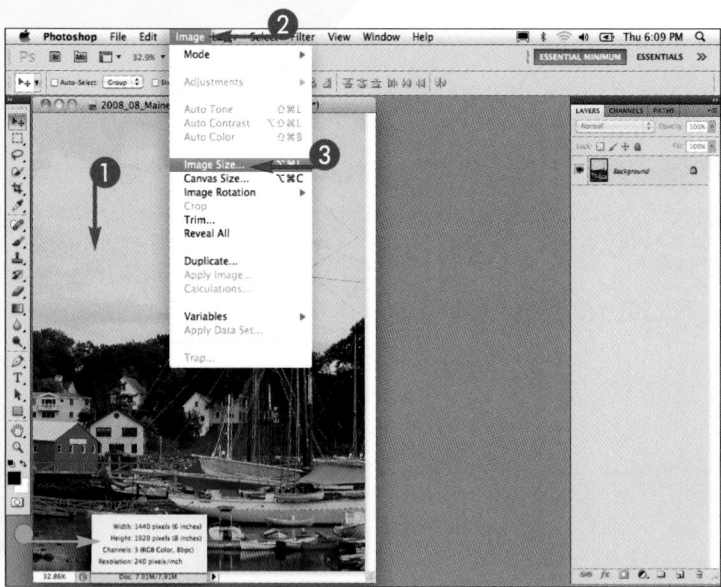

1 Open a photo that you want to enlarge.

● The current size of the image as shown on-screen appears here.

2 Click Image.

3 Click Image Size.

The Image Size dialog box appears, showing the current size of the opened image.

4 Make sure that the Resample Image check box is selected.

5 Double-click in the Width box to highlight the contents.

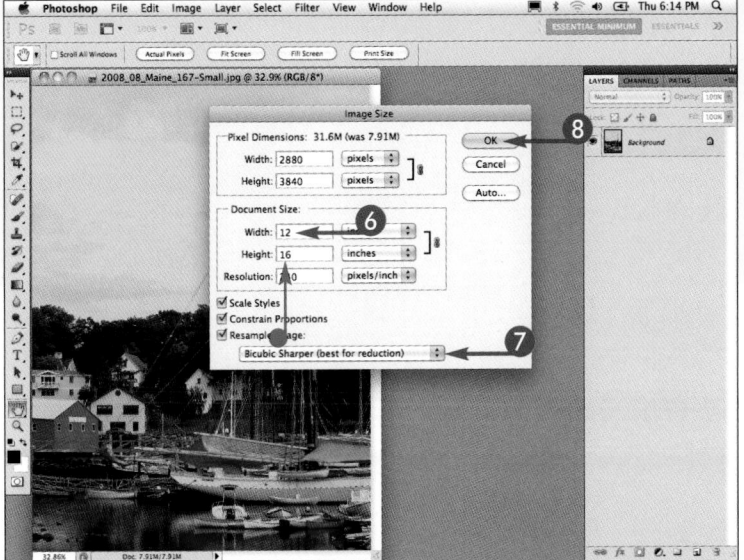

6 Type the width that you want for the final printed image.

● The height automatically adjusts proportionally.

7 Click here and select Bicubic Sharper (Best for Reduction).

8 Click OK.

A progress bar may appear depending on the speed of the computer's processor and the size of the image as Photoshop processes the enlargement.

The enlarged photo appears.

9 Click here to check the file size in the window frame.

Test It!

Make two copies of an image. Enlarge the first using Bicubic Smoother and the second using Bicubic Sharper. Crop the same 4-×-6-inch section on both enlargements and paste these into two new documents. Because resampling may reduce detail and sharpness, you can apply the Smart Sharpen filter with the same settings to each new document and print them for comparison.

Did You Know?

A resolution of 150 to 360 ppi is generally recommended for inkjet printing. Images for on-screen viewing need only a resolution of 72 ppi. Images intended for a printing press require a resolution of twice the *line screen* of the press, referring to the number of lines of dots that appear per linear inch (lpi) on the printed piece. If the line screen is 133 lpi, the resolution should be 266 ppi. Rounding up to 300 ppi is generally recommended.

Retouch Portraits

You can use Photoshop to give your subjects a digital makeover and make them look more beautiful, younger, and healthier. However, it is so easy to alter images in Photoshop that new users often overdo it and make people look like plastic versions of themselves. You are trying to enhance a person's best features and minimize other areas, not turn him or her into someone else. If your subject looks at his photo and thinks that he looks good, you have done your job well.

You can use the tools in Photoshop CS5 to remove blemishes and red eye, enhance the eyes, whiten teeth, soften the face, and more. You can also change a model's hair color or eye color to fit a client's request. You can add a catchlight to the eyes even if it was not captured by the camera to enhance a portrait. You can

even reduce wrinkles and smooth the skin without plastic surgery.

Applying the enhancements on separate layers enables you to preserve the original image as well as blend or reduce the changes, making them appear more natural. You should always work on a duplicate of the original file even when you make minor enhancements. To finalize the image, select Flatten Image from the Layer menu before saving it with a new name. Like a magician, you should not reveal your tricks or show the original unretouched photo to the subject!

Because these enhancements should be subtle, a pen tablet is particularly useful when retouching portraits.

Top 100

REMOVE BLEMISHES
and improve the skin

You can greatly improve a portrait with some simple steps in Photoshop CS5. You can remove skin imperfections such as blemishes and liver spots. You can remove them all, or leave some while making them less obvious.

As with many other projects in Photoshop, you can use a variety of tools to reduce or remove blemishes. Depending on the areas that need to be retouched, the Clone Stamp tool, the Patch tool, and the Healing Brush can all be used; however, the Spot Healing Brush is the most effective tool for removing small

imperfections. The Spot Healing Brush automatically samples the areas around the spot to be removed and blends the pixels so you do not need to specify the source sample. The key to using the Spot Healing Brush on skin is to work in stages on separate layers and to adjust the brush as you work such that the brush size is just slightly larger than the blemish.

You can then change the opacity of each layer and make the changes less obvious. If you do not like the changes, you can simply discard the layers.

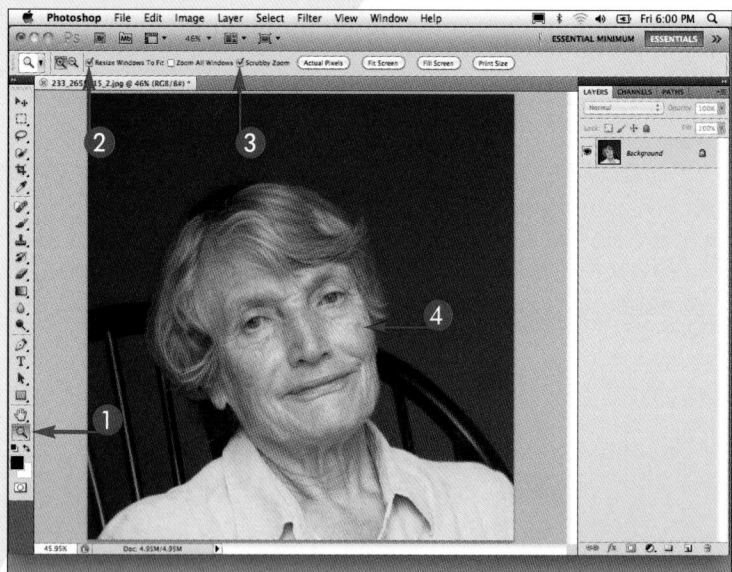

1 With the image open, click the Zoom tool.

2 Click Resize Windows To Fit (☐ changes to ☑).

3 Click Scrubby Zoom (☐ changes to ☑).

4 Click and drag over the blemish areas to zoom in.

The image is enlarged and fills the screen.

5 Click the New Layer button to add a new empty layer.

6 Click the Spot Healing Brush.

7 Click Sample All Layers (☐ changes to ☑).

8 Click Content-Aware (☐ changes to ☑).

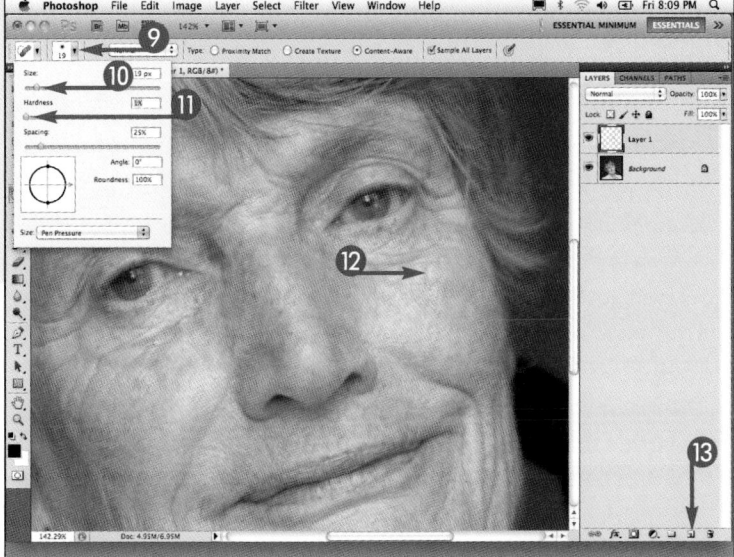

9 Click here to open the Brush picker.

10 Move the Size slider to set a brush just larger than the blemish you want to remove.

11 Move the Hardness slider to 0% for a soft brush.

12 Click each of the worst blemishes of a similar size first.

Photoshop removes the blemishes and blends the surrounding skin area.

13 Click the New Layer button to add another empty layer.

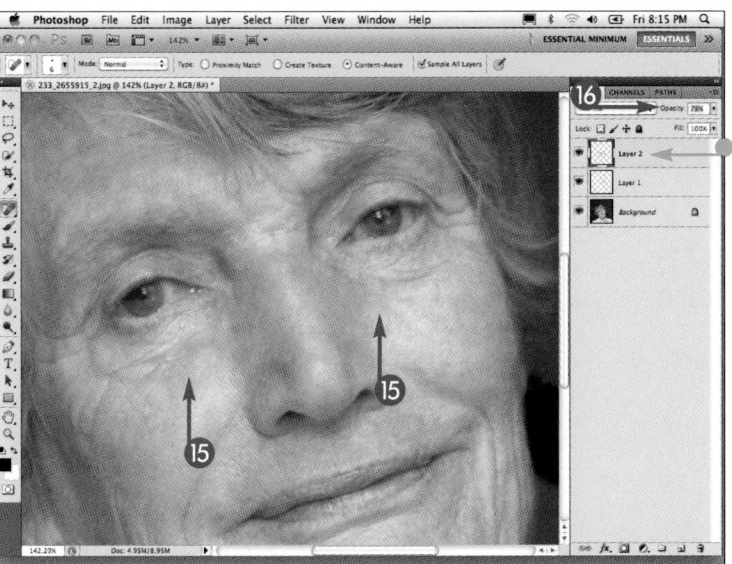

14 Press the left bracket key to reduce the size or the right bracket key to increase the brush size.

15 Click the other blemishes.

● Layer 2 should be highlighted in the Layers panel.

16 With Layer 2 selected, click Opacity and drag to the left until the skin looks natural.

36

TIPS

More Options!

Once you have finished removing the blemishes, you can combine the blemish-repair layers by selecting the top one and pressing ⌘+E (Ctrl+E) leaving just one blemish layer and the original Background layer. You can then quickly compare the before and after images by turning on and off the Eye icon (👁) for the blemish layer.

Did You Know?

If you use a pen tablet rather than a mouse, you can set the size in the Brush picker to respond to Pen Pressure. Then set the initial brush size to be just larger than the largest blemish. To vary the size as you brush, press harder to remove large blemishes and press lightly to remove smaller blemishes.

REMOVE BLEMISHES
and improve the skin

The Spot Healing Brush generally removes blemishes and imperfections and makes the skin appear cleaner. However, the blemishes often discolor the surrounding skin tone, and removing the blemishes can leave spots or streaks of mismatched colors on your subject. You can easily improve the overall skin tone and smooth any blotches the Healing Brush may have left using the skin-smoothing technique, as taught by Jane Conner-ziser.

Known as one of the best photo retouchers in the professional photography industry, Jane teaches

classes in portrait photography, facial retouching, and fine-art portrait painting at her Digital Art School in Florida, as well as across the United States and internationally. You can learn more about Jane's many classes and seminars at www.janesdigitalart.com.

This technique adds a special dodge and burn layer to your image. You can control the amount of tonal adjustment and improve the skin without making the photo appear retouched and without altering your original file.

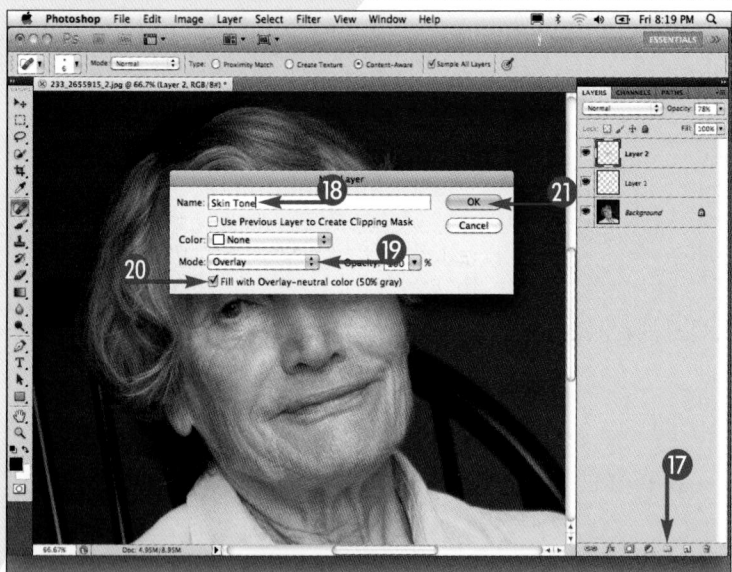

17 Press Option (Alt) and click the New Layer button.

The New Layer dialog box appears.

18 Type a name such as Skin Tone in the Name field.

19 Click here and select Overlay for the mode.

20 Click Fill with Overlay-Neutral Color (50% Gray) (☐ changes to ☑).

21 Click OK.

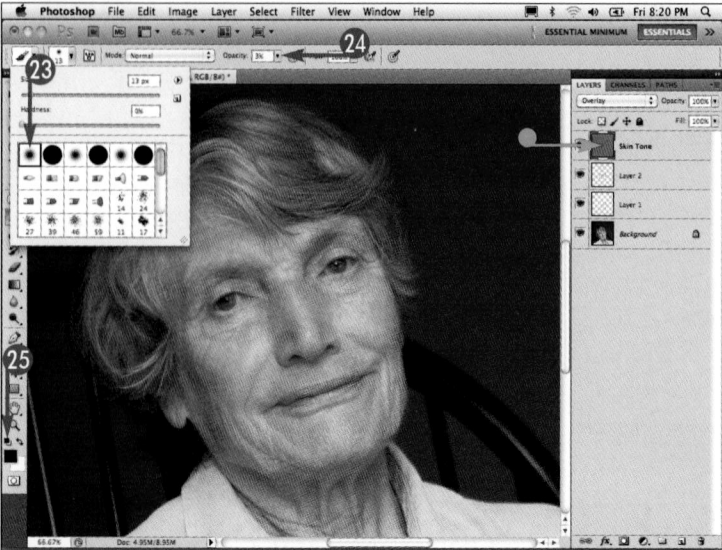

● A gray layer in Overlay mode appears in the Layers panel.

22 Click the Brush tool (🖌).

23 Click the Brush picker and click a soft-edged brush.

24 Click Opacity and drag to the left to reduce the brush opacity to about 3%.

25 Click the Default Colors icon to reset the default colors to black and white.

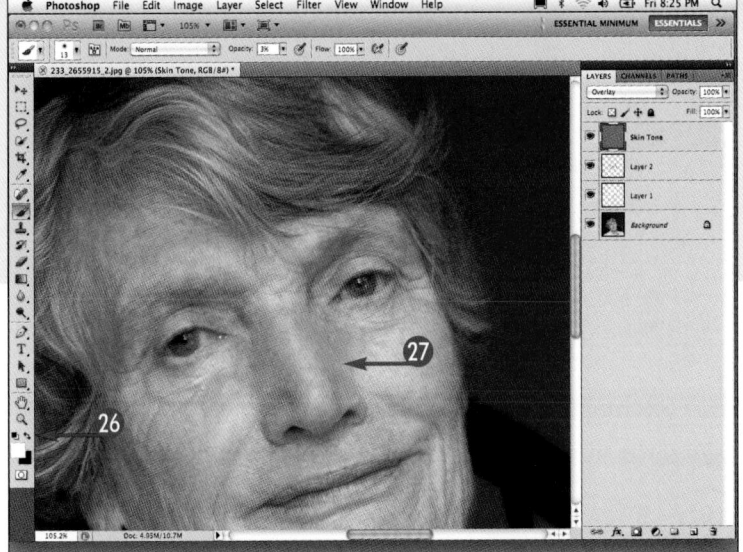

26 Click the Switch Colors icon to reverse the colors, making white the foreground color.

27 Paint over any dark spots in the image to smooth the skin.

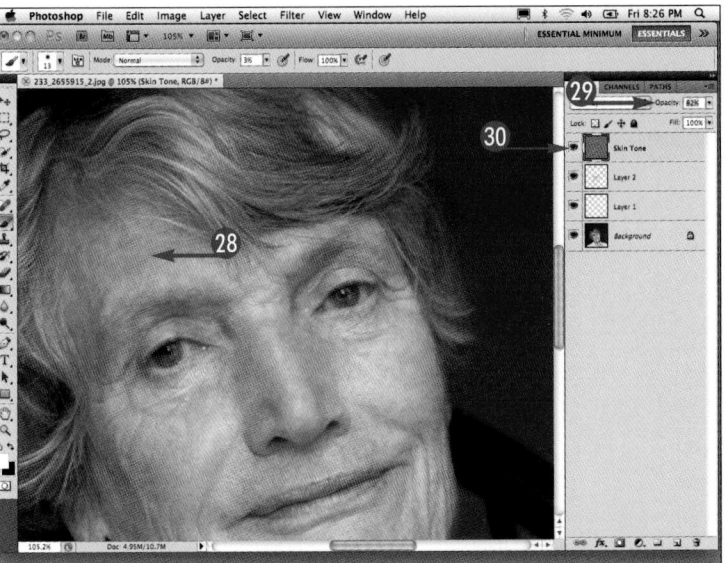

The skin tone appears smoother.

Note: The skin tone changes are very subtle and should be more visible on your monitor and on a printed photo than in the photo on these pages.

28 Continue painting over any dark areas, adjusting the size of the Brush tool as necessary.

29 Click Opacity and drag to the left to reduce the effect for a more natural look.

30 Click the Eye icon for the gray layer multiple times, turning it off and on to compare the image before and after the adjustment.

The skin tone is smoothed and appears natural rather than over-corrected.

More Options!

You can press X to reverse the background and foreground colors and paint with black to darken any areas that appear too light. However, if your image starts to appear unnatural, open the History panel and click back several steps to undo the changes. Then continue painting until the skin tone appears natural.

Attention!

You may not see much of a change as you paint with the brush opacity set to 3%; however, when you turn off the Eye icon (👁) for the layer, you will definitely see the changes. You can increase or decrease the brush opacity one or two percent, brush over an area, and then check the changes by toggling on and off the Eye icon.

REDUCE WRINKLES
with a soft touch

You can remove wrinkles with Photoshop in a variety of ways, and with a variety of Photoshop tools. However, if you remove all the wrinkles and give a person perfectly smooth skin, the effect is not believable. By using the Spot Healing Brush tool and separate layers, you can maintain more control over the corrections and give your subject a rejuvenated yet natural appearance.

You can modify the Spot Healing Brush to a medium softness and change its shape and angle so that your brush strokes are not as visible when you literally paint away the wrinkles. The effect appears more realistic if you use a pressure-sensitive pen tablet and set the Spot Healing Brush to respond to pressure.

You can create multiple layers and remove the wrinkles on one area of the face on each layer. After you brush away the years, you can change the opacity of the altered layers individually to reintroduce just enough wrinkles to appear natural.

1. Click the Zoom tool and zoom in to enlarge the areas with wrinkles.

2. Click the New Layer button to add a new empty layer.

3. Click the Spot Healing Brush tool.

4. Click Sample All Layers (☐ changes to ☑).

5. Click Content-Aware (○ changes to ◉).

6. Click here to open the Brush picker.

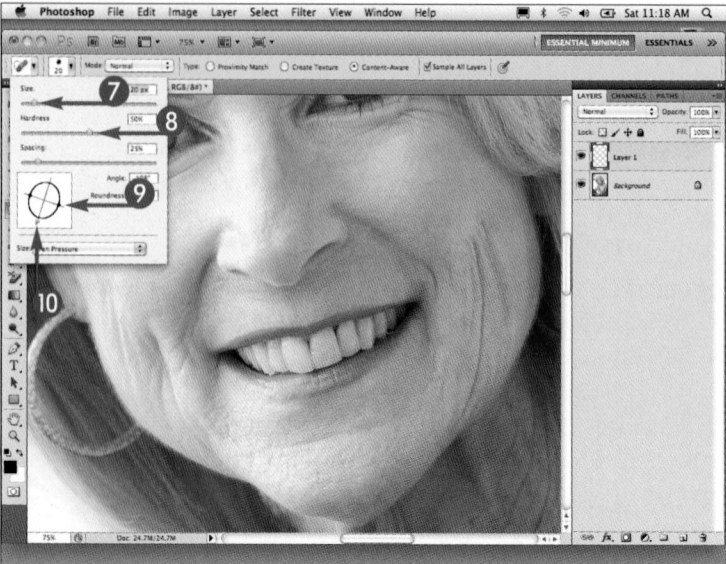

7. Click and drag the Size slider to change the brush width to cover the deepest wrinkles.

8. Click and drag the Hardness slider to the midpoint to build a brush with slightly soft edges.

9. Click here and drag toward the center to change the roundness of the brush.

10. Click and drag the arrowhead to change the angle of the stroke in the direction of the deepest wrinkles.

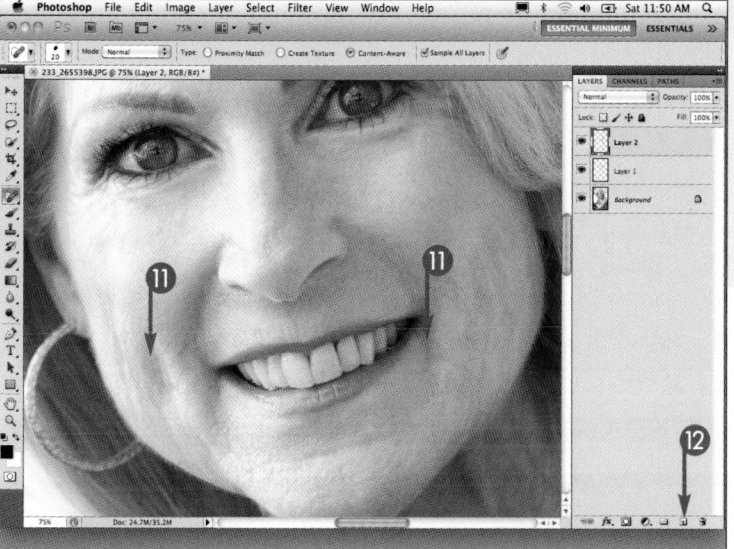

#37

11 Click and drag directly on the deepest wrinkles to paint them away.

12 Click the New Layer button to add a new empty layer.

13 Repeat steps 6 to 10, changing the brush angle and roundness for smaller wrinkles.

14 Press ⌘+Option (Ctrl+Alt) and click and drag in the image to zoom out.

15 With the top layer selected, click Opacity and drag to the left until the wrinkles appear diminished and still natural.

16 Repeat step 14 for any other wrinkle layers.

The wrinkles on the face are less pronounced, and the person appears slightly rested and younger.

TIPS

Did You Know?

If you use many small strokes rather than one larger one and change the size and angle of the brush according to the area of the wrinkle, the skin tones match more closely, and the results appear more natural.

More Options!

You can create a special wrinkle-removing brush by changing attributes in the Brush picker in the Options bar and saving your wrinkle remover as a Brush Preset in the Brush picker.

Try This!

You need to zoom in and out often when removing wrinkles. Instead of changing tools when the Spot Healing Brush is selected, press ⌘+spacebar (Ctrl+spacebar) and click to zoom in. Press Option+spacebar (Alt+spacebar) to zoom out. Although on a Mac the Spotlight feature momentarily opens with the same keystrokes, using ⌘+spacebar in Photoshop CS5 still zooms in.

REMOVE RED EYE
to quickly improve any photo

You can remove the red-eye effect from your photos quickly using either the Red Eye tool in Photoshop or the Red Eye Removal tool in Camera Raw.

Red eye is caused by the reflection of a camera flash in a person's retina. When you shoot in a darkened room, the subject's irises are wide open and his or her pupils enlarged, increasing the chances for red-eye photos. Using a camera with the flash mounted directly above the lens also causes more red eyes than using a bounce flash or a flash unit positioned away from the camera lens.

The default settings for pupil size and darken amount for both tools are the same and can be adjusted to fit your image. You can quickly apply the Red Eye tool in Photoshop to one eye. If necessary undo the correction, adjust the darken amount in the Options bar, and apply the tool again. In Camera Raw, you can more easily control the effect as you apply the Red Eye Removal tool by adjusting the correction on each eye individually.

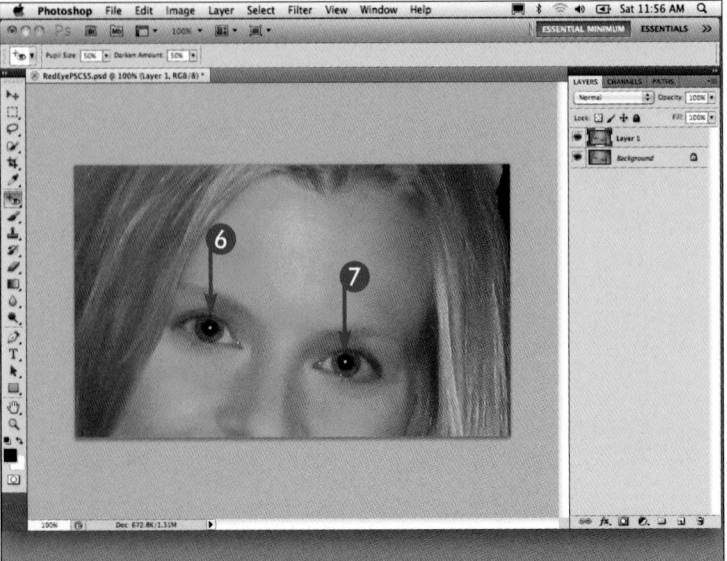

Remove Red Eye in Photoshop

1 In Photoshop, open a photo that has a red-eye effect.

2 Press ⌘+spacebar (Ctrl+spacebar) and click and drag over the eyes to zoom in.

Note: Although on a Mac the Spotlight feature momentarily opens with the same keystrokes, using ⌘+spacebar in Photoshop CS5 still zooms in.

3 Press ⌘+J (Ctrl+J) to duplicate the Background layer as a safety step.

4 Click and hold the Spot Healing Brush tool to see the other tools.

5 Click the Red Eye tool.

6 Click and drag over one eye.

The red is replaced by a dark gray.

7 Repeat step 6 for the other eye.

38

Remove Red Eye in Camera Raw

1 In Photoshop, click File.

2 Click Open.

3 Navigate to the red-eye photo in the Open dialog box.

4 Click here and select Camera Raw.

5 Click Open.

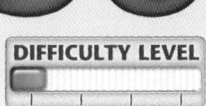

DIFFICULTY LEVEL

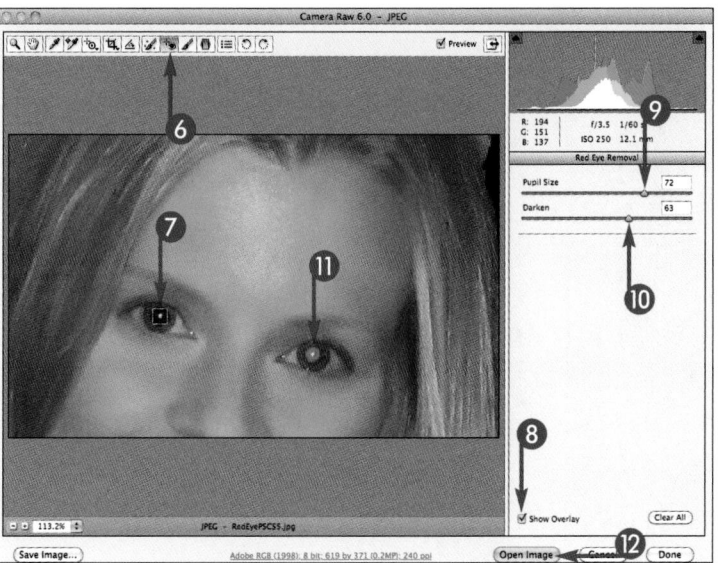

The photo opens in the Camera Raw dialog box.

6 Click the Red Eye Removal tool.

7 Click and drag an area across one eye, including some of the surrounding face in the selection rectangle.

The red is replaced by a neutral gray.

8 Click Show Overlay to deselect it (☑ changes to ☐).

9 Click and drag the Pupil Size slider to adjust the size of the gray area covering the pupil.

10 Click and drag the Darken slider to adjust the strength of the gray area.

11 Repeat steps 7 to 10 for the other eye.

12 Click Open Image to open the image in Photoshop.

Try This!

In Photoshop, press J to select the Spot Healing Brush tool (🖌). Then press Shift as you press J again three times to select the Red Eye tool (👁).

More Options!

You can remove the red-eye effect from all photographs, whether they are scanned from film or prints or start out as digital files.

Did You Know?

You can often avoid red eye by using the red-eye reduction feature included with some cameras. This feature minimizes the red-eye effect by firing several flashes an instant before the photo is taken, forcing the pupils to close slightly just as the final flash and shutter are released.

CHANGE EYE COLOR
digitally

The eye color often appears grayer or darker in photos than the actual color of the eyes when you look at the person directly. You can improve many photos by adding a little color to the iris of the eyes. You can simply add a little more color or you can change the color to a different hue.

When you colorize the eyes, you are looking for a natural eye color. You can also select any color as the foreground color and paint in the irises. If you have another photo of the same person where the eye color appears more natural, you can sample the eye

color from the first photo and paint it into the one with the grayed eyes. The specific brush options you set in the Options bar are key to colorizing the eyes to appear natural.

You can also use the same technique to apply one person's eye color to another subject's eyes. Agencies often request a specific eye color for a model to better blend into the color scheme of an advertising piece. You can save time by using Photoshop to change the eye color in the original photo and avoid finding and photographing a different model.

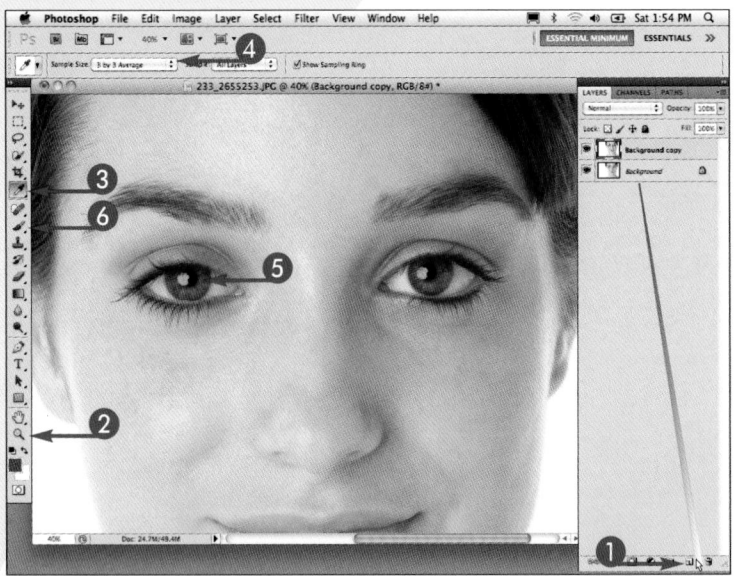

① Click and drag the Background layer over the New Layer button to duplicate the layer as a safety step.

② Click the Zoom tool and zoom in to enlarge the eyes.

③ Click the Eyedropper tool.

④ Click here and select 3 by 3 Average.

⑤ Click in the iris to set a reference color as the foreground color.

⑥ Click the Brush tool.

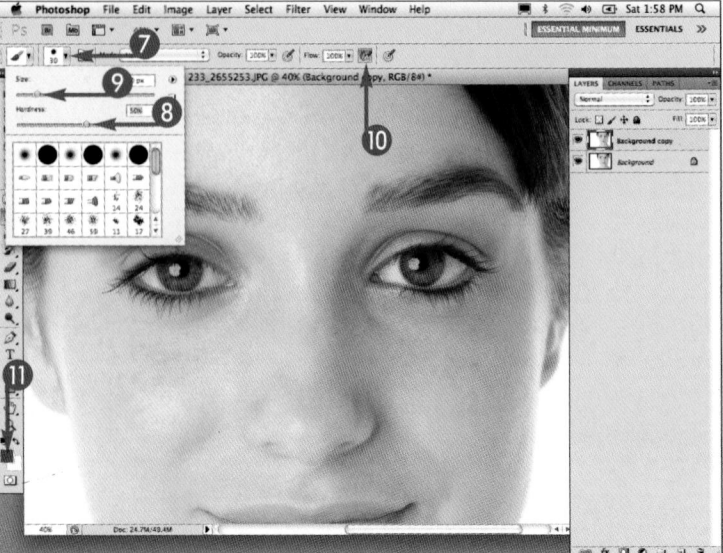

The Options bar changes.

⑦ Click here to open the Brush picker.

⑧ Click and drag the Hardness slider to 50% so there is only a slightly soft brush edge for better blending.

⑨ Adjust the brush size just smaller than one-half the iris using the left and right bracket keys on the keyboard.

⑩ Click the Airbrush button to enable it.

⑪ Click the Foreground Color box in the Tools panel.

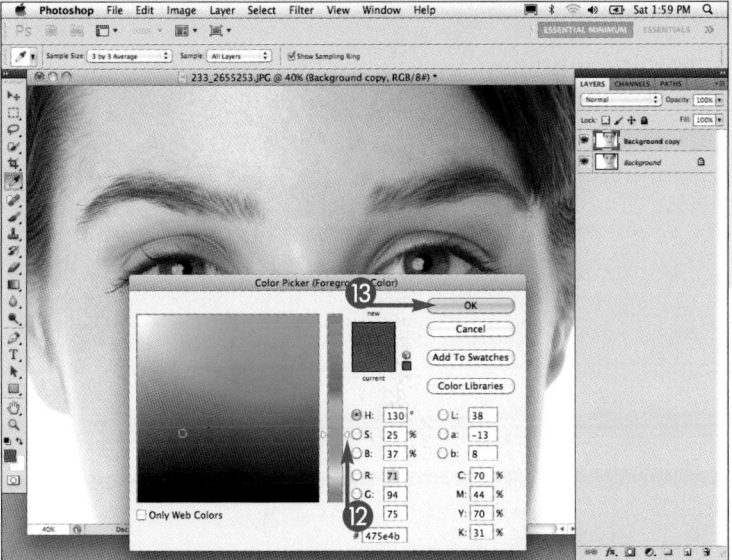

The Color Picker appears.

⑫ Click and drag the Hue slider to another color.

⑬ Click OK to close the Color Picker.

#39

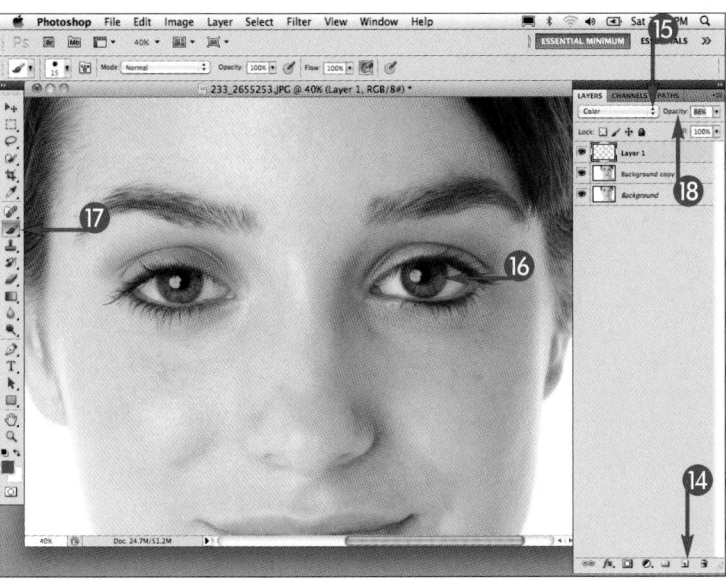

⑭ Click the New Layer button to add a new empty layer.

⑮ Click here and select Color for the layer blend mode.

⑯ Click and drag over both irises to paint in the new color.

⑰ Click the Eraser tool and erase if you paint over other areas.

⑱ Click Opacity and drag to the left until the eye color appears natural.

The irises of the eyes are now a different color.

TIPS

More Options!

If you have another photo with an appropriate eye color, you can use the Color Replacement tool instead of the standard Brush tool. The tools are in the same group in the Tools panel. Option+click (Alt+click) in the first photo using the Color Replacement tool (🖌) to sample the color of the eyes that you want to use. Then apply the color on the empty layer of the image you are correcting using a soft-edged brush.

Did You Know?

Dog and cat eyes often show a greenish or white eye when they are photographed with a flash. The Red Eye Removal tool (🔴) does not remove that effect. You can, however, paint in the eye color using the techniques described in this task.

Add a gradient layer to
LIGHTEN THE IRISES

The eyes are generally considered the most important feature in a portrait. You can add interest to the eyes and draw the viewer in by giving the eyes a digital brightening effect. You can improve the eyes in a variety of ways in Photoshop. Some methods work better on one image than another, so learning and trying various techniques lets you improve your images according to your subject and the project's requirements.

You must apply the gradient on a separate layer, not only to protect the original image and make it easy to undo the effect, but also so you can adjust the strength of the eye brightening to fit your photo and make it look natural. You adjust the layer opacity as you view the effect on-screen before flattening the layers and saving the file. This technique is very quick and often gives just enough sparkle to an otherwise dull eye.

Like all portrait retouching, the effect should be subtle and yet still brighten the subject's eyes.

① Click the New Layer button in the Layers panel to add a new layer.

② Click the Default Colors icon to reset the default colors to black and white.

③ Press X to reverse the default colors, making the foreground color white.

④ Click the Zoom tool and zoom in to enlarge the eyes.

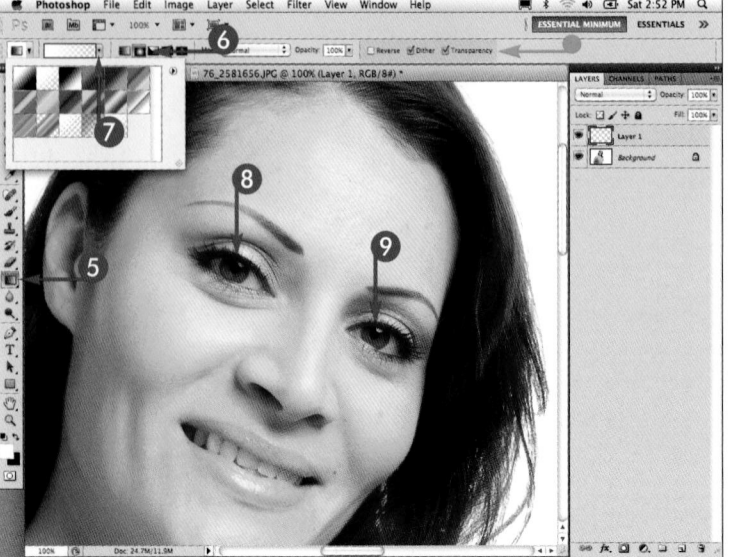

⑤ Click the Gradient tool.

   The Options bar changes.

⑥ Click the Radial gradient.

⑦ Click here and select the Foreground (White) to Transparent gradient.

● Reverse should be unchecked; Dither and Transparency should be checked.

⑧ Click in the center of one pupil and drag to the edge of the iris.

⑨ Repeat step 8 for the second eye.

⓵⓪ Click here to change the layer blend mode to Overlay.

The bright white spots blend into and lighten the irises.

⓵⓵ Click Opacity and drag to the left to reduce the layer opacity until the eye color appears lighter but still natural.

The irises of the eyes are now brighter.

⓵⓶ Click the Eye icon for Layer 1 to turn it off and compare the before and after views.

TIP

Did You Know?

The default gradient always uses the current foreground and background colors in the toolbar. Set the foreground color before you select the Gradient tool and then press G to quickly select the Gradient tool. You can also access the other tools in the Tools panel by pressing a specific letter, such as V for the Move tool or Z for the Zoom tool. When multiple tools are grouped together, like the Spot Healing Brush, the Healing Brush, the Patch tool, and the Red Eye tool, you can press the one-letter keyboard shortcut to access the first tool and then repeatedly Shift+press the letter to cycle through all the grouped tools.

BRIGHTEN THE EYES
by lightening the whites

You can quickly enhance any portrait by lightening the whites of the eyes. The eyes are the most important feature of the face and the key to a person's individuality. Whether the whites of the eyes are bloodshot or just appear dull, lightening them can enhance the whole face. Lightening and removing red or yellow areas in the white area brightens the subject's eyes.

Lightening the whites of the eyes is a multistep and multilayer process and can be done in various ways. You can paint directly on the whites of the eyes or start by selecting the whites. You can remove the redness or yellow areas using a Hue/Saturation adjustment layer and a layer mask. Then you can lighten the eyes by duplicating the Hue/Saturation adjustment layer and layer mask, adjusting the lightness, and changing the blend mode. You can reduce the adjustment layer opacity to give a more natural look.

The whites of people's eyes are not completely white, so you need to zoom in and out to view the entire photo as you apply the changes. Using adjustment layers, you can easily go back and modify the changes to keep the subject looking natural.

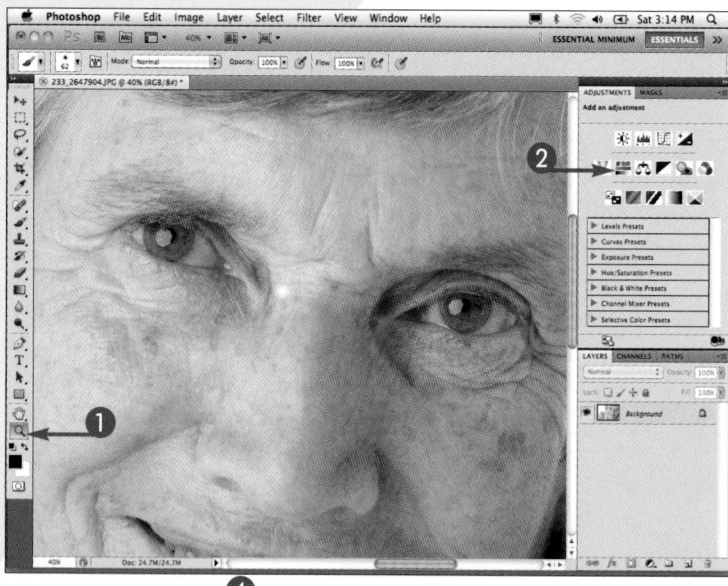

① Click the Zoom tool and zoom in on the eye area.

② Click the Hue/Saturation button to create a new adjustment layer.

The panel changes to the Hue/ Saturation panel, and a Hue/ Saturation layer appears in the Layers panel with the layer mask selected.

③ Click and drag the Saturation slider to the left to reduce the discoloration in whites of the eyes.

Note: *The whole image turns gray.*

④ With the layer mask selected, click Edit.

⑤ Click Fill.

The Fill dialog box appears.

⑥ Click here and select Black.

⑦ Click OK.

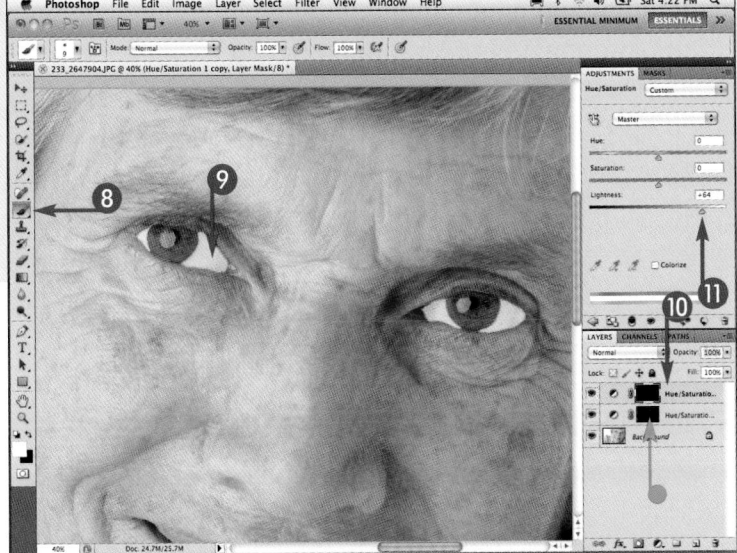

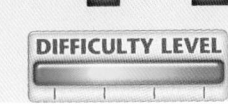

● The layer mask turns black and hides the Saturation adjustment.

⑧ Click the Brush tool.

⑨ With white as the foreground color, carefully paint over the whites of the eyes to remove the discoloration.

⑩ Press ⌘+J (Ctrl+J) to duplicate the Hue/Saturation layer and layer mask.

⑪ Click and drag the Lightness slider for this adjustment layer to the right and the Saturation slider to 0.

⑫ Press ⌘+0 (Ctrl+0) to zoom out and view the whole face.

⑬ Click here and change the blend mode for the top adjustment layer to Soft Light.

⑭ Click Opacity and drag to the left to reduce the effect until the eyes look brighter but still natural.

TIPS

More Options!

Instead of painting directly over the whites of the eyes on the mask, you can apply the same technique to a selection of the eye whites. Start by selecting the white areas with a selection tool such as the Quick Select tool as in task #21. With the selection tool still active, Control+click (right-click) the selection area. A contextual menu appears, listing options such as Feather and Select Inverse. Click Feather, and then apply the first Hue/Saturation adjustment layer as in step 2. The selected area appears on the layer mask automatically.

Try This!

Press Shift as you select with a selection tool to add to a selected area or add a separate selection. Press Option (Alt) as you drag over a selected area to remove areas from that selection.

ADD DEPTH TO THE EYES
to emphasize them

Removing red eye and lightening the whites of the eyes improves any portrait photograph. You can also make your subject more interesting by adding other adjustments that emphasize the eyes. You can add more contrast to the iris by lightening some areas and darkening others. You can add depth to the eyes by darkening the eyelashes and the natural outline of the eyes. This digital technique is similar to dodging and burning in the darkroom.

Instead of using Photoshop's Dodge and Burn tools on the image, however, you can use the Brush tool on separate empty layers and vary the opacity of each layer to control the adjustments. Painting with white lightens areas. Painting with black darkens areas, lengthens the eyelashes, and adds definition to the eyes. Using the Opacity setting in the Layers panel, you can fine-tune the adjustments before you finalize the image.

Making the eyes sparkle by using a variation of digital dodging and burning in Photoshop helps draw the viewers' attention to the eyes and engages them in the photo.

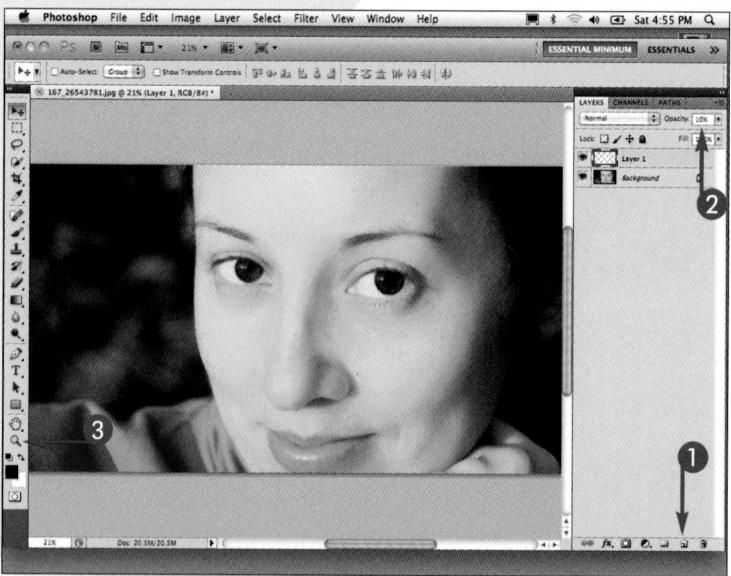

① Click the New Layer button.

② Double-click in the Opacity field and type **10** to view a more realistic adjustment as you work.

   Note: You can increase or decrease the opacity before saving the file.

③ Click the Zoom tool and click and drag across both eyes to zoom in.

④ Click the Default Colors icon to reset the foreground and background colors to the defaults.

⑤ Click the Switch Colors icon to reverse the foreground and background colors and set the foreground to white.

⑥ Click the Brush tool.

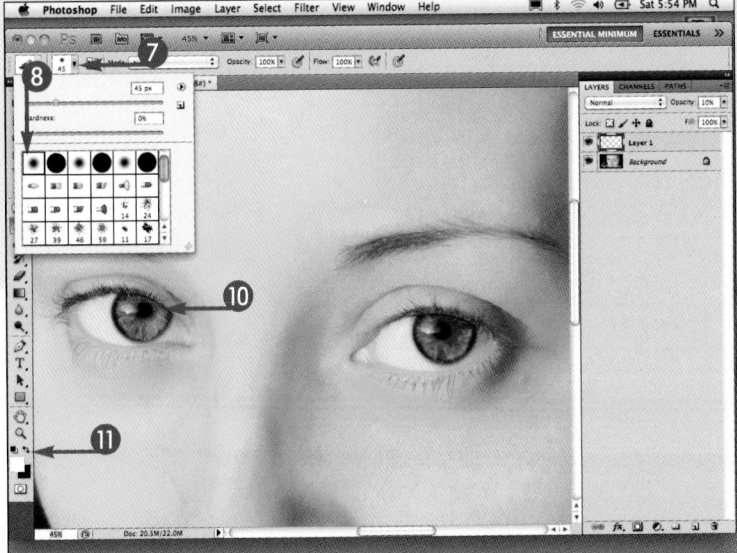

7 Click here to open the Brush picker.

8 Click a soft-edged brush.

9 Click the left or right bracket keys to find a brush size that fits inside the iris.

10 Paint over the center of each iris.

11 Click the Switch Colors icon to reverse the foreground and background colors and set the foreground to black.

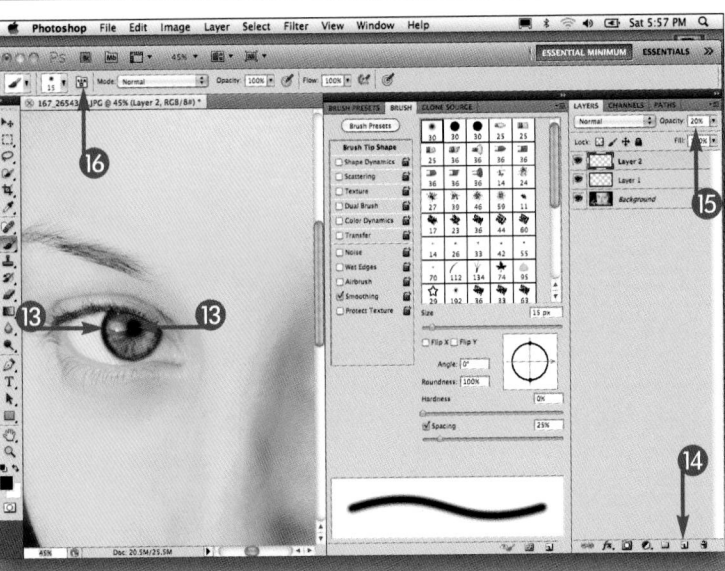

12 Press the left bracket key to reduce the brush size.

13 Paint with black around the edges of the irises and in the pupils.

14 Click the New Layer button to add a second empty layer.

15 Double-click in the Opacity field and type **20** to view a more realistic adjustment on this layer as you work.

16 Click the Brushes button, or press F5 to open the Brushes panel.

42

DIFFICULTY LEVEL

TIPS

Did You Know?
You can save and reuse an eyelash brush. With the settings that you create for Brush Tip Shape (see steps 18 to 21), click the panel menu button ( ) on the right in the Brushes panel. Click New Brush Preset. Type a name in the dialog box and click OK.

Try This!
Press D to set the foreground and background colors to the default black and white. Press X to quickly switch the foreground and background colors as you digitally dodge and burn.

Try This!
To lighten dark brown eyes, try setting the foreground color to a dark red or burgundy color instead of white. Paint in the irises on a separate layer and adjust the opacity. Adding red to dark brown eyes softens the look.

ADD DEPTH TO THE EYES
to emphasize them

Retouching portraits is always tricky. You want to improve the image and still preserve the person's character. Because the eyes can define personality, enhancing the eyes almost always helps the overall portrait and helps the viewer focus on the subject.

When you work on any portrait and especially when you work on the eyes, you need to make small changes. Large changes are too often obvious, and your subjects want to see themselves and be seen at their best, not different. Make small changes and repeat these on several layers. You can easily adjust the opacity of each layer independently, creating more variations in brush strokes and colors. With adjustments on multiple layers, it is also easier to change or delete enhancements that do not seem natural.

Using a pressure-sensitive pen tablet also gives more variety to brush strokes. Use light brush strokes instead of heavy ones. Many of the brush options can be set to respond to pressure or tilt, allowing you to alter brush styles with fewer trips to the Brushes panel.

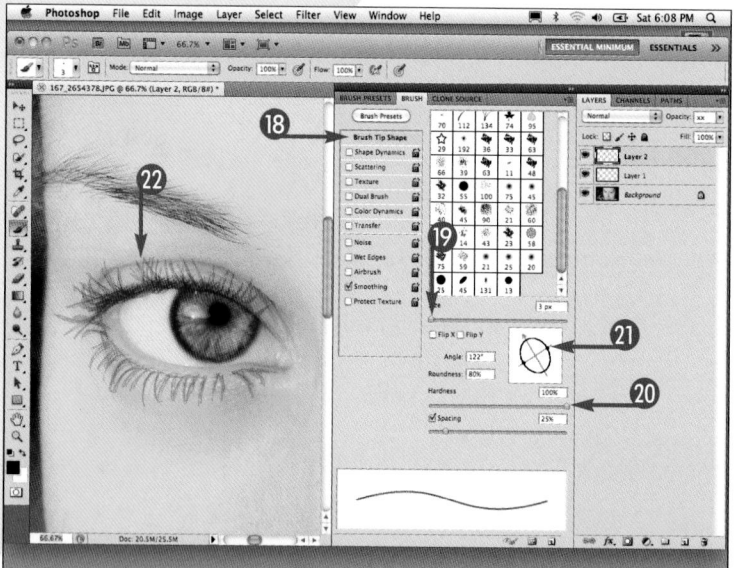

⑰ Press ⌘+spacebar (Ctrl+spacebar) and then click in the image to zoom in to see the eyelashes.

⑱ Click Brush Tip Shape.

⑲ Select a very small brush to match the size of the eyelashes.

⑳ Click and drag the Hardness slider to 100% to build a completely hard-edged brush.

㉑ Drag the brush angle and the dots on the roundness icon to conform the brush shape to the eyelashes of one eye.

㉒ Paint over the eyelashes one at a time to darken them.

㉓ Repeat steps 21 and 22 to adjust the brush for different-angled eyelashes.

㉔ Press the spacebar and click and drag in the image to move to the other eye.

㉕ Repeat steps 21 to 23, adjusting the brush to fit the shape of the lashes of the other eye.

㉖ Click the Brushes button to close the Brushes panel.

㉗ Press Option+spacebar (Alt+ spacebar) and click in the image to zoom out to see the whole face.

28. Click Layer 1 to highlight it.

29. Click in the Opacity data field.

30. Press the keyboard up or down arrows to increase or decrease the layer opacity until the irises look natural.

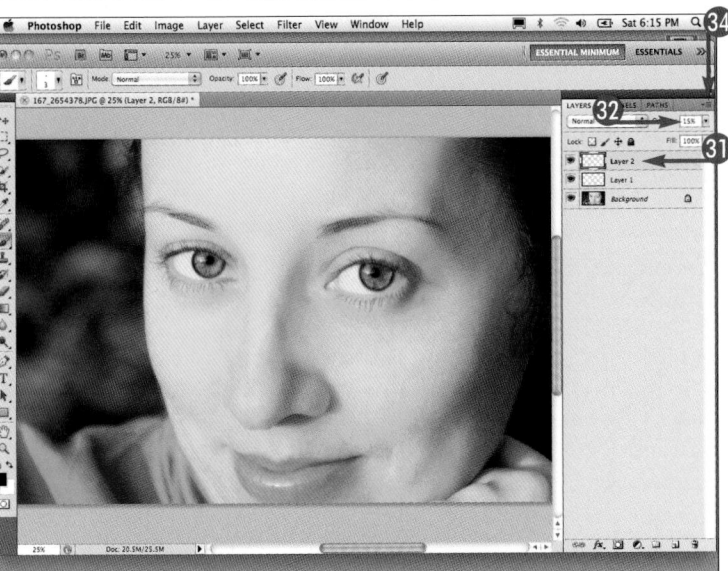

31. Click Layer 2 to highlight it.

32. Click in the Opacity data field.

33. Press the keyboard up or down arrows to increase or decrease the opacity until the eyelashes look darker but still natural.

    The eyes now appear stronger and still natural and help focus the viewer's eyes.

34. Click the panel menu button and select Flatten Image from the menu to finalize the photo.

TIPS

More Options!

You can add eyeliner to the eyes in a photograph. First add another layer. Click Opacity and drag to the left to lower the opacity to about 18%. Paint with black at the edge of the eyelashes on each eye. Click in the Opacity field and use the keyboard up and down arrows to increase or reduce the opacity of the layer until the eyeliner looks natural.

Did You Know?

You can use the same technique shown in this task to enhance light eyebrows. Add a layer and reduce the opacity to 8%. Open the Brushes panel and click Brush Tip Shape. Set the hardness to 0% and change the size, angle, and roundness to match the shape of the eyebrows. Paint a few smooth strokes over both eyebrows using black. Change the layer's opacity as needed.

ADD A CATCHLIGHT
to make the eyes come alive

When the light source — whether it comes from a camera flash, side lighting, or a natural light source — reflects in the subject's eyes, it forms a catchlight. A *catchlight*, also called a *specular highlight*, in a subject's eyes adds life and sparkle to the subject and brightens the overall photograph. More importantly, it draws attention to the subject's eyes and engages the viewer.

If the subject in a photograph does not have any specular highlights in the eyes or if the subject's eyes

appear somewhat dull, you can use Photoshop to add catchlights. The trick is to make them look real.

Jane Conner-ziser, one of the most experienced and well-respected portrait retouching masters, teaches this technique in her classes and instructional videos. Jane creates catchlights with diffused edges and emphasizes the use of two separate layers, one for the glow and the other for the sparkle of catchlights. By placing them on separate layers, you can adjust the catchlights to achieve a natural, realistic look.

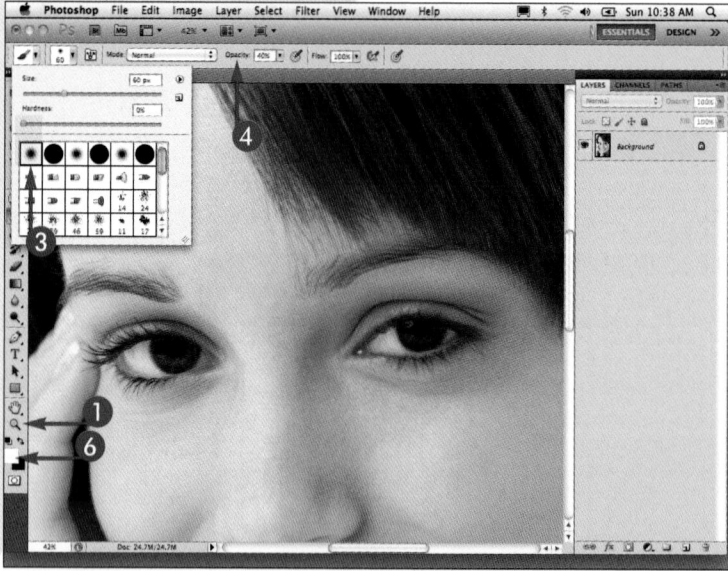

① Click the Zoom tool and zoom in on the eye area.

② Click the Brush tool (🖌).

③ Click the Brush picker and select a soft-edged brush, with the Hardness slider at 0%.

④ Click Opacity in the Options bar and drag to the left to reduce the brush opacity to 40%.

⑤ Press D to reset the foreground and background colors.

⑥ Press X to reverse the colors, making white the foreground color.

⑦ Press the left or right bracket keys to adjust the brush size to be slightly larger than the final catchlight.

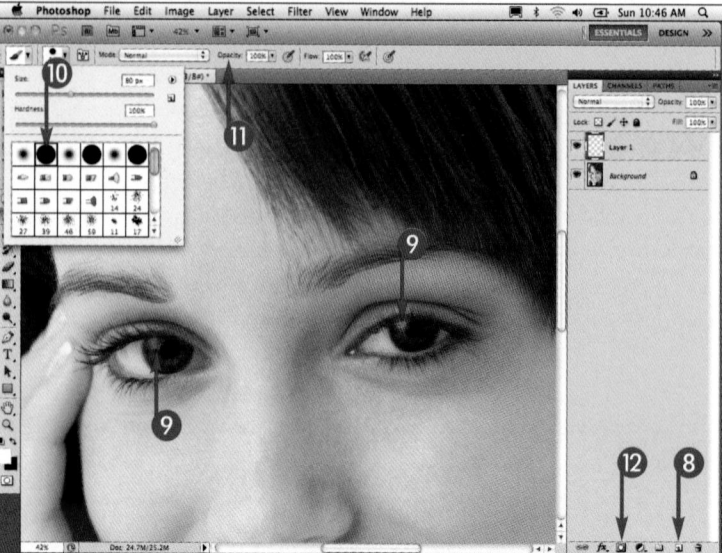

⑧ Click the New Layer button to add a new empty layer.

⑨ Click once in each eye to create the catchlights.

⑩ Click the Brush picker to change to a hard-edged brush.

⑪ Click Opacity in the Options bar and drag to the right to 100%.

⑫ Click the Layer Mask button to add a layer mask.

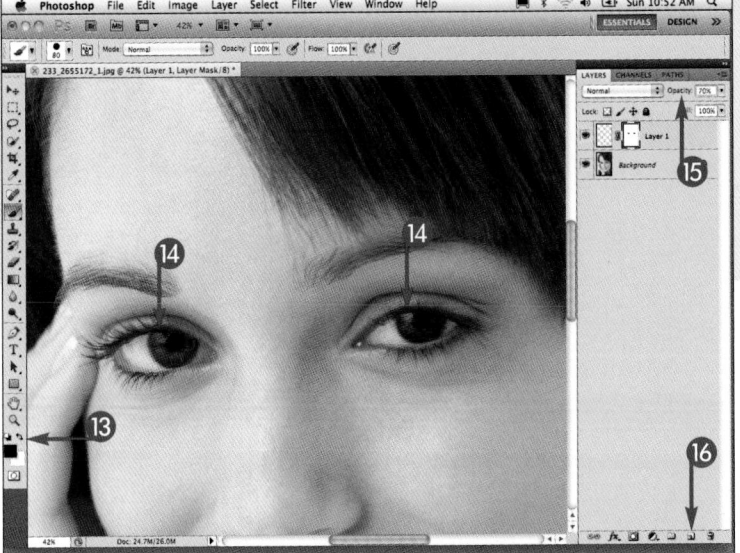

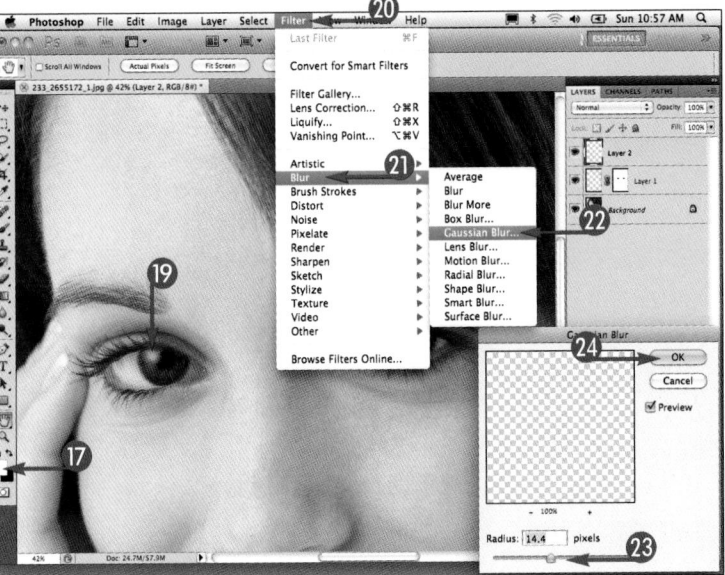

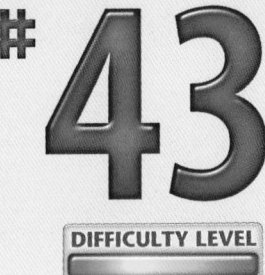
⑬ Click the Switch Colors icon to make black the foreground color.

⑭ Paint over the top of the catchlight so that it conforms to the upper eyelid.

⑮ Click Opacity and drag to the left to reduce the layer opacity to about 70% to slightly better blend the effect.

⑯ Click the New Layer button.

⑰ Press X to make white the foreground color.

⑱ Press the left bracket key multiple times to reduce the brush size to about half the previous size.

⑲ Click once in the center of each catchlight.

⑳ Click Filter.

㉑ Click Blur.

㉒ Click Gaussian Blur.

The Gaussian Blur dialog box appears.

㉓ Click and drag the Radius slider to soften the edges.

㉔ Click OK.

A soft-edged catchlight with a sparkle in the center appears in each eye.

TIPS

More Options!

You can refine the catchlights more by viewing the whole face at once. Press Option+spacebar (Alt+spacebar) and click to zoom out. Click and drag the Layer Opacity slider for each of the catchlight layers until you see a bright sparkle with a natural diffused edge.

Important!

The catchlights must correspond to the natural direction of the light to appear natural. If the light is coming from the right, the catchlights should be on the right side of the pupils, just slightly above the center.

Did You Know?

Studio portrait lighting is often arranged to intentionally create catchlights to help draw attention to the eyes. Different types of photographic lighting produce different styles of catchlights.

SELECTIVELY SHARPEN JUST THE EYES
to add focus

The final step to enhancing the eyes in a photograph is to sharpen the eye area. You want to add focus and draw the viewer into the photo, but you may not want to sharpen the rest of the face or the skin. You can selectively sharpen the eyes by using a Sharpen filter and then applying the filter with the History panel and History Brush.

You can use not only the Unsharp Mask filter for sharpening, but also the Smart Sharpen filter. This filter is not only easier to use, but it also has added features including a much larger preview.

After sharpening the entire portrait, you hide the effect using the History panel to go back to a version of the photo before the sharpening was applied. Then, using the History Brush, you can paint the sharpening effect specifically on the eye area where you want to draw the focus.

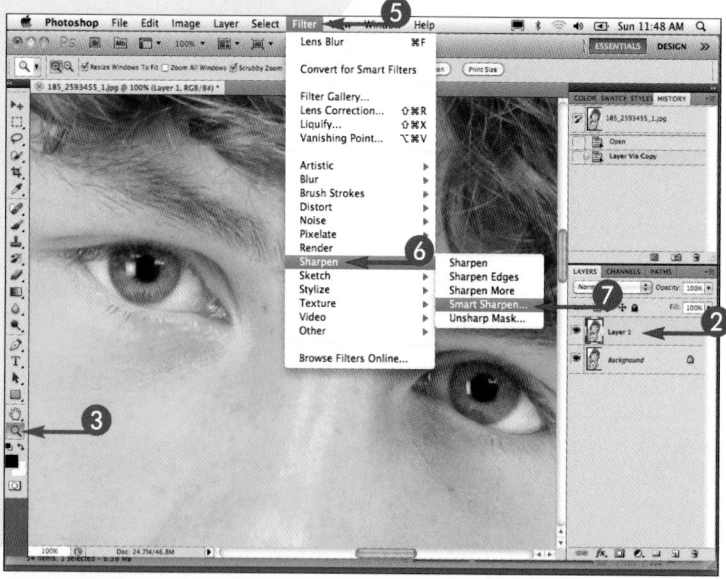

1 Arrange the workspace panels to see both the Layers panel and the History panel.

2 Press ⌘+J (Ctrl+J) to duplicate the Background layer.

3 Double-click the Zoom tool to view the image at 100%.

4 Press the spacebar, click in the image, and move it to see the eyes.

5 Click Filter.

6 Click Sharpen.

7 Click Smart Sharpen.

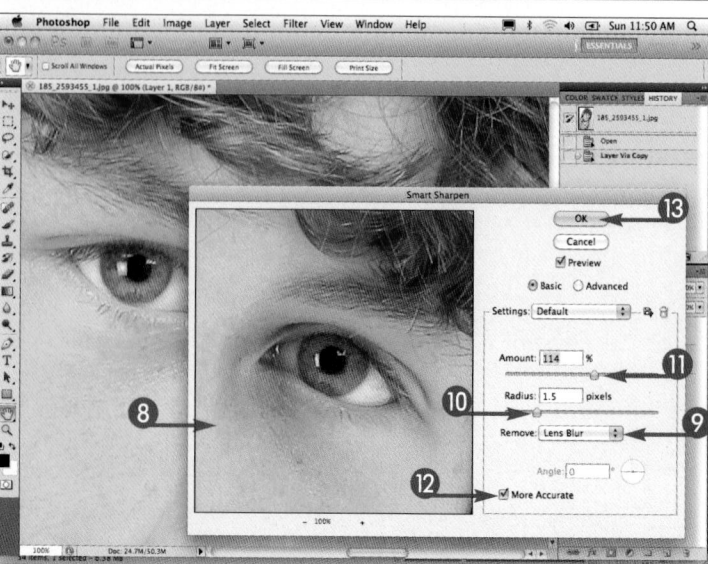

The Smart Sharpen dialog box appears.

8 Click in the Preview window and drag to see the eyes area.

9 Click here and select Lens Blur.

10 Click and drag the Radius slider to 1.5 to increase the area to be sharpened.

11 Click and drag the Amount slider to sharpen the eye, generally between 80 and 115 percent.

12 Click More Accurate (☐ changes to ☑).

13 Click OK to apply the sharpening.

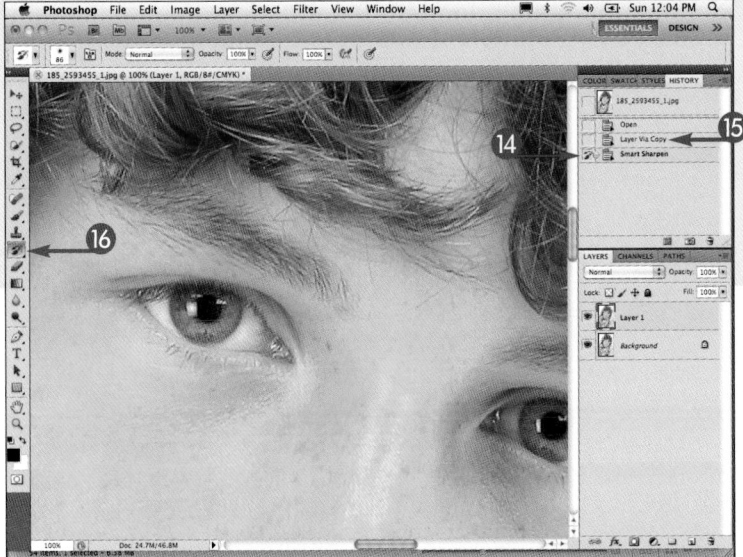

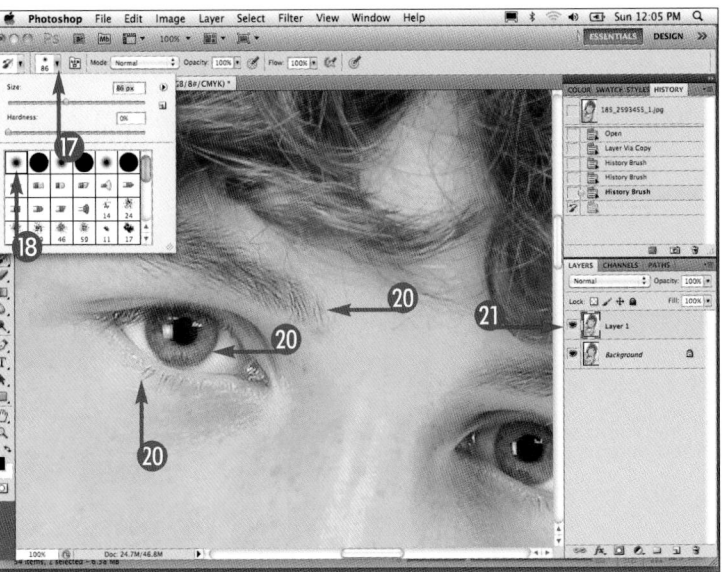

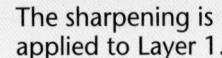

The sharpening is applied to Layer 1.

⑭ In the History panel, click the box to the left of the Smart Sharpen step to set the source for the History Brush.

⑮ In the History panel, click the previous state named Layer Via Copy.

⑯ Click the History Brush tool.

DIFFICULTY LEVEL

⑰ Click the Brush picker.

⑱ Click to select a soft-edged brush (0%).

⑲ Press the left or right bracket keys to adjust the brush size to be large enough to cover the edge of the eyes.

⑳ Paint over the eyes, eyelashes, and eyebrows with the History Brush to apply the sharpening.

㉑ Click the Eye icon for Layer 1 on and off to compare before and after sharpening.

The sharpening is applied only to the eye areas.

TIPS

Attention!

The Smart Sharpen filter applies only to one layer. If you have made other adjustment layers, you must merge them before applying the sharpening. Press ⌘+Option+Shift+E (Ctrl+Alt+Shift+E). The adjustment layers and the Background layers merge in the new layer. All the adjustment layers, Background copy or Layer 1, and original Background layers remain unchanged.

Did You Know?

Always view the image at 100% magnification when you use a sharpening filter to get the most accurate view on-screen of your changes. Still, the amount of detail visible in a print may be slightly different than what you see on the screen. The amount of detail can vary depending on the type of printer and paper used.

WHITEN TEETH
to improve a smile

You can greatly improve every portrait in which the subject is smiling by applying a little digital tooth-whitening. Yellow teeth always dull a smile as well as the overall look of the photo.

You first select the teeth and soften the selection, to avoid a visible line between the lightened areas and the rest of the image. Although you can make a selection in Photoshop in many ways, using the Quick Mask mode or the Quick Selection tool as described in

Chapter 2 works well when making a detailed selection such as selecting a person's teeth.

After the teeth are selected, whitening is a two-step process. You have to remove the yellow and then brighten the teeth by adjusting the saturation. As in previous tasks, zoom in to make the detailed selection, and then zoom out to see the whole image before adjusting the color. Digital tooth-whitening should be a subtle adjustment to keep the smile and the person looking natural.

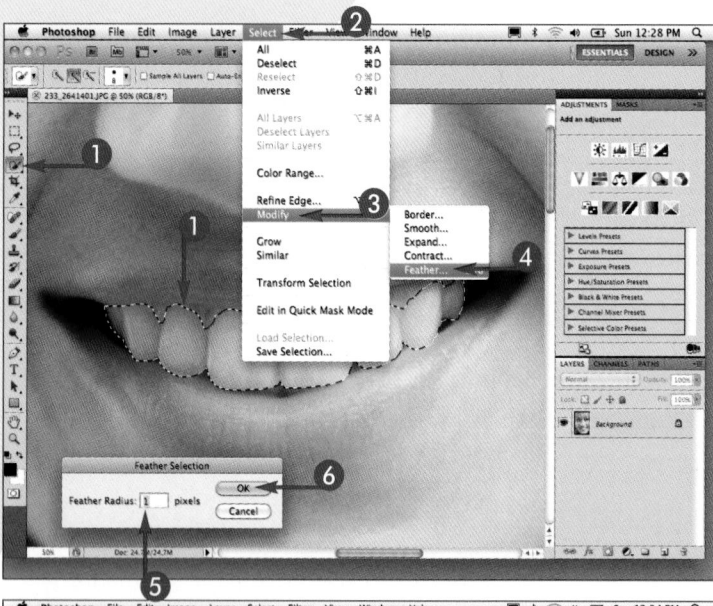

Note: Arrange the panels to see both the Layers and the Adjustments panels.

① Zoom in and make a selection of the teeth using the Quick Mask mode or the Quick Selection tool.

Note: To use the Quick Mask mode, see task #23. To use the Quick Selection tool, see task #21.

② Click Select.

③ Click Modify.

④ Click Feather.

The Feather Selection dialog box appears.

⑤ Type **1** in the Feather Radius field to slightly soften the edge of the selection.

⑥ Click OK.

⑦ Click the Zoom tool and zoom out to see the whole image.

⑧ Press ⌘+H (Ctrl+H) to hide the selection marquee.

The selection marquee is no longer visible, but the teeth are still selected.

⑨ Click the Hue/Saturation button to create a new adjustment layer.

The Hue/Saturation pane appears in the Adjustments panel, and a Hue/Saturation layer is created in the Layers panel.

⑩ Click here and select Yellows.

⑪ Click and drag the Saturation slider slowly to the left to remove the yellow.

⑫ Click here and select Master.

⑬ Click and drag the Lightness slider slowly to the right to brighten the teeth.

⑭ Press ⌘+D (Ctrl+D) to deselect the teeth.

⑮ Press ⌘+Shift+E (Ctrl+Shift+E) to merge all the visible layers into one layer.

TIPS

Try This!

When zooming in on an image, press and hold the spacebar; the pointer temporarily changes to the Hand tool. You can click and drag around your image with the Hand tool and easily move to the area that needs to be adjusted. When you release the spacebar, you change back to the tool that was previously selected.

Did You Know?

Feathering softens the edge of a selection and smoothes the transition between two distinct areas. You can also click Select and click Refine Edge to feather the selection edge. The default settings of the Refine Edge dialog box include a one-pixel feather. Click OK in the dialog box and continue lightening the teeth as shown here.

Enhance Colors, Tone, and Sharpness in Photos

Color is the heart of Photoshop. Whether you work on a design or a photograph, you often adjust the hue, saturation, and brightness of an image. Using Photoshop, you can fine-tune shadows and highlights or completely alter the overall tone of a photograph. You can transform a color photograph into a grayscale image, colorize an old grayscale image, or make a color image look like an antique colorized photograph. You can also tone a photo as photographers used to do in the darkroom by digitally dodging and burning. And you can create these effects in many different ways.

Because some pixel information is discarded whenever you make color and tonal adjustments, you should apply corrections on a duplicate layer, on separate layers, or on a Smart Object layer. Photoshop CS5's adjustment layers and the new

Adjustments panel also help you make some changes without permanently altering pixel values. In addition, opening or converting an image or a layer to a new Smart Object enables you to apply most filters as Smart Filters, making them continuously editable and nondestructive. Even when you sharpen a photograph to remove the softness created by the camera's processor, you can use a Smart Filter, so you can reedit the changes without altering pixels until you flatten the image.

Whenever you make color or tonal adjustments, start by calibrating and profiling your monitor as discussed in task #13. Otherwise, you may be changing colors that are not really in the image, and what you see on your monitor can look very different when it is printed.

Top 100

Improve an underexposed photo in
TWO STEPS

You may find a photograph that is perfect for your project or has the subject just the way you want, but the picture is underexposed. Although most of the details of a digital photograph are in the highlights, and as a rule it is better to overexpose than underexpose, you can still improve an underexposed photograph using a variety of tools in Photoshop. Sometimes you can make a quick correction using a duplicated layer and altering the layer blend mode as in task #16. You can also use Photoshop CS5's Adjustments panel and

quickly try an Exposure adjustment preset before you work with more complicated methods.

Depending on the photo, the exposure may appear corrected when you apply the Plus 1.0 or Plus 2.0 presets. For other images, you may need to add a bit more or less exposure using the sliders. You can even change the blend mode of the adjustment layer to increase the exposure and then dial it down and reduce the effect by changing the Opacity slider of the layer.

① With an underexposed photo open in Photoshop, click the disclosure triangle in the Adjustments panel to open the Exposure Presets.

② Click Plus 1.0.

● An Exposure adjustment layer is added and the photo appears lighter.

Note: The photo may look fine this way, or you can continue to vary the adjustment as in steps 3 and 4.

③ Click here and change the layer blend mode to Screen.

The photo appears even lighter.

④ With the adjustment layer selected, click Opacity and drag to the left until the underexposed image is improved.

● You can optionally click and drag the Exposure slider slowly to the right to increase the adjustment.

Improve an overexposed photo in
THREE STEPS

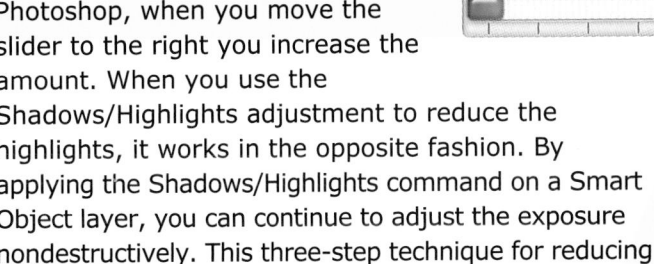

DIFFICULTY LEVEL

An overexposed photograph is impossible to salvage with traditional darkroom techniques. Too much light means that there is nothing in the film to print. However, the image sensor in a digital camera sees more of the lighter values, and it records more tonal differences in the brighter areas, or the right side of the histogram. As long as the highlights are not completely blown out or showing no information, you can improve an overly bright photograph with Photoshop CS5.

You can use the Shadows/Highlights command in the basic mode to effectively reduce the highlights.

With most dialog boxes in Photoshop, when you move the slider to the right you increase the amount. When you use the Shadows/Highlights adjustment to reduce the highlights, it works in the opposite fashion. By applying the Shadows/Highlights command on a Smart Object layer, you can continue to adjust the exposure nondestructively. This three-step technique for reducing the highlights and improving an overexposed photo is always worth testing before spending time with other methods or discarding the photo.

① Open an overexposed photo.

② Click Layer, Smart Objects, and Convert to Smart Object from the menu.

● The Background layer is converted to a Smart Object as in task #24.

③ Click Image.

④ Click Adjustments.

⑤ Click Shadows/Highlights.

The Shadows/Highlights dialog box appears.

⑥ Click and drag the Shadows slider to the left to 0%.

⑦ Click and drag the Highlights slider to the right until the image looks the way you want.

● You can optionally click Show More Options (☐ changes to ☑) to refine the adjustment using the other sliders.

⑧ Click OK.

The image exposure is improved.

REMOVE A COLORCAST
to improve the overall color

Whether you have a scanned image or one from a digital camera, your image may show a colorcast due to improper lighting, white balance settings, or other factors. A *colorcast* often appears as a reddish, bluish, or greenish tint over the whole image. Photoshop has many tools that you can use to remove colorcasts, including the White Balance setting in Camera Raw, and sometimes you may need to try different ones, depending on the photograph. Using the Match Color command as shown here to remove a colorcast is simple and often works well.

Intended for matching the colors between two images, the Match Color command uses advanced algorithms to adjust the brightness, color saturation, and color balance in an image. Because you can adjust the controls in different combinations, using this command on just one image gives you better control over the color and luminance of the image than many other tools.

When using the Match Color command on a duplicated layer, you can use the layer's Opacity slider to blend the results with the Background layer to achieve the best color for your image, as well as compare the before and after images.

1 Press ⌘+J (Ctrl+J) to duplicate the Background layer.

2 Click Image.

3 Click Adjustments.

4 Click Match Color.

The Match Color dialog box appears.

5 Click Preview (☐ changes to ☑).

6 Click Neutralize to remove the colorcast (☐ changes to ☑).

The overall colorcast is removed.

7 Click and drag the Fade slider slowly to the right to reduce the effect, if necessary.

8 Click and drag the Color Intensity slider to the right to increase the color range, if necessary.

9 Click and drag the Luminance slider to the right to increase the luminance, if necessary.

10 Click OK to apply the change.

11 Click Opacity and drag to the left to adjust the overall effect, if necessary.

The colorcast is removed and the colors appear more natural.

TIPS

Did You Know?

You can view the floating Histogram panel and see the color changes as they are made. Click Window and click Histogram to display the Histogram panel. Click and drag the Histogram panel so that you can keep it open and still see the image and your other panels.

More Options!

If there is an area in the image that is normally neutral gray, you can also correct a colorcast using the Levels command. Click the Levels button (▦) in the Adjustments panel to create a new adjustment layer. Click the Gray Point eyedropper, the middle eyedropper in the Levels pane. Click in the part of the image that should be neutral gray to neutralize the colorcast. If necessary, click another area until the colors appear natural.

COLORIZE
a black-and-white photograph

Hand-coloring a photograph can be a difficult process using traditional paints and traditional film photos. With Photoshop, hand-coloring an old black-and-white image is much easier. You can use any black-and-white photo, called a *grayscale image,* and paint areas using any colors that you choose.

You can start with larger areas and then focus in on specific parts to colorize individually and on additional layers. By making selections of detailed areas and then applying the colors, you can be as precise as necessary to achieve the effect. Zoom in to select and

paint detailed areas and then zoom out to see the overall effect. Continue making different selections and choosing other colors until the whole image is colorized. After the entire image is painted, you can lower the opacity of each colored layer as a final touch.

You can vary the size of the Brush tool as you paint using the left and right bracket keys. If you are using a pressure-sensitive stylus and tablet, open the Brushes panel, click Shape Dynamics, and set the Control to Pen Pressure.

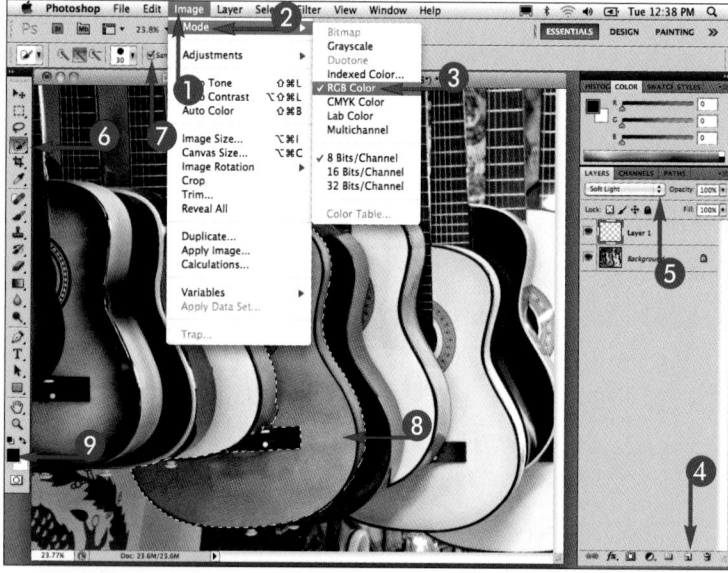

① Click Image.

② Click Mode.

③ Click RGB Color.

The color mode changes, but the image on the screen does not.

④ Click the New Layer button in the Layers panel.

⑤ Click here and select Soft Light.

⑥ Click the Quick Selection tool.

⑦ Click Sample All Layers in the Options bar (☐ changes to ☑).

⑧ Click in an area to make a selection.

Note: You can optionally use any of the other selection tools to complete the selection.

⑨ Click the foreground color in the Tools panel.

The Color Picker appears.

⑩ Click and drag the Color slider to select a color range.

⑪ Click in the Color Preview box to select a color.

⑫ Click OK to close the dialog box.

49

DIFFICULTY LEVEL

⑬ Press B to select the Brush tool.

⑭ Click here to open the Brush picker.

⑮ Click the soft-edged brush.

⑯ Press the left or right bracket keys to adjust the brush size.

⑰ Paint over the selected areas to apply the color.

⑱ Click Opacity and drag to the left to adjust the color for the layer.

⑲ Repeat steps 4 to 17 until the entire image is painted.

The black-and-white photo now appears in color.

TIPS

Try This!

Instead of clicking the foreground color, simply click in the Set Foreground Color box in the Color panel to open the Color Picker without changing tools. You can also position the cursor over the Color panel and click in the color ramp to select a color — all without changing tools. Click and drag the RGB sliders to adjust the colors.

More Options!

You can select realistic colors for a grayscale image by sampling the colors from a color image that has similar subjects. Keep the other image open on the screen while you are colorizing the grayscale photo. With the Color Picker open, position the cursor outside the dialog box to sample real colors from the color image. Then paint in the grayscale image with those colors.

CUSTOM GRAYSCALE PHOTO

You can convert a color image to black and white using many different tools and techniques in Photoshop, and because there are no fixed rules on which colors in an image should match specific levels of gray, you can create a variety of different grayscale images from just one color photograph.

The Black and White adjustment in Photoshop CS5 offers a powerful conversion method with complete visual control. You interactively determine what shade of gray is applied to any particular color range in the image by moving the sliders in the Adjustments

panel. And because you are editing using a nondestructive adjustment layer, the original image data is preserved.

Although you can access the Black and White adjustment layer from the menu, using the Adjustments panel in Photoshop CS5 is faster. In addition, the Black and White pane of the Adjustments panel includes a number of presets that you can use or modify, or you can create and save your own preset.

① Click Window and Adjustments to make sure the Adjustments panel is open.

② Open an image to convert to grayscale.

③ Click the Black and White adjustment layer button.

The image converts to a default grayscale image.

④ Click Auto to see the changes.

The grays in the image change.

Note: *The Auto function in the Black and White Adjustments pane maps the colors to grays differently from the Default setting.*

⑤ Click and drag any of the sliders to vary the grays according to the colors in the image.

The gray tones change.

 **50**

⑥ Click here and select one of the presets, such as Infrared.

The grayscale image changes accordingly.

⑦ Click and hold the View Previous State button to temporarily view the previous black-and-white conversion.

⑧ Click and drag any of the sliders to customize the preset settings.

TIPS

Important!

Converting a color image to grayscale is not the same as changing the mode to grayscale, which in effect throws away image data. When you convert a color image to grayscale, you map individual colors to different shades of gray, preserving the same complete tonal range that exists in the color image. The image remains in RGB mode.

Change It!

You can select a color to tone the grayscale image. Click the Tint check box in the Black & White pane (☐ changes to ☑). The color box next to the check box fills with a color. Click the color box to open the Select Target Color dialog box. Click any color and the image updates dynamically.

More Options!

You can also convert a color image to a grayscale image using the LAB Black & White Technique action in the Actions panel. Click Window and click Actions to open the panel. Then click the LAB Black & White Technique and click the start button on the Actions panel to automatically convert your image.

ADD A CREATIVE TOUCH
with a little color

You can hand-color an old grayscale photograph with Photoshop to create an antique look. You can also start with a color image, convert it to grayscale as in task #50, and then colorize it to get a very different look; this type of colorization is much easier to accomplish. You can colorize the entire photo or just one area for effect. You can brush the color into specific areas and even create a more or less muted colorized effect by changing the opacity of the brush as you paint. Start with a low opacity setting and bring the original color back gradually.

If you have already saved a grayscale version of the photo without the original layers, you can still use the method shown here. First open both the original color image and the converted grayscale photo. Using the Move tool, press and hold Shift as you click and drag the grayscale version onto the original color photo. Then follow steps 4 to 14 of this task using the Eraser tool instead of the Brush tool to paint a very creative image.

① Open a color photo.

② Follow steps 3 to 5 of task #50 to apply a black-and-white adjustment layer.

The photo appears in grayscale.

● The color photo is the Background layer. The Black & White adjustment layer with a white mask appears as the second layer.

③ Click the mask thumbnail in the Layers panel to select it.

④ Click the Default Colors icon to reset the foreground to black and background to white.

⑤ Click the Brush tool (▨).

⑥ Click here to open the Brush picker.

⑦ Click the soft-edged brush.

8 Click the Airbrush button.

9 Double-click here and type **20** to lower the opacity.

10 Paint over the area to be colorized.

11 Double-click here again and type **40** to increase the opacity.

12 Press the left bracket key several times to reduce the brush size.

13 Paint over parts of the colored area to increase the color.

The image is selectively colorized and the viewer's attention is drawn to the perfect spot.

TIPS

Keyboard Shortcut!

You can change the size of the Brush tool by pressing the right bracket key to increase the size and the left bracket key to reduce the size. With a Wacom pen tablet, you can click the Tablet Pressure Controls Size and the Tablet Pressure Controls Opacity buttons in the Options panel (and). You can then press harder for more opacity and a larger size brush and vice versa.

Did You Know?

You can also vary the hardness or softness of the Eraser or Brush tools using the keyboard instead of the Brush picker. Click the Eraser or Brush tool to select it. Press and hold Shift as you repeatedly press the right bracket key to increase the hardness or the left bracket key to increase the softness.

DODGE AND BURN
with a special layer

Dodging and burning are photographic techniques describing the traditional darkroom methods for brightening and darkening tones in an image. You can effectively dodge and burn a digital image in Photoshop.

Although Photoshop CS5 includes digital dodge and burn tools, these tools directly affect the pixels on the layer, making your edits permanent and destructive. Using a separate layer and the Brush tool to dodge and burn not only adjusts the image nondestructively, it also gives you greater control over the adjustment.

You can digitally dodge and burn on a separate layer with two different methods. One uses a separate

empty layer in the Soft Light blend mode. The other uses a separate layer filled with neutral gray in the Overlay blend mode. You can use the method that you prefer or that works best on your particular image. With either type of layer, you dodge by painting with white and burn by painting with black on the layer. By setting the brush opacity to about 30% to start, you can increase the effect as you work by brushing over an area multiple times.

Both methods give you complete control over dodging and burning digitally.

Use a Layer in the Soft Light Blend Mode

① Click the Default Colors icon to reset the foreground and background colors to black and white.

② Click the New Layer button to create a new empty layer.

③ Click here and select Soft Light for the layer blend mode.

④ Click the Brush tool (⬛).

⑤ Click here to open the Brush picker.

⑥ Select the soft-edged brush.

⑦ Double-click here and type **30** to set the brush opacity to 30%.

⑧ Click and drag to paint with black in the light areas of the image to darken, or digitally burn them.

⑨ Click the Switch Colors icon to reverse the foreground and background colors, making the foreground color white.

Note: You can also press X to reverse the foreground and background colors.

⑩ Click and drag to paint with white in the dark areas of the image to lighten, or digitally dodge them.

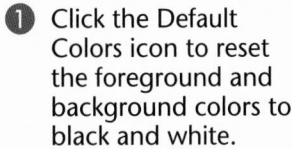

Use a Layer in the Overlay Blend Mode

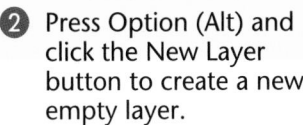
① Click the Default Colors icon to reset the foreground and background colors to black and white.

② Press Option (Alt) and click the New Layer button to create a new empty layer.

The New Layer dialog box appears.

③ Click here and select Overlay.

④ Click Fill with Overlay-Neutral Color (50% Gray) (☐ changes to ☑).

⑤ Click OK.

● A new layer appears filled with gray in the Layers panel, but the image in the main window is unchanged.

⑥ Repeat steps 4 to 10 in the Soft Light blend mode method described in the first part of this task.

More Options!

You can even create separate layers for dodging and burning using either method. Name one layer Burn and the other Dodge. You can then adjust the layer opacity of the dodge or burn layer individually to give you even more control and use the Layers panel's Opacity slider to adjust the effect.

Try This!

If the darkening or lightening is not as strong as you want, you can just release the mouse button and click and paint over the same area again. Because you are using the brush at a low opacity to start, you can paint over an area multiple times to increase the effect.

Did You Know?

When you use a layer filled with 50% gray in the Overlay blend mode, the layer displays a gray thumbnail in the Layers panel, but appears as a transparent layer over the image in the main window.

Chapter 5: Enhance Colors, Tone, and Sharpness in Photos

Increase saturation subtly using a
VIBRANCE ADJUSTMENT LAYER

Vibrance is similar to saturation in that it increases or decreases the intensity of the colors. Unlike saturation, vibrance affects only the less saturated areas and minimizes any effect on the more saturated areas in the image, thus increasing the intensity of the colors while maintaining a more natural appearance. The Vibrance adjustment also improves skin tones better than the Saturation adjustment, which saturates all the colors in the image.

You can increase the intensity of the colors in an image without altering the original pixels by using a Vibrance adjustment layer. You can apply the

adjustment by clicking Layer, selecting New Adjustment Layer, and selecting Vibrance. However, you can also use the Adjustments panel, which enables you to quickly apply a variety of image modifications as nondestructive adjustment layers. The panel includes one-click buttons as well as a number of presets for the various options.

You can adjust both the vibrance and the saturation using the sliders in the Adjustments panel's Vibrance pane to increase the intensity of the colors in your image.

1 Open an image.

2 Click Window.

3 Click Adjustments to open the Adjustments panel.

Note: You can optionally click Essentials to have the Adjustments panel included in right panel dock.

4 Click the Vibrance button.

The Vibrance adjustments pane appears.

5 Click and drag the Vibrance slider to the right to increase the intensity of the colors.

6 Click and drag the Saturation slider slightly to the right to increase all the colors if necessary.

The colors in the image intensify.

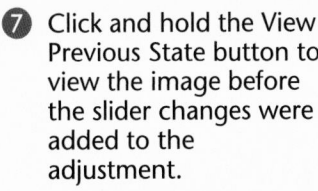
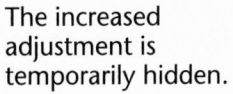

7 Click and hold the View Previous State button to view the image before the slider changes were added to the adjustment.

The increased adjustment is temporarily hidden.

8 Release the mouse button to view the adjustment again.

9 Click and drag to adjust the sliders to increase or decrease the vibrance and saturation.

10 Click the Return to Adjustment List arrow to view all the options in the Adjustments panel, and apply more adjustments if desired.

TIPS

Did You Know?
You can selectively increase the vibrance of an area in an image by clicking the Sponge tool (🔘), selecting Saturate for the Mode in the Options bar, and then clicking Vibrance in the Options bar (☐ changes to ☑).

More Options!
You can remove the Vibrance adjustment layer and return to the list of Adjustments by clicking the trash can (🗑) in the Adjustments panel.

You can return to the list of adjustments by clicking the Return to Adjustment List arrow (◀) any time without removing the adjustment you just applied.

Try This!
Click the Eye icon (👁) in the Adjustments panel to hide the effect of the adjustment layer. Click the Previous State button (🔘) in the Adjustments panel or press the backslash key to temporarily view the previous adjustment state. Click the Reset button (🔄) to reset the adjustment to the default settings.

SHARPEN THE PHOTO
to correct digital softening

Whether your photos are scanned in or come from a digital camera, most images can benefit from some sharpening. Image softness is inherent to digital capture. The sensor technology in digital cameras and scanners automatically introduce softness when recording images. Digital cameras require a blurring filter in front of the light-capturing sensor to average the details into pixels. Most digital cameras then apply some automatic sharpening during in-camera processing to counteract the softness. However, because images are most pleasing when they are sharp, you can sharpen photos as the final editing step.

You can use various Photoshop tools to sharpen a digital photo. The Sharpen, Sharpen Edges, and Sharpen More filters offer less control than the Smart Sharpen and Unsharp Mask filters. The Unsharp Mask filter can require more experimentation when printing because it often displays a stronger sharpening effect on-screen than when the image is printed at a high resolution. The Smart Sharpen filter has a large preview box and lets you control the amount of sharpening in shadow and highlight areas; it is often the best filter to use for digital sharpening.

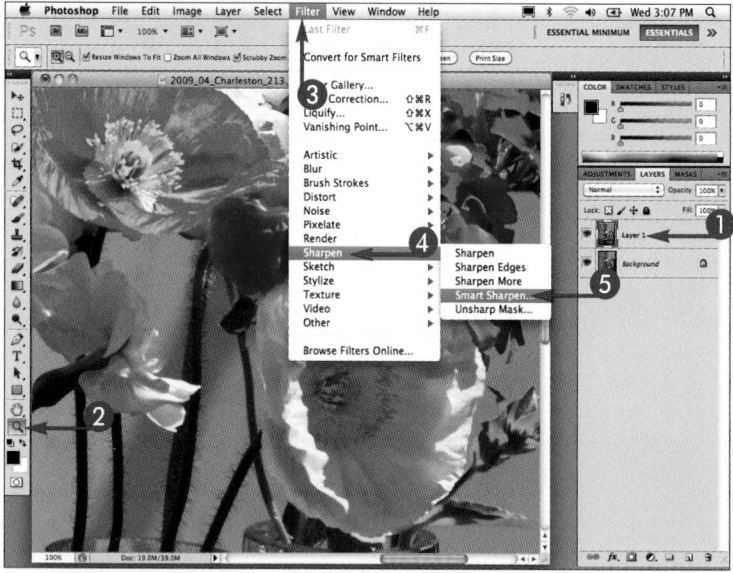

① Press ⌘+J (Ctrl+J) to duplicate the Background layer.

② Double-click the Zoom tool to zoom the image to 100%.

③ Click Filter.

④ Click Sharpen.

⑤ Click Smart Sharpen.

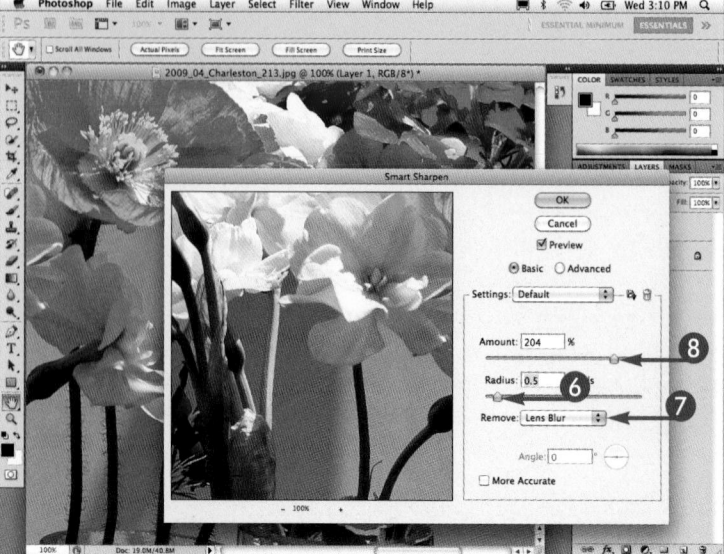

The Smart Sharpen dialog box appears.

⑥ Click and drag the slider to reduce the default radius amount to 0.5 as a starting point.

⑦ Click here and select Lens Blur.

Note: *Lens Blur finds the edges and detail and produces a sharper effect with fewer halos.*

⑧ Click and slowly drag the Amount slider to the right until you see halos on the edges.

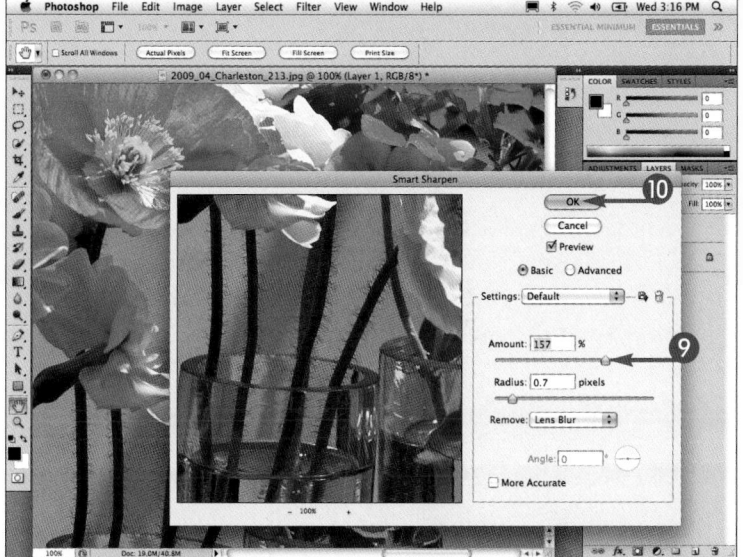

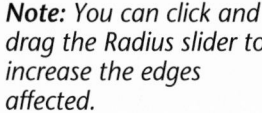

⑨ Click and drag the Amount slider slowly to the left just until the halos are no longer visible.

Note: *You can click and drag the Radius slider to increase the edges affected.*

⑩ Click OK.

DIFFICULTY LEVEL

The image appears sharper.

⑪ Press and hold the spacebar and click and drag in the image to view different areas.

⑫ Click Fit Screen to view the whole image.

TIPS

Did You Know?

Digital sharpening is actually an illusion. It does not actually sharpen anything but rather exaggerates edges by increasing the contrast of adjacent pixels. Sharpening cannot correct an image blurred from camera shake or a moving subject.

More Options!

You can sharpen the photo as a whole, use a selection, or paint on a layer mask to sharpen only target regions in the image. You can use the Sharpen tool to paint directly over specific areas to sharpen them. You can even sharpen individual color channels, such as the red and green channels, to avoid exaggerating the noise in the third channel.

Important!

The amount of sharpening to apply is often a matter of personal choice. However, oversharpening creates a halo effect around the edges. To sharpen images for viewing on-screen, sharpen until the image looks pleasing on your calibrated monitor. To sharpen images for print, add just enough sharpening so the image looks slightly oversharpened on the monitor.

APPLY HIGH PASS SHARPENING
to increase edge sharpness

You can increase the sharpness on edges in an image using a combination of the Unsharp Mask filter and the High Pass filter. With this technique you first apply a sharpening to a duplicated layer, then duplicate the sharpened layer and apply the High Pass filter. This filter has the opposite effect of the Gaussian Blur filter. Instead of blurring edges, the High Pass filter removes any details or pixels without strong edges and retains the details where the sharpest color transitions occur.

You should generally sharpen your image in small amounts and at different times in the editing process. You first sharpen to correct the capturing blur caused by scanning or the digital camera. After resizing and color-correcting the image, you can sharpen a copy of the image for your intended type of output, that is, for viewing on a monitor or for printing.

If you sharpen your image on a separate layer, you can apply a different type of sharpening when you want to use the photo for a different type of output.

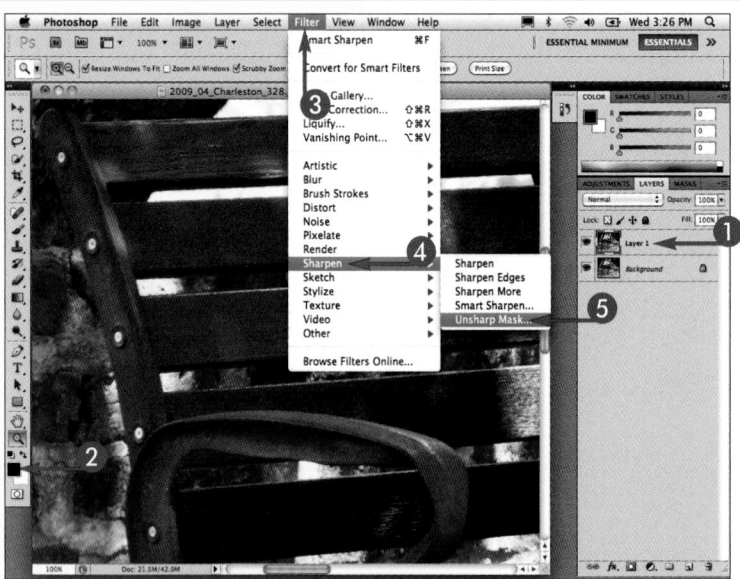

1. Press ⌘+J (Ctrl+J) to duplicate the Background layer.

2. Double-click the Zoom tool to zoom the image to 100%.

3. Click Filter.

4. Click Sharpen.

5. Click Unsharp Mask.

The Unsharp Mask dialog box appears.

6. Click and drag the Radius slider to reduce the default radius amount to 0.5 as a starting point.

7. Click and drag the Threshold amount to 2.

   Note: Threshold determines how much contrast pixels must have from adjacent pixels before they have sharpening applied as edge pixels. The default Threshold value (0) sharpens all pixels in the image. Try Threshold values between 2 and 20 to avoid introducing noise or posterization.

8. Click and slowly drag the Amount slider to the right until you see halos on the edges.

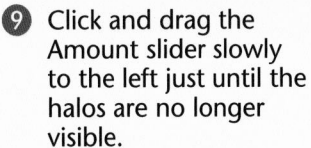

⑨ Click and drag the Amount slider slowly to the left just until the halos are no longer visible.

Note: *Click the image in the preview window and hold down the mouse to see how the image looks without the sharpening. Drag in the preview window to see different parts of the image, and click + or – to zoom in or out.*

⑩ Click OK.

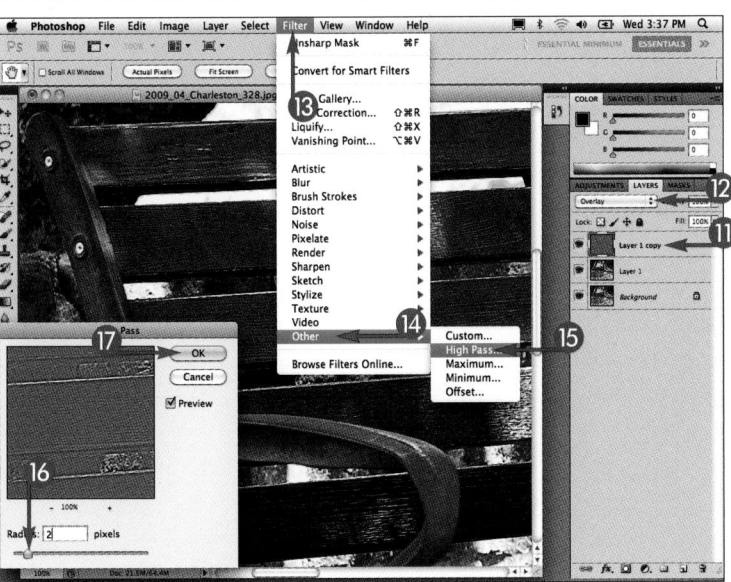

The image appears sharper.

⑪ Press ⌘+J (Ctrl+J) to duplicate the sharpened layer.

⑫ Click here and change the blend mode to Overlay.

⑬ Click Filter.

⑭ Click Other.

⑮ Click High Pass.

The High Pass filter dialog box appears.

⑯ Click and drag the Radius slider to 2 as a starting point and increase as necessary.

⑰ Click OK.

**TIPS**

Important!
If the image contains noise, sharpening can make the noise more pronounced. You can reduce the image noise before applying any form of sharpening.

More Options!
After applying the High Pass filter, you can use the Eraser tool (⌹) and set the Brush Opacity in the Options bar to 50%. Then brush over edges that seem too sharp in the image to reduce or soften the effect.

Did You Know?
Sharpening sometimes shifts the colors along the edges in the image. When you use a duplicate layer to sharpen your image, you can change the layer's blending mode to Luminosity and avoid the changed edge colors.

Process Photos in Camera Raw

Camera Raw is a plug-in automatically included with Photoshop CS5. RAW is a file format, such as CR2 on advanced Canon cameras or NEF or Nikon's advanced cameras.

All digital cameras first record the raw data on the sensor, then the camera's internal processor converts the data into the file you see on the back of the camera. If you shoot in the JPEG file format, the camera's built-in processor applies the manufacturer's predetermined settings, and it decides what capture data to keep and what data to throw away to create a pleasing image. It also automatically compresses the file. When you make any changes to a JPEG or even a TIFF file, either with Camera Raw or Photoshop, you are changing pixels that have already been processed and compressed inside the camera.

If you shoot in the RAW format, the RAW file includes all the original uncompressed captured data. You can then process the file with Camera Raw in your computer, so you can control the desired tonal rendition, color balance, saturation, and other characteristics of the final image.

You can edit JPEG and TIFF files as well as RAW files with Camera Raw, and the interface makes many types of edits easy. When you make adjustments with Camera Raw, the edits are nondestructive — all the image data in the file, whether it is a JPEG, TIFF, or RAW file, is preserved and the adjustments are stored as metadata, in a separate small file, called a sidecar XMP data file.

Top 100

SET THE PREFERENCES
to open any image in Camera Raw

DIFFICULTY LEVEL

Most digital cameras can create JPEGs and sometimes TIFF files. Advanced digital cameras can also write a manufacturer's proprietary camera RAW format, such as NEF or CR2. The DNG file format, an open format created by Adobe, is also a RAW file.

The RAW file format is the most direct representation of what the camera sensor captured because the data is not processed or compressed in the camera. Such proprietary RAW files require specific software to convert the file in the computer. Photoshop CS5 includes the Camera Raw plug-in to convert RAW

images. However, Camera Raw is a powerful image editor on its own.

Camera Raw automatically launches whenever you open a manufacturer's proprietary RAW file. However, you can set the Camera Raw preferences to automatically open both JPEGs and TIFFs as well and take advantage of the Camera Raw editing tools.

You can then open any photo using Camera Raw and make specific adjustments. The edits are visible in the image on your monitor; however, they are actually saved as data. You have not altered any of the pixels in the file.

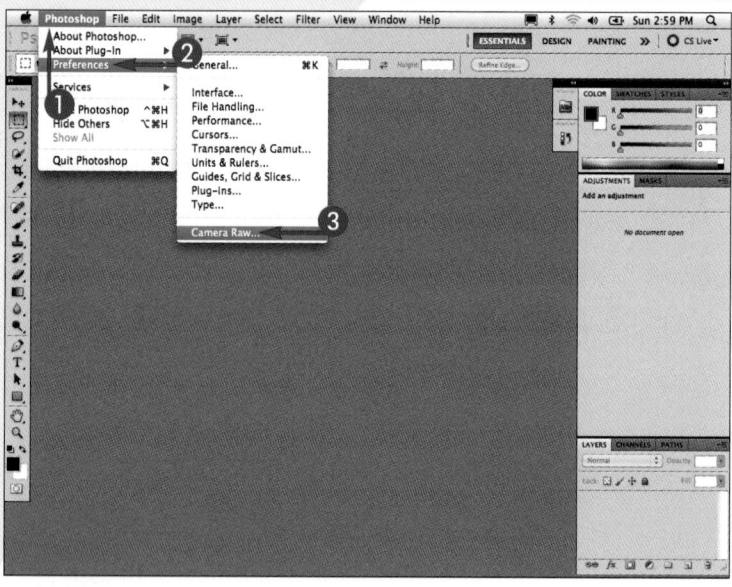

Set the Camera Raw Preferences to Open JPEGs and TIFFs

1 Click Photoshop (Edit).

2 Click Preferences.

3 Click Camera Raw.

The Camera Raw Preferences dialog box appears.

4 Click here and select Automatically Open All Supported JPEGs.

5 Click here and select Automatically Open All Supported TIFFs.

6 Click OK to save the Camera Raw preferences.

CROP AND STRAIGHTEN #57
in Camera Raw

Although you can straighten and crop an image in two simple steps using the Ruler tool and then the Crop tool in Photoshop, you can actually straighten and crop an image in one step in Camera Raw.

If you straighten and crop an image with Photoshop, the cropped areas are permanently deleted from the file. With Camera Raw, you can go back to the original photo and make changes.

Using Camera Raw's Straighten tool, you can click and drag along what should be the horizon or a horizontal line in the image. You can also draw along

what should be a vertical line in the image. When you let go of the mouse or raise the Wacom pen, the image is automatically straightened and the crop rectangle surrounds the largest available area.

You can then open the image in Photoshop to continue making adjustments, and you can save the image in other file formats, such as DNG, JPEG, TIFF, or PSD. However, although you can use Camera Raw to open and edit the original RAW file from the camera, you cannot save an image in that original file format.

① Follow the steps in the previous task.

② From Photoshop, Bridge, or the Mini Bridge, open a photo that needs to be straightened.

   The file automatically opens in Camera Raw.

③ Click the Straighten tool.

④ Click and drag a line across an element that should be horizontal or vertical.

⑤ Release the mouse or lift the Wacom pen.

   The image is automatically straightened and shows the crop rectangle around it.

● The Crop tool is automatically selected.

⑥ Click and drag on a corner anchor to rotate more if necessary.

⑦ Click Open Image.

   The cropped version of the image opens in Photoshop.

● You can optionally click Save Image and select the location and file type in the Save Options dialog box.

RECOVER HIGHLIGHTS
with Camera Raw

The Recovery slider is one of the many valuable tools in Camera Raw. The Recovery slider can often reduce or remove the clipped highlights. Clipped or blown highlights print as completely white areas because the image has no pixel information in these areas. Clipped highlights can ruin an otherwise good photograph and are often difficult to control with other tools.

With an image open in Camera Raw, you can see the blown-out highlights by clicking the Highlight Clipping warning triangle in the histogram. The highlights

without any colored pixels appear in red. Conversely, clicking the Shadow Clipping warning triangle in the histogram makes the overly dark shadow areas or completely black areas with no tonal range appear in blue.

The Recovery slider works in combination with the Exposure slider. Using both sliders, you can improve the exposure and prevent most of the highlights from being completely blown out. The Exposure and the Recovery sliders are located on the Basic tab.

① With the Camera Raw Preferences set as in task #56, open a photo from Photoshop, Bridge, or the Mini Bridge.

The file automatically opens in Camera Raw.

Note: You can also open most camera manufacturers' RAW files by double-clicking the file in any folder or in Bridge.

② Click the clipped highlights button to view the overexposed highlights.

The blown-out highlights appear in red.

③ Click the clipped shadows button to view any underexposed shadows.

The underexposed shadows appear in blue.

Note: Underexposed shadows can be adjusted using the Exposure or Fill Light sliders depending on the image.

④ Click and drag the Recovery slider to the right.

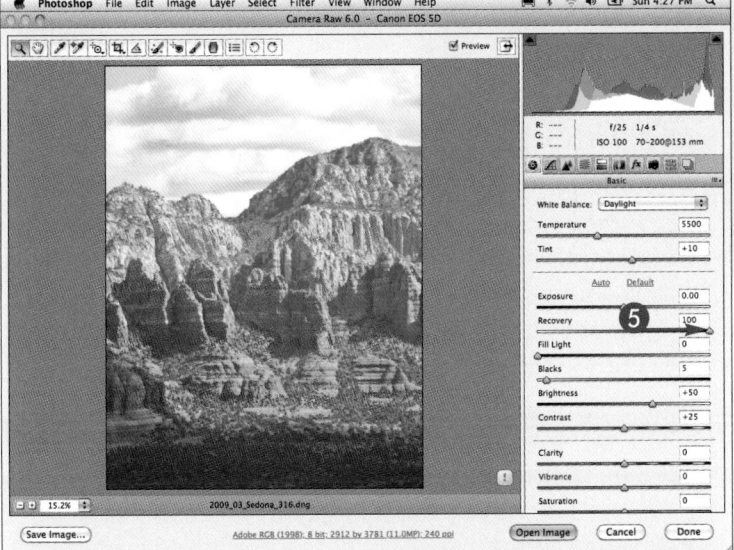

The red-colored highlights are reduced or removed.

⑤ Click and drag the Recovery slider slowly back to the left just until there are no more red-colored highlights.

#58

DIFFICULTY LEVEL

The blown highlights are removed and the photo displays a better exposure.

⑥ Click Open Image to open the image in Photoshop.

Note: You can optionally click Save Image to save the image with the new adjustments without opening the image.

TIPS

Did You Know?
The latest version of Camera Raw includes an Adjustment Brush tool (🖌) so you can selectively paint Exposure, Clarity, Brightness, and other adjustments onto specific areas of a photo. You can then refine the amount of the adjustments by moving the appropriate sliders. You can also use the Graduated Filter tool (▢) in Camera Raw to apply a gradual blend of selected adjustments over specific areas of the photo.

Try This!
You can quickly access the Camera Raw preferences from within Camera Raw by clicking the Open Preferences Dialog button (▤) in the Camera Raw toolbar.

More Options!
The Fill Light slider in Camera Raw performs changes similar to the Shadows/Highlights adjustment in Photoshop CS5. The Fill Light slider brightens only the shadows without changing other values. The Blacks slider changes the black points in the photo, darkening it.

CHANGE THE WHITE BALANCE
to a group of images in Camera Raw

A digital camera records the white balance setting as metadata. This data is applied when you open the file in the Camera Raw dialog box. You can easily adjust the white balance by using the White Balance tool and specifying an object that should be white or gray, or clicking a gray card if you included one in an image. Camera Raw then determines the color of the light in which the scene was shot and automatically adjusts the colors in the image to make those objects appear neutral-colored.

One of the benefits of opening all the images in Camera Raw is that you can not only edit one photo at a time, but you can work on one photo and then apply the identical changes to multiple images opened at the same time. This is particularly useful in adjusting the white balance of a group of photos taken at the same time and under the same lighting conditions.

You can select photos of the same or different file types from the Open dialog box, Bridge, or the Mini Bridge. When they open in Camera Raw, you make the edits to one photo and then synchronize that edit with other open images in the Camera Raw dialog box.

① From Photoshop, Bridge, or the Mini Bridge, ⌘+click (Ctrl+click) multiple images captured in the same light and open them.

The images all appear in Camera Raw.

② Click to select an image with a white or gray reference.

Note: The image shown here uses the Digital GrayCap white balance card from www.sjphoto.com/ graycap.html.

The central image changes.

③ Click the White Balance tool.

④ Click the reference area or an area that should be white or neutral gray.

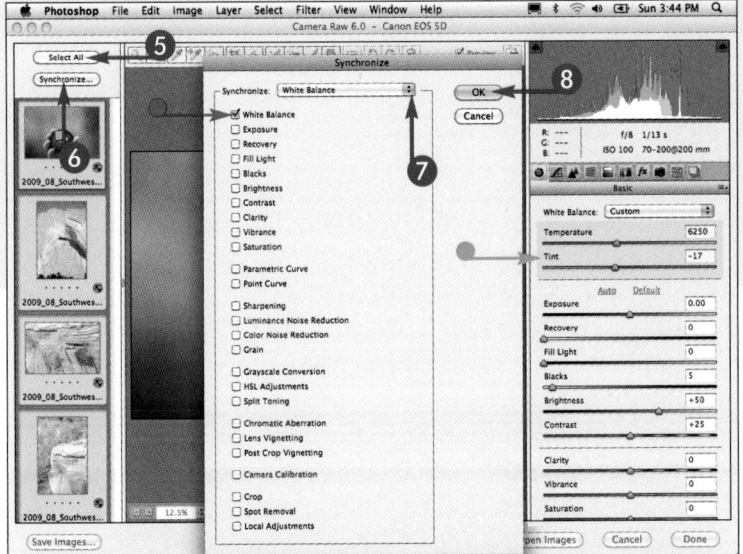

● The white balance changes and the Temperature and Tint sliders adjust accordingly.

⑤ Click Select All or Shift+click the other images in the Camera Raw dialog box.

⑥ Click Synchronize.

The Synchronize dialog box appears.

⑦ Click here and select White Balance.

● Only the White Balance check box remains checked.

⑧ Click OK.

● The white balance changes in all the other selected images.

TIPS

More Options!

You can convert most RAW files from the various camera manufacturers into DNG files using the Adobe DNG converter, available on Adobe. com. You will then be able to open them in the future even if the manufacturer no longer supports the older file formats.

Important!

The Temperature and Tint sliders adjust to make the selected color as neutral as possible. When you select and click a white area, avoid clicking a highlight area that contains a specular highlight. You can always double-click the White Balance tool (🖊) to reset White Balance to As Shot and try a different area.

Did You Know?

After you process and edit a camera RAW file using the Camera Raw plug-in, an Edit icon (🔳) appears on the image thumbnail in Bridge. If the image has been cropped, the Crop tool icon (🔳) appears.

Use the Targeted Adjustment tool in
CAMERA RAW

Think of a camera RAW file as your photo negative. When you process the photo in Camera Raw, you can reprocess the file at any time because although changes are viewable, you have not altered any pixels, so you can continue to make changes to render the image as you want it to appear.

Once you have made adjustments in the Basic tab, you can fine-tune the image using the other tabs in the Camera Raw dialog box. You can click the Tone Curve tab to make adjustments to the values in specific tonal ranges in the image. With the

Parametric Curve, the curve on the graph in the Parametric tab, you can adjust areas of highlight, lights, darks, or shadows depending on where you move the split arrows at the bottom of the graph. The light and dark regions affect the central areas of the curve and the tones in the image, whereas the highlights and shadows affect the edges of the tonal range. You can make changes by dragging the specific sliders. You can also use the Targeted Adjustment tool and click and drag in specific areas directly on the image.

① Open an image in Camera Raw and make White Balance and Basic changes as in previous tasks.

② Click the Tone Curve tab.

The pane changes to the Tone Curve.

③ Click the Targeted Adjustment tool.

④ Click an area in the image that should be lighter and drag the tool slowly up.

The light areas are brightened and the tone curve changes.

The Highlights and Lights sliders also adjust accordingly.

⑤ Click an area in the image that should be darker and drag down.

The image shows more contrast and the tone curve changes.

The Darks and Shadows sliders also adjust.

⑥ Click and drag any of the region sliders to expand the area of the curve.

⑦ Click and drag the sliders slowly to make detailed adjustments in those regions.

The image changes more in regions affected by the sliders.

⑧ Click Open Image to open the image in Photoshop.

Note: *You can optionally click Save Image to save the image with the new adjustments without opening the image.*

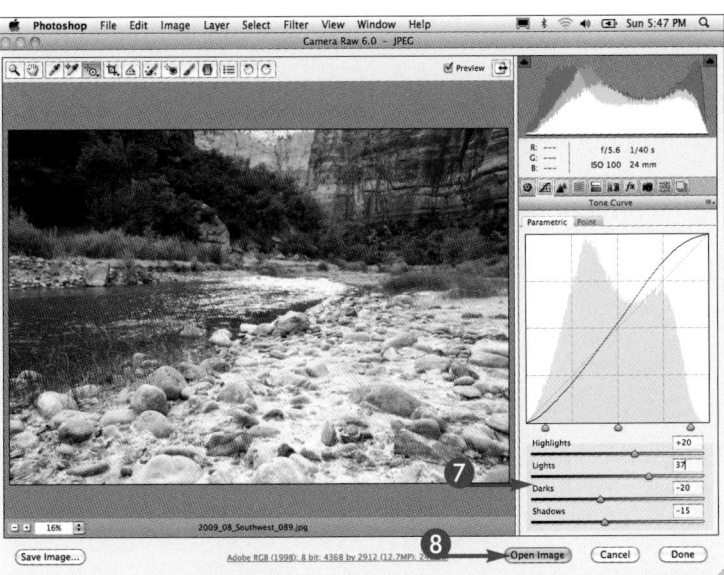

60
DIFFICULTY LEVEL

TIPS

Important!
If your camera displays a histogram on the LCD, this is the histogram of the file after it has been processed in-camera using the camera's default settings. It is a histogram of the conversion to JPEG, and not the histogram of the original RAW file.

Attention!
The on-camera histogram often tells you that your highlights are blown when, in fact, they may not be because most cameras apply a fairly strong S-curve to the raw data so that the JPEGs appear more like traditional film.

Did You Know?
After you process and edit a camera RAW file using the Camera Raw plug-in, an icon appears in the image thumbnail in Bridge.

IMPROVE A SKY
with the Camera Raw graduated filter

When you first open an image in Camera Raw, the tools in the Basic tab help you adjust the tone, white balance, and saturation of the overall image. On other tabs, you can adjust different tones and colors individually, make lens corrections, alter colors in the image, sharpen and reduce noise, and even save some of your settings as presets so that you can reapply them to similar images.

The Graduated Filter tool in the Camera Raw dialog box enables you to apply tonal changes similar to a

photographic graduated filter. For example, you can easily dramatize an open sky in a landscape photo by changing the exposure, saturation, clarity, and color of the sky or a large area and completely change the mood of the image.

You can open any file from Camera Raw as a Smart Object in Photoshop. Then you can easily reopen the Camera Raw dialog box and change the settings as you work before you save the file in Photoshop.

① Open an image with a large sky area in Camera Raw.

② Click the Graduated Filter tool.

The Graduated Filter options appear under the histogram.

③ Click Show Overlay (☐ changes to ☑).

④ Press and hold Shift and click and drag from the top of the image to where the sky meets the foreground.

● The Graduated Filter overlay appears with two adjustment pins on the image.

⑤ Click and drag the Exposure slider to the left to darken the sky.

⑥ Click and drag the other sliders on the Graduated Filter panel to increase the intensity of the sky.

⑦ Click the Color box.

The Color Picker appears.

⑧ Click a color to apply to the sky.

⑨ Click OK.

The sky in the photo changes.

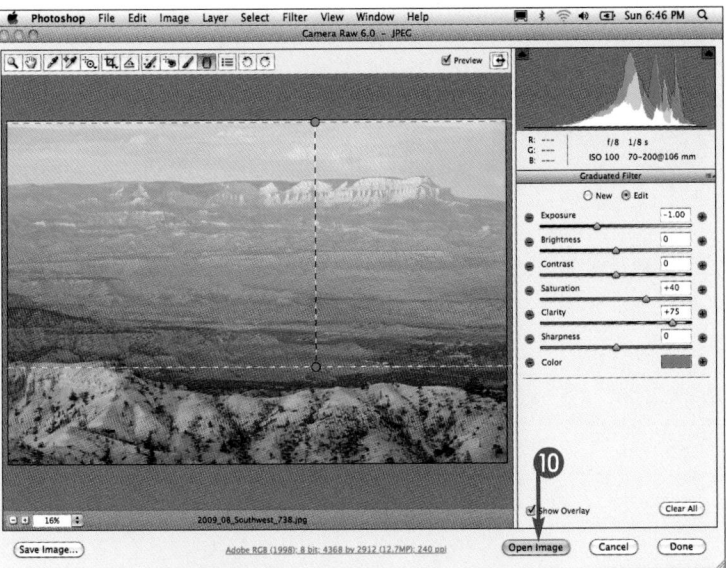

⑩ Shift+click the Open Image button.

The button changes to Open Object and the image opens as a Smart Object in Photoshop.

Note: You can optionally click Save Image to convert and save the image with the Graduated Filter adjustment, or click Done to apply the changes and close the dialog box without opening the image in Photoshop.

TIPS

More Options!

Once you have applied the Graduated Filter settings, you can continue to adjust the image in Camera Raw. Click the Zoom tool (🔍) to return to the Basic panel. The adjustments you applied with the graduated filter remain on the image.

Try This!

You can apply multiple Graduated Filter adjustments to an image by applying one and then selecting New (○ changes to ◉) to start another one. You can always go back and edit any adjustment. Make sure that Show Overlay is selected and click the Graduated Filter pin on the image.

Important!

With Camera Raw, you control the colors in the image by what you see on the screen, so it is essential to work with a properly calibrated and profiled monitor as discussed in task #13.

CREATE A SPLIT TONE
for a special effect in Camera Raw

Creating split tone effects in the traditional darkroom was difficult and labor-intensive. With Camera Raw included with Photoshop CS5, you can easily create a split tone look, in which a different color is applied to the shadows and highlights. You can also visually add or remove tones while previewing the image.

This feature of Camera Raw lets you associate hue and saturation with the lightest colors separately from the hue and saturation values associated with the darkest colors in the image. You can then adjust the

Balance slider to emphasize the tone of the highlights or the tone of the shadow areas.

Because you create the split tone in Camera Raw, the alteration to the image is completely nondestructive. The original image always remains intact. You can reopen Camera Raw to change the color or saturation amounts at any time to adjust the effect.

You can apply a split tone to either a grayscale or a color image; however, the toning is often most effective on a grayscale photo with high contrasts.

1 Open an image in Camera Raw.

2 Make any adjustments as in the previous tasks.

3 Click the Split Toning tab.

The Split Toning pane appears.

4 Click and drag the Highlights Saturation slider to 100.

5 Click and drag the Highlights Hue slider to select the color for the highlights.

134

The highlights in the image appear in a fully saturated color tone.

62

⑥ Click and drag the Shadows Saturation slider to 100.

⑦ Click and drag the Shadows Hue slider to select the color for the shadows.

The shadow areas in the image appear in a fully saturated color tone.

⑧ Click and drag the Balance slider to the right to shift the toning more into the highlights or to the left to emphasize the tones in the shadows.

⑨ Click and drag both the Highlights and the Shadows sliders to adjust the split tone effect.

⑩ Repeat steps 8 and 9 to adjust the split tone image.

The grayscale image appears as a split tone image with tinted shadows and highlights.

TIPS

Did You Know?

You can automatically open any image from Camera Raw as a Smart Object in Photoshop. Press Shift to change the Open Image button to Open Object. Once in Photoshop, you can double-click the Smart Object layer to reopen the image in Camera Raw and edit the settings.

More Options!

If you add a split tone to a color image, you can still convert it to grayscale after applying split toning by clicking the HSB/Grayscale tab in Camera Raw (▦). You can also change the effects of the split toning.

Try This!

Leave the Saturation slider set to 0 and press Option (Alt) as you drag the Hue sliders. The preview shows a 100% saturation of that hue. After you select the hue, move the Saturation sliders to the amount that you want.

Make Magic with Digital Special Effects

Since Photoshop's inception, photographers and graphic designers alike have been using the application for digital imaging and photo manipulation. Photoshop can transform an average shot into a good photograph, a good photograph into a great one, and a great image into creative fine art. Photoshop CS5 adds even more power and control to digital image editing. Just as with the previous versions, there are many different ways to create a design or enhance a photograph. You can use the new tools alone or in combination with the older techniques to create, improve, or completely alter any image.

You can simulate the effect of using traditional photographic filters to enhance the colors or change the areas in focus in an image. You can draw attention to one part of the image using a vignette or change the point of focus digitally after the shot has been captured. Using the Merge to HDR feature, you can combine multiple exposures to realize a photo with a wider range of tones than the camera can capture in one shot. You can use the flexibility of Smart Objects to edit images and then modify the changes you made previously and create a different type of final result. You can remove elements from a photograph and make it look like they were never there.

Photoshop CS5 offers newer and better tools for altering images than previous versions.

Top 100

APPLY A PHOTO FILTER
for dynamic adjustments

63

Different lighting conditions produce different color temperatures on photographic images. The Photo Filter adjustment in Photoshop enables you to change the color balance and color temperature of an image whether it is digital or scanned from film, just as a film photographer would use colored filters in front of the lens. The Photo Filter adjustment offers different and creative ways to visually enhance an image. Because Photoshop considers the Photo Filter an adjustment rather than a filter, you find the Photo Filter adjustment under both the Image ⇨ Adjustments and Layer ⇨ New Adjustment Layer menus. However, using the Adjustments panel is the quickest and easiest way to access this adjustment.

Using a Photo Filter adjustment can visually change the time of day in the photo, turning midday into sunset. You can turn a bland photo into a dramatic one by applying a blue or violet filter across the entire image, or warm a cool photo by applying a warming filter. You can optionally apply the filter selectively by painting on the adjustment mask that is automatically applied with a Photo Filter adjustment layer.

① Open a photo in the Essentials workspace or with the Adjustments panel visible.

② Click the Photo Filter adjustment layer.

Note: Using a Photo Filter adjustment layer does not alter the original image until you flatten the layers.

The Photo Filter options appear in the Adjustments panel.

● Make sure that Preserve Luminosity is selected.

③ Click here and select a colored filter.

④ Click and drag the Density slider to the right to increase the effect if necessary.

The Photo Filter adjustment is applied to the entire image.

Note: You can duplicate the layer to increase the effect or change the layer blend mode to Hue to soften the effect.

Add a vignette effect to
FOCUS ON THE SUBJECT

A dark vignette around the edges of a photograph is often due to the light falloff in the camera lens. Intentionally darkening the edges of an image can help focus the viewer's eye on the subject. For other images, a darkened edge can simulate the look of an old photograph. Used on a portrait, a dark vignette can create a more dramatic look, and a light vignette can create an entirely different image. With a landscape, you can simulate a burned-in edge, essentially enhancing the center of the image.

You can remove a camera lens vignette or create a vignette effect in many ways with Photoshop. Most methods involve separate layers and multiple steps. Controlling the vignette in Camera Raw offers more flexibility. You can easily add either a lighter or darker edge to an image, and the vignette can even be appropriately applied to a cropped image. Also, when you apply or remove the vignette in Camera Raw, the pixels in the file are not altered.

① Open an image in Camera Raw as described in task #56.

② Click the Lens Corrections tab.

③ Click and drag the Amount slider to the left for a dark-edged vignette effect.

Note: You can optionally click and drag the Amount slider to the right for a light vignette or to correct an unwanted dark vignette.

④ Click and drag the Midpoint slider to control how far the darkened areas extend into the photograph.

⑤ Click Open Image to open the file in Photoshop for final editing or output.

Add action with a
SIMULATED MOTION BLUR

You can add a sense of movement to action shots by using a filter to simulate the motion of the subjects. Photoshop includes a number of blur filters, including one for motion blur. Unlike the Gaussian Blur filter, which blurs pixels in clusters, the Motion Blur filter blurs pixels in both directions along straight lines. You can choose the angle of movement and the distance in pixels that are affected by the blur in the filter dialog box to simulate both the direction and speed of motion of the subject of the photo.

The Motion Blur filter blurs the entire image, removing all details. Both the subject matter and the background are blurred, making the photo look as though the camera and not the subject was moving when the shot was taken. By adding a layer mask filled with black to hide the motion blur, you can then selectively paint in white over certain areas to create the illusion of movement while keeping the main subject and the background in focus. Apply the filter as a Smart Filter on a previously converted Smart Object layer, and you can edit the amount of blur after applying it for even more visual control.

① With the image as a Smart Object layer (see task #24), click Filter.

② Click Blur.

③ Click Motion Blur.

The Motion Blur dialog box appears.

④ Click and drag the straight line in the circle to simulate the angle of the motion in the photo.

⑤ Click and drag the Distance slider to adjust the amount of blur.

⑥ Click OK.

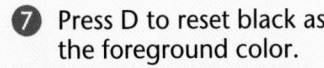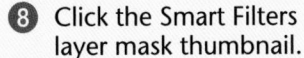

The filter is applied to the Smart Object layer.

⑦ Press D to reset black as the foreground color.

⑧ Click the Smart Filters layer mask thumbnail.

The mask appears with a line around it, and the default foreground color changes to white.

⑨ Press ⌘+Delete (Ctrl+Backspace) to fill the Smart Filter layer mask with black.

The motion blur effect is hidden and the mask is filled with black.

⑩ Click the Brush tool.

● Make sure the foreground color is white.

⑪ Click here and select a large soft-edged brush from the Brush picker.

⑫ Paint in the image over the areas where you want the motion blur to appear.

The motion blur is applied to the specific areas and the subject appears to be moving through the background.

TIPS

Did You Know?

You can also use the Wind filter for a linear motion effect. Instead of selecting the Motion Blur filter, click Filter, Stylize, and then Wind. Click From the Right or From the Left to select the direction of the movement. Click OK to close the dialog box. Then follow steps 7 to 12 in this task to selectively paint in the appropriate motion.

More Options!

After applying Motion Blur as a Smart Filter, you can instead leave the blur over the entire image and paint back the subject and foreground to bring them back into focus. Click the mask to select it as in step 8 and press X if necessary to reverse the foreground and background colors so that black is the foreground color. Paint with black over the areas that you want in focus.

Remove image elements with a
CONTENT-AWARE FILL

In previous versions of Photoshop, you were able to use the Clone tool, Spot Healing Brush tool, or Patch tool to selectively remove objects from a photograph to transform the photo into the image you wanted. You might also have blended multiple photographs and used masks or other techniques to remove unwanted image elements. Most such tasks were difficult and time-consuming.

Photoshop CS5 introduces a new fill option called Content-Aware. Selecting an area and applying a

Content-Aware fill, you can not only remove an element in a photo but also replace it with pixels that match and blend into the surrounding areas. The selected area is replaced with elements that match the lighting, tone, and even the noise of the adjacent areas so the replacement appears more natural. For smaller areas you can also use the Content-Aware Fill setting along with the Spot Healing Brush to brush away the element you want to remove. You can then easily use the other tools to refine the edited areas.

Remove an Area with a Content-Aware Fill

1 Press ⌘+J (Ctrl+J) to duplicate the background layer.

   Note: You can optionally press ⌘+spacebar (Ctrl+spacebar) to zoom in if necessary.

2 Click the Lasso tool.

   Note: You can use any selection tool.

3 Click and drag to select an area to be removed.

4 Click Edit.

5 Click Fill.

   The Fill dialog box appears.

6 Click here and select Content-Aware.

7 Click OK.

   The selected area is removed and filled with pixels from surrounding areas.

8 Press ⌘+D (Ctrl+D) to deselect the area.

9 Click the Clone Stamp tool or the Healing Brush tool.

10 Option+click (Alt+click) to select a clone source and clone or heal any areas to blend them in.

Remove an Area with the Spot Healing Brush and Content-Aware Option

1 Click the New Layer button to add a new blank layer.

2 Click the Spot Healing Brush (□).

3 Click here to open the Brush picker and select a soft-edged brush slightly larger than the area you want to fix.

4 Click here and select Replace.

5 Click Content-Aware (○ changes to ◉).

6 Click Sample All Layers (□ changes to ☑).

7 With the blank layer highlighted in the Layers panel, click and drag the area in the image to be removed.

The unwanted item is removed and the area is filled with content from adjacent areas.

TIPS

Did You Know?

By adding a new empty layer and making the edits on that layer, you do not alter the original file until you flatten the layers.

More Options!

Selecting Replace for the Mode in the Options bar helps to preserve noise, film grain, and texture at the edges of the brushed areas.

Important!

Both the Spot Healing Brush and the Healing Brush paint with pixels from a sampled area and match the texture, lighting, transparency, and shading. The Spot Healing Brush automatically samples from the surrounding areas. The Healing Brush requires you to Option+click (Alt+click) to specify an area to sample.

SCALE AN IMAGE
without distorting the subject

When you scale an image to make it fit a different aspect ratio, all the pixels in the image are affected and stretched uniformly. Although distorting a sky or a grassy field when adjusting an image to improve composition or fit a layout may not be noticeable, you cannot easily scale images with people or recognizable objects.

Photoshop now includes the Content-Aware scaling feature so you can more easily upscale or downscale an image, or even change its orientation, without distorting the main subject.

You can stretch a sky, increase the length of a wall, and expand the area around the main visual content and keep a natural aspect ratio to some areas while adapting the image to a new aspect ratio. For example, you can expand the sky in a photograph to extend upward for a magazine cover layout to allow room for the title text, without distorting the items or people in the foreground.

Depending on the image, Content-Aware scaling may require creating a selection or repositioning reference points around which to stretch the image.

① Create a new blank document with the desired final dimensions.

② Open an image.

③ Click and drag the image over the tab for the blank document.

● The image appears as a layer on the blank document.

Note: *Steps 4 to 7 are optional depending on the subject matter and areas to scale.*

④ Click the Lasso tool.

⑤ Click and drag around the content to protect.

⑥ Click the Channels tab.

⑦ Click the Layer Mask button to save the selection as a channel.

● The selection is saved as Alpha 1.

⑧ Press ⌘+D (Ctrl+D) to deselect.

⑨ Click Edit.

⑩ Click Content-Aware Scale.

A bounding border surrounds the image.

⑪ Click here and select Alpha 1.

● You can optionally click the Protect Skin Tones button to protect people in the image.

⑫ Click and drag a handle on the bounding border to scale the image, as far as needed or until the main content starts to stretch.

The image scales, leaving the main content at its original proportions.

⑬ Click the Commit button to apply the scaling.

Note: Content-Aware scaling works best when scaling in moderate amounts.

Note: You can optionally repeat steps 9 to 13 to scale the image more.

TIPS

Did You Know?
Although Content-Aware scaling can be applied to individual layers or selections, you cannot use it on the Background layer, adjustment layers, layer masks, individual channels, Smart Object layers, layer groups, or multiple layers at one time.

More Options!
You can combine normal scaling with Content-Aware scaling when resizing your image by specifying the ratio amount of Content-Aware scaling to be combined using the option in the Options bar.

More Options!
The default scaling reference point is the center of the image. You can set reference points or specify the fixed point around which the image is called by clicking a square on the reference point locator.

BLEND SEPARATE PHOTOS
for the best group shot

Photoshop CS5 includes an Auto-Align Layers command to help you combine separate photos for panoramas or for composites. Auto-Align Layers analyzes edges and common elements in each image and brings them into alignment with each other. This tool works very well when combining multiple photos of a group so that everyone looks their best in the final photo.

You can drag all the separate images onto one of the images, making multiple layers. When you run the

Auto-Align Layers command, Photoshop matches each layer with the others so that the similar shapes and forms match as much as possible. You can then add a layer mask to the layers to merge the images, erasing the unwanted parts of each layer. For group shots, you erase the closed eyes or grimaces to reveal the best expressions of everyone in the group.

1. Open the photos to combine.

2. Click the Move tool.

3. Click and drag one photo on top of the other.

   Note: In Photoshop CS5 you can drag a layer from one image onto the tab for another image.

4. Click to close the photo that you just dragged.

5. Press Shift and click both layers to select them.

6. Click Edit.

7. Click Auto-Align Layers.

   The Auto-Align Layers dialog box appears.

8. Click a projection style, depending on the elements in the photos (○ changes to ⦿).

   Note: In this example, you are trying to align people in a group shot; Auto Projection will work best.

9. Click OK.

- Photoshop aligns the photos by the content and renames the layers Layer 0 and Layer 1.

⑩ Click the top layer to select it.

⑪ Click Opacity and drag to the left to 60% to see the shapes below.

⑫ Click the Brush tool.

⑬ Click here and select a soft-edged brush.

⑭ Click the Layer Mask button to add a layer mask to the top layer.

⑮ Click the Switch Colors icon to set the foreground color to black.

Note: The top layer's mask should still be selected.

⑯ Paint with black on the top layer to show the best group shots.

- The mask displays the painted areas in black.

⑰ Click Opacity and drag to the right back to 100%.

The final image blends the preferred subjects from both images.

⑱ Click the Crop tool and crop the image to the final size.

TIPS

Caution!
Make sure that the top layer's mask is still selected and that the foreground color is set to black when you paint on the photo to reveal the parts of the image on the layer below.

Did You Know?
Photoshop automatically selects one alignment projection option (see step 8) based on the contents of the images you are combining. You can try it and then press ⌘+Z (Ctrl+Z) to undo the auto-alignment and try a different option.

More Options!
The Auto-Blend Layers command blends separate layers and tries to reduce or eliminate the perspective differences as well as the differences in colors or luminance without leaving a seam. This command works well for scenic photos.

MERGE MULTIPLE PHOTOS
into an image with high dynamic range

Dynamic range in a photo refers to the ratio between the dark and bright areas. The human eye can adapt to different brightness levels, but the camera cannot. You can merge multiple photos of the same scene but with different exposures into a *high dynamic range* (HDR) image, displaying luminosity levels beyond what the human eye can see, and with more shades of color than any camera can capture in a single photo. Photoshop CS5's Merge to HDR Pro command enables the still photographer to create a detailed photo with a wide dynamic range, and customize the settings for a realistic or more stylized final image.

The Merge to HDR Pro command works best on a series of photos taken with a tripod so that only the lighting of the image differs and nothing is moving. The aperture and ISO of the images should be the same in each photo. The shutter speed should vary from one to two f-stops in each direction. You can merge to HDR with at least three photos; however, you can include more photos with varying shutter speeds so your photos have a large variation in the image tones.

Open Merge to HDR from Bridge

1 In Bridge, ⌘+click (Ctrl+click) to select the images to merge.

Note: Photos taken specifically to use with the Merge to HDR Pro command would normally appear in sequential order.

2 Click Tools.

3 Click Photoshop.

4 Click Merge to HDR Pro.

Note: Continue the steps starting with step 5 below.

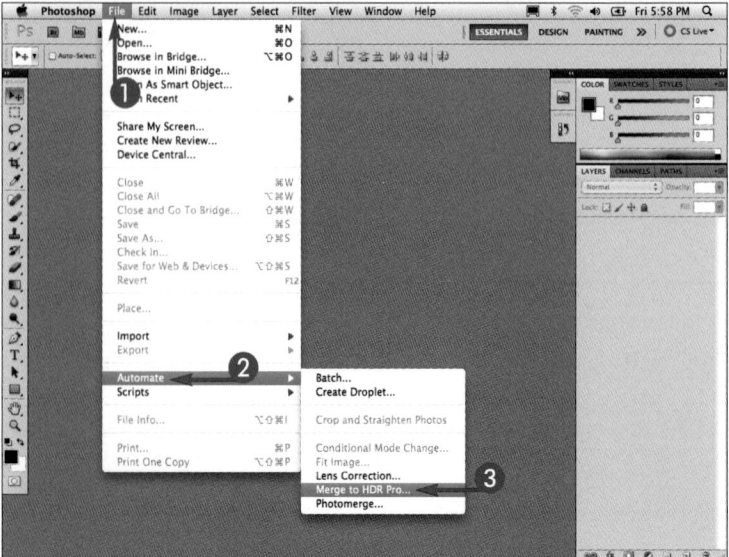

Open Merge to HDR Pro from Photoshop

1 In Photoshop, click File.

2 Click Automate.

3 Click Merge to HDR Pro.

4 Continue with step 5 below.

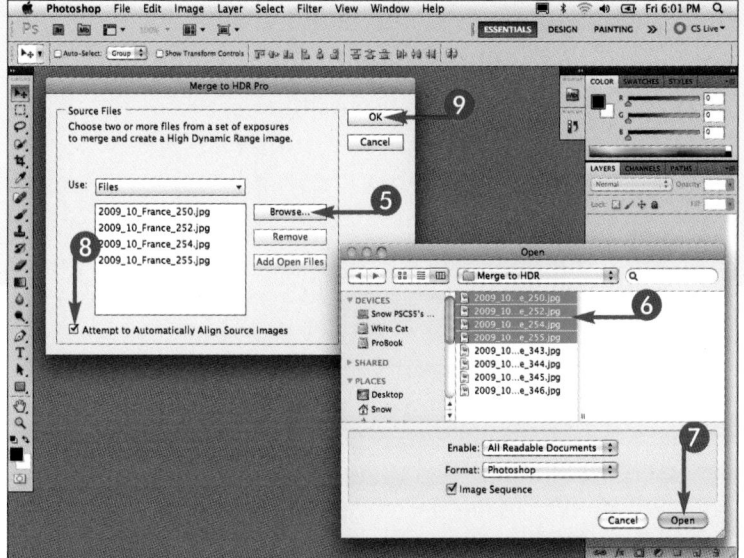

The Merge to HDR dialog box appears.

⑤ Click Browse.

The Open dialog box appears.

⑥ Navigate to and ⌘+click (Ctrl+click) to select the images to use.

⑦ Click Open.

● The files appear in the list box.

⑧ Click Attempt to Automatically Align Source Images (☐ changes to ☑).

⑨ Click OK.

Photoshop opens, analyzes, aligns, and combines the images into one multilayered file.

The larger Merge to HDR Pro dialog box appears.

⑩ For 16-bit images, click and drag the sliders to customize the edge glow, tones, and detail.

Note: For 32-bit images, click and drag the slider to adjust the white point of the preview image.

⑪ Click and drag to adjust the Vibrance and Saturation.

⑫ Click the Curve tab to adjust the contrast.

⑬ Click OK.

Photoshop merges the files into a document named Untitled_HDR.

More Options!

If your images have items in slightly different positions from one image to the next, such as moving foliage, you can click Remove Ghosts (☐ changes to ☑) in the Merge to HDR Pro dialog box. Photoshop selects the items with the best tones and hides the overlapping areas on the other images.

Important!

You can output the merged image as a 32-, 16-, or 8-bit image; however, only the 32-bit image can store all the high dynamic range data. You can convert from 32 bit to 16 or 8 bit after the image has been merged by clicking Image, Mode, 16 or 8 bit/channel and adjusting the exposure and contrast for the resulting HDR image.

Did You Know?

You can open all the images in Camera Raw first. You can make adjustments such as white balance or chromatic aberration to one image, then select all, synchronize the settings, and click Done. Select the images in Bridge, and from the Tools menu, click Merge to HDR Pro. The Camera Raw adjustments remain in the final HDR image.

USE A PUPPET WARP
to alter your subject

Photoshop CS5 includes a completely new tool for recomposing images or parts of an image. The Puppet Warp tool enables you to click and drag any element or selection and reposition it within the image. You can push and pull to shift the pixels and Photoshop adjusts the image to fit.

The Puppet Warp tool applies a visual mesh to your image. You can click specific areas, creating drop pins that act as anchor points, and then move specific areas to warp an area or element separately from the background. You can reposition one item in a photograph or apply the Puppet Warp to manipulate a graphic element in a design. You can make simple adjustments to better position a distracting strand of hair or completely alter an item to give it a new position or shape, such as moving a person's hand or distorting a flower into a design. You can also apply the Puppet Warp to a Smart Object so all your distortions are nondestructive and no pixels are permanently altered.

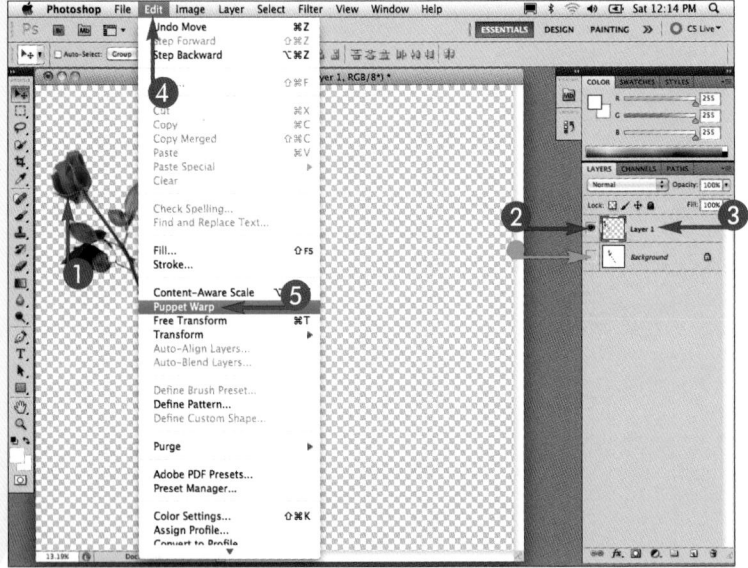

1 Select the item to warp.

2 Press ⌘+J (Ctrl+J) to place the item on its own layer.

3 Click the layer in the Layers panel.

4 Click Edit.

5 Click Puppet Warp.

● You can optionally click the Eye icon for the bottom layer to hide it.

The Puppet Warp mesh covers the selected subject.

6 Click here and select Distort.

Note: Distort mode enables more elastic and less rigid style of warping.

7 Click here and select Fewer Points to change the spacing of the mesh points.

Note: Fewer Points is less precise but takes less time for processing.

8 Click here and drag to increase or decrease the size of the mesh around the subject.

9 Click the image to add a transformation pin.

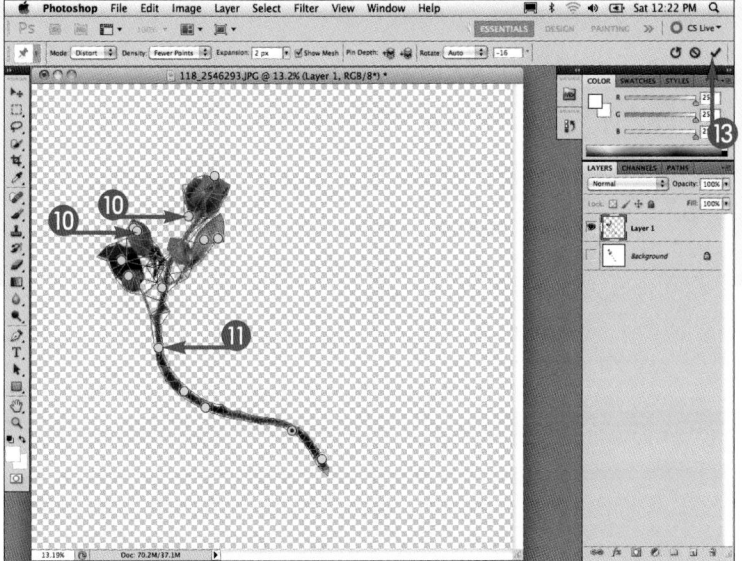

⑩ Repeat step 9 to add pins for both distorting and anchoring areas.

⑪ Click and drag the points to reshape the item.

⑫ Repeats steps 10 to 11 as necessary.

Note: *Shift+click multiple pins and press Shift as you drag to move the selected pins at one time.*

Note: *To delete the pin, press Option (Alt) as you position the cursor over a pin and click when the scissors icon appears.*

⑬ Click the Commit button to apply the Puppet Warp.

● You can optionally press ⌘+J (Ctrl+J) to duplicate the warped item layer and move the items to create a design.

TIPS

Did You Know?
The Options bar includes two buttons to move overlapped items, one for setting the Pin Depth forward (🖼) and one for setting it backward (🖼). Click the Remove All Pins button (🔘) to delete all the pins at once.

More Options!
The Distort mode setting in the Options bar enables you to distort the item with a more fluid movement. The Rigid mode gives you precise or more geometric bending around a drop pin.

Important!
You can apply the Puppet Warp tool to items on individual image layers, text layers, and shape layers, as well as to layer masks and vector masks.

ALTER DEPTH OF FIELD
with a Lens Blur filter

You can draw the attention of the viewer into an image by narrowing the depth of field, or defining the in-focus part of the image and blurring other areas. Photographers control the depth of field by changing the aperture setting on the camera. A small opening results in a greater depth of field with more of the image in focus. A larger aperture creates an image with less depth of field and only the center of the image in focus. For previously captured images you can create a similar effect using Photoshop's blur filters to selectively adjust the depth of field.

Use the Lens Blur filter and a white-to-black gradient on an *alpha channel*, a special type of channel for saving a selection, to create a smooth transition from the focused areas to the out-of-focus areas in the photo. Click one area in the image to set the main focal point. Areas with the same level of gray in the alpha channel as the selected area are now in focus. All other areas are blurred depending on the level of gray in the alpha channel.

① With a photo open, click the Channels tab in the Layers panel.

② Click the New Channel button to add a new black alpha channel.

The image is covered with black, and the channel is named Alpha 1.

③ Click the Eye icon for the RGB channel to see the image.

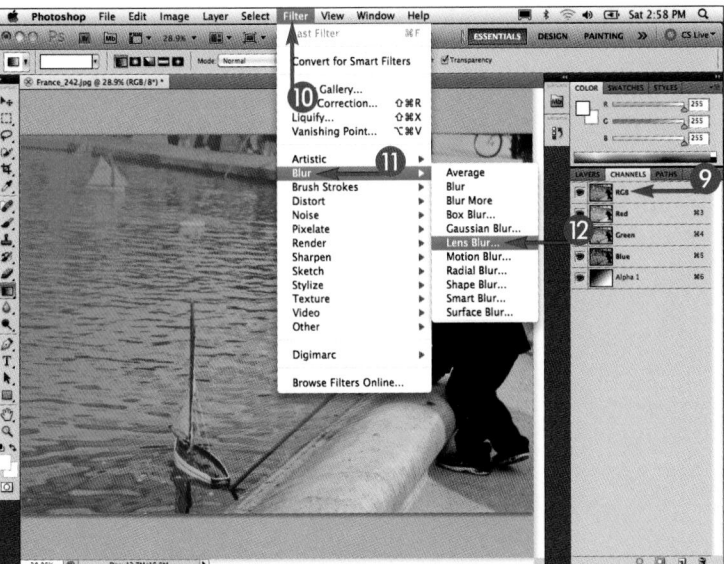

All the channels are visible, and a red mask covers the image.

④ Click the Alpha 1 channel to select it.

⑤ Press D to reset the default foreground and background colors.

⑥ Click the Gradient tool.

⑦ Click the Linear gradient.

⑧ Press and hold Shift as you click and drag in the image from the background toward the foreground.

Note: You can click and drag diagonally, from bottom to top, or from side to side.

The red mask area appears as a red gradient.

⑨ Click the RGB channel to highlight it.

⑩ Click Filter.

⑪ Click Blur.

⑫ Click Lens Blur.

More Options!

You can keep a selected area in focus when you apply the Lens Blur. Make a selection. Click Select and then Save Selection. Type a name in the data field in the Save Selection dialog box and click OK. Next, click the Channels tab and deselect the Eye icon (👁) of the new channel. Click the RGB channel to select it and click the Layers tab. Now when you apply the Lens Blur filter everything in the selection remains in focus.

Try This!

You can create a channel with two selections, one for the main subject and the second for an area slightly farther in the background. Fill the first selection with white and the second with a light gray. Apply the Lens Blur filter with this channel as the source. Your image now has areas with three distinct levels of focus.

ALTER DEPTH OF FIELD
with a Lens Blur filter

All Photoshop's blur filters can soften or blur either a selected area or the entire image. The Lens Blur filter works well for simulating depth of field in a photo because it can use a depth map to determine the position of the pixels to blur. Using the Lens Blur filter with a separate alpha channel or a layer mask as the source enables you to specify exactly what is in sharp focus and how much depth of field effect to apply. The Lens Blur filter also enables you to determine the shape of the iris to control how the blur appears.

Dragging the Blade Curvature slider smoothes the blur, dragging the Rotation slider rotates the blur, and dragging the Radius slider increases the amount of blur. The Brightness slider increases the brightness of the highlights, and the Threshold slider limits the brightness for specular highlights. You can even add noise without changing the colors in the image by clicking Monochromatic noise and dragging the Amount slider.

The Lens Blur dialog box appears.

⑬ Click and drag all the sliders to the left to remove any blur effect.

⑭ Click here and select Alpha 1.

⑮ Click the main subject in the image to assign the point of focus.

⑯ Click and drag the Radius slider to the right to blur the background.

⑰ If necessary, click Invert to set the blur to the background (☐ changes to ☑).

⑱ Click and drag the Blur Focal Distance slider to adjust the point of focus.

Note: *The Blur Focal Distance number corresponds to the level of gray at the targeted point in the alpha channel.*

⑲ Click OK.

The Lens Blur filter is applied to the image in the areas covered by the red gradient.

⑳ Click the Eye icon on the Alpha 1 channel to deselect it and hide the red mask.

㉑ Click the Layers tab.

The main subject in the image is sharp, whereas the rest of the image gradually blurs out of focus as it gets farther away from the focal point.

TIPS

Attention!

Film grain and noise are removed when the Lens Blur filter is applied. You can replace some of the noise and make the image look more realistic. First, zoom in to see the image at 100%. Click and drag the Amount slider in the Noise section of the Lens Blur dialog box until the image appears less changed and click OK.

Did You Know?

Applying a Lens Blur filter rather than a Gaussian Blur filter preserves more of the geometric shapes in the original image. Highlights in the image also reflect the Shape setting that is chosen in the Iris section of the Lens Blur dialog box. You can smooth the edges of the iris and rotate it by changing the Blade Curvature and Rotation settings.

Use the Auto Blend tool to create
GREATER DEPTH OF FIELD

The depth of field you can capture depends on the type of camera, the aperture, and the focusing distance. Larger apertures, or smaller f-stop numbers, and closer focal distance produce images with a shallower depth of field, or less of the image in focus. Using smaller apertures, or larger f-stop numbers, produces photos with greater depth of field or more of the overall image in focus.

Sometimes you cannot use as small an aperture as you would need to create a photo with a very large depth of field because of the distance involved, or because of the lighting conditions. You can combine multiple shots and blend them together using the capabilities in Photoshop CS5 to create a larger depth of field.

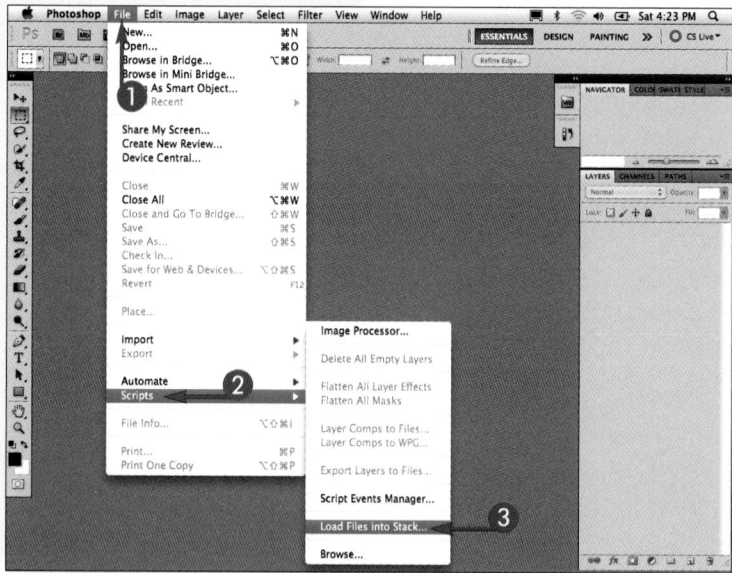

1 Click File.

2 Click Scripts.

3 Click Load Files into Stack.

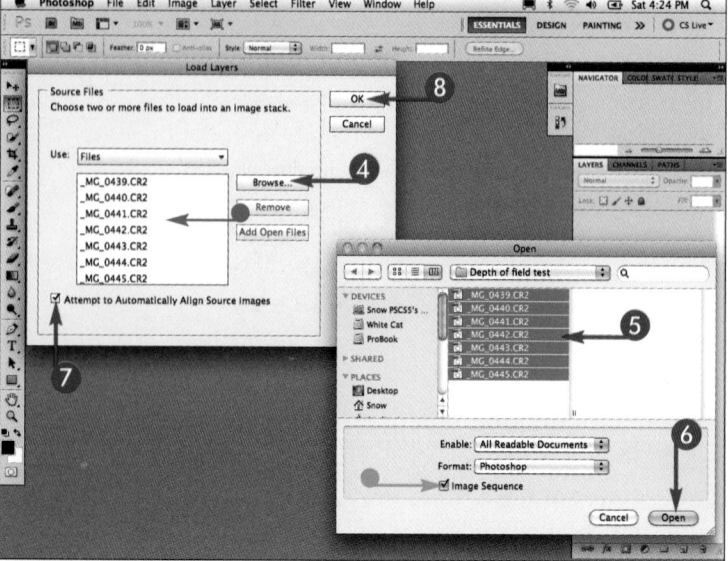

The Load Layers dialog box appears.

4 Click Browse.

The Open dialog box appears.

5 ⌘+click (Ctrl+click) multiple photos to select them.

● You can optionally click Image Sequence to have the images load in order (☐ changes to ☑).

6 Click Open.

● The files appear in the Load Layers dialog box.

7 Click Attempt to Automatically Align Source Images (☐ changes to ☑).

8 Click OK.

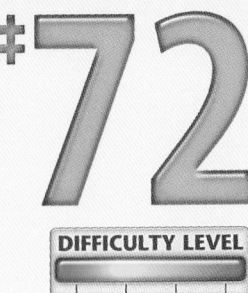

● The images all open as individual layers of one file named *Untitled1*.

⑨ Click the first layer and Shift+click the last layer to select all the layers at once.

⑩ Click Edit.

⑪ Click Auto-Align Layers.

TIPS

Did You Know?
Depth of field occurs as a gradual transition, with everything in front of and behind the focusing distance of the camera lens losing sharpness.

Try This!
You can also start by selecting the files and opening them all as separate files. Then click File, Scripts, and Load Files into Stack. In the Load Layers dialog box, click Add Open Files to select all the currently open files and click OK, and then continue with step 9 above.

Did You Know?
The Auto-Align Layers command aligns the layers based on similar content, such as corners and edges, in each of the different layers.

Use the Auto Blend tool to create
GREATER DEPTH OF FIELD

To create the best blend for extending the depth of field of the final image, you should use a tripod and use the manual focus of the camera. With the full image in the viewfinder or on the camera's LCD, manually focus on the area closest to the camera and take the first shot. Then change only the focus point to see the next area over in sharp focus. Continue taking photos until all the areas are in focus in at least one shot.

The Auto-Blend Layers command works only with RGB or Grayscale images and does not work with Smart Object layers or Background layers. And although the Auto-Blend dialog box does have an option for blending multiple images into a panorama, the Photomerge command generally produces better photo blends for panoramas.

You can use as many photos as required to capture each area of the scene in sharp focus.

The Auto-Align Layers dialog box appears.

⑫ Click a projection option (○ changes to ◉).

Note: The Auto Projection option, in which Photoshop analyzes the images for content and positions them in the layout, generally works well when blending images with overlapping areas to increase depth of field.

● You can optionally click Vignette Removal and/or Geometric Distortion (☐ changes to ☑) to have Photoshop recognize the lens type in the metadata and attempt to correct for these defects.

⑬ Click OK.

A progress bar appears as the layers are automatically aligned.

Note: You may not see a noticeable change on-screen.

⑭ With all the layers still selected, click Edit.

⑮ Click Auto-Blend Layers.

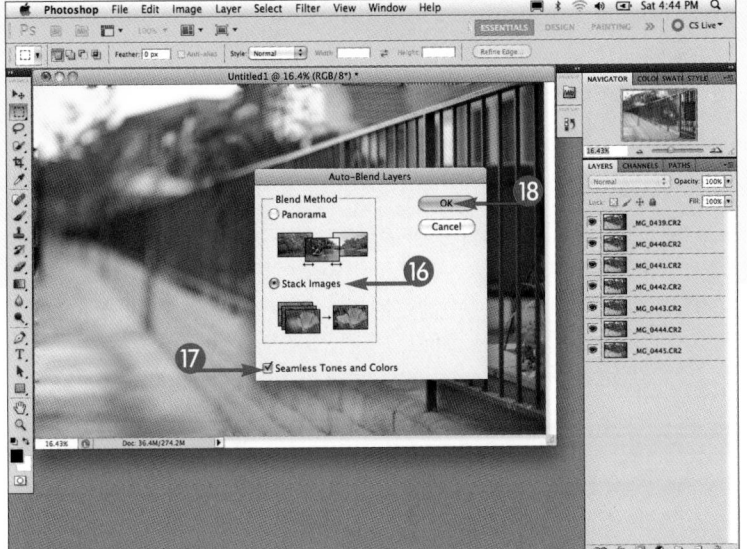

The Auto-Blend Layers dialog box appears.

⑯ Click Stack Images (○ changes to ◉).

⑰ Click Seamless Tones and Colors (☐ changes to ☑).

⑱ Click OK.

A progress bar appears as the layers are blended based on the content, and layer masks are created.

The layers are blended using the layer masks, and the depth of field is increased, reflecting all the points in sharpest focus from each layer.

TIPS

More Options!
The Auto-Blend Layers command can also be used to create a correctly illuminated composite from multiple images of a scene with different over- or underexposed areas.

Attention!
Although you selected Attempt to Automatically Align Source Images in the Load Layers dialog box (step 7), the Auto Blend Layers command generally works best if you apply the Auto-Align Layers command before attempting to auto-blend the layers.

More Options!
You can also convert video frames shot against a static background into layers and then use the Auto-Align Layers command to combine these frames and add or delete specific areas from the frames.

EDIT IN PERSPECTIVE
with the Vanishing Point filter

The Vanishing Point filter helps Photoshop recognize the third dimension of objects so that you can manipulate items in perspective. Using the Grid tool, you create a grid over a rectangular area, making sure to align the anchor points of the grid precisely with the corners of a rectangular area in the photo. With the first grid area set, you can extend the grid by pulling on the anchor points to cover a larger area with a blue grid in the same perspective.

Once the grid is in place, you can change the look of the image by erasing items, copying objects from one area of the image to another, or adding items from other images, all while keeping the perspective in the original photo.

By creating a separate layer in Photoshop before applying the Vanishing Point filter, you can more easily adjust areas once you are back in the main Photoshop window.

Using the Vanishing Point filter, you can change the words on street signs or add doors and windows to buildings. Just be sure to copy the item to be added to the clipboard *before* you choose the Vanishing Point filter on the main image.

Add Items in Perspective

① Open an image to copy and a main image.

② Select an area to be copied from the image.

③ Press ⌘+C (Ctrl+C) to copy the image to the clipboard.

④ Click the main image tab.

⑤ With the main image visible, click the New Layer button to add a new layer.

⑥ Click Filter.

⑦ Click Vanishing Point.

The Vanishing Point dialog box appears.

● The Create Plane tool is automatically selected.

⑧ Click four corners of an area that shows the perspective of the photo to create a blue grid.

⑨ Click the Edit Plane tool.

⑩ Click and drag the center points of the grid marquee to extend the plane if necessary.

⑪ Press ⌘+V (Ctrl+V).

- The pasted image appears in a corner of the Vanishing Point dialog box.

⑫ Click and drag the second image over the perspective plane.

- The second image snaps into perspective on the plane.

⑬ Click the Transform tool.

⑭ Shift+click and drag the corners of the second image to adjust it into position.

⑮ Click OK.

The copied element is added to the main image in perspective.

TIPS

More Options!
You can pull a secondary plane around a 90-degree corner and add items in perspective to different sides of a structure. You can even rotate a secondary plane by any amount to fit an angled area of a structure such as a roof.

Did You Know?
When you are in the Vanishing Point dialog box, you can use the Zoom tool (🔍) to enlarge the area where you plan to apply the anchor points of the plane. You can also zoom in temporarily as you are placing or adjusting the anchor points by pressing and holding X.

Important!
You can use the Vanishing Point filter to increase the size of the building beyond the boundaries of the existing photo. Increase the canvas size first by clicking Image and Canvas Size, and then add width or height to one side of the existing image.

EDIT IN PERSPECTIVE
with the Vanishing Point filter

You can also use the Vanishing Point filter in Photoshop CS5 to help you remove items in an image while maintaining perspective.

You can edit the image in Photoshop before and after using the Vanishing Point filter. When you save the edited image as a PSD, TIFF, or JPEG, the perspective planes are saved with the file. You can then reopen the file, reapply the Vanishing Point filter, and continue to erase or edit in perspective at a later date.

Using the Vanishing Point grids takes a little practice. The first grid is the most important and must be accurate. A blue grid shows a correct perspective plane. A red or yellow grid must be adjusted using the anchor points until the grid turns blue. However, even with a blue grid, you may need to readjust the anchor points to fit the perspective of the building or the subject after you extend the grid.

Erase Items in Perspective

1 Click the New Layer button in the Layers panel to add an empty layer above the Background layer.

2 Click Filter.

3 Click Vanishing Point.

The Vanishing Point dialog box appears.

● The Create Plane tool is automatically selected.

4 Click four corners of an area that shows the perspective of the photo to create a blue grid.

5 Click the Edit Plane tool.

6 Click and drag the points of the grid to extend the plane.

The grid expands to fit the area.

7 Click the Stamp tool.

8 Option+click (Alt+click) in an area in the perspective plane to establish the sampling point.

9 Click and drag carefully using short strokes in the area of the photo to be erased.

10 Repeat steps 8 and 9, resampling several times to keep the look natural.

11 Click OK.

The edits are applied to the top layer.

Important!
When erasing with the Vanishing Point Stamp tool (□), Option+click (Alt+click) a straight line in the area to be sampled. Then click along the same line in the area to be removed to help align the parts you will be cloning.

More Options!
Set the Heal mode in the Stamp tool options to On to blend the cloned strokes with the texture of the sampled image. Setting the Heal mode to Luminance blends the cloned strokes with the lighting of the surrounding pixels.

Try This!
You can save Vanishing Point grids on a separate layer in the Photoshop document. Add a new layer before using the Vanishing Point filter and create the grids. Click the Settings and Commands for Vanishing Point button (▾≡) in the Vanishing Point dialog box. Click Render Grids to Photoshop. Click OK, and the grids appear on the top layer of the file.

Use the Clone Stamp tool to
SIMULATE A REFLECTION

You can create a reflection or a mirror image of the subject in a photo using a variety of techniques and different tools in Photoshop CS5. Creating a perfectly mirrored reflection of the subject is tricky and can involve many techniques and tools for selecting objects, duplicating and transforming layers, adjusting opacity, and more. However, you can quickly create a simulated mirror image of the subject in a photo using the Clone Stamp tool and the Clone Source feature of Photoshop CS5.

The Clone Source tabbed panel enables you to see the reflection as a guide before you paint it; however, this panel must be moved away from the main image window to function correctly as a preview of what you are painting. You create the reflection on a separate layer so you can adjust the look using the layer opacity or a blended layer mask, or both.

Depending on the subject matter, angle of the subject, and intended use of the photo, your mirrored image can be convincingly realistic.

① Click Window and select Clone Source to open the Clone Source panel.

② Click the Clone Stamp tool.

③ Click the New Layer button on the Layers panel to create a new layer.

④ Click here and select All Layers.

⑤ In the Clone Source panel, click to uncheck Clipped, Auto Hide, and Invert if these are selected (☑ changes to ☐).

⑥ Click and drag the Clone Source panel so it does not touch the image window.

⑦ Click Show Overlay (☐ changes to ☑).

⑧ Make sure the Maintain Aspect Ratio link is not selected.

⑨ Click Flip Vertically.

⑩ Click Opacity and drag to the left to reduce the preview opacity to 50% or lower so you can see both the reflection and the original subject as you work.

⑪ Press Option (Alt) and click at the bottom of the subject to be mirrored to sample it.

⑫ Move the cursor away from the image window.

The reflection appears as an overlay on the image.

⑬ Click and drag using the Clone Stamp tool and a large brush to paint in the reflection.

Note: Start painting close to the spot you originally sampled in step 11.

⑭ Click Show Overlay to turn off the overlay (☑ changes to ☐).

⑮ Click and drag with the Clone Stamp tool to finish painting the reflection.

⑯ Click the Layer Mask button to add a layer mask.

⑰ Press D to reset the foreground and background colors to white and black.

Note: The foreground color should be white.

⑱ Click the Gradient tool.

⑲ Click the Linear gradient.

⑳ Click and drag from the bottom of the original subject to the bottom of the reflection using a white-to-black gradient.

The reflection appears to fade away from the subject.

㉑ Click Opacity and drag to make the reflection appear realistic.

#74

DIFFICULTY LEVEL

TIPS

Did You Know?
The Clone Stamp reflection technique works well on product shots and can also be used as a creative tool for special effects with rasterized type.

More Options!
The Clone Source feature works with the Healing Brush tool (🖌) as well as with the Clone Stamp tool.

Try This!
You can change the offset values in the Clone Source panel to change the distance of the reflection from the subject. You can also vary the angle of the reflection by clicking and dragging the angle icon (◢) or typing a set number of degrees in the Clone Source panel.

Blend one image into another with a
DISPLACEMENT MAP

You can paste one image onto another and blend the pasted image into the Background layer by changing the blend mode. The layer blending modes control how the colors in the top image combine with the pixels in the underlying image. They do not affect the texture of either image. To make the top image blend into the texture of the base image and make the final image appear more realistic, you can use the Distort filter and a special file called a *displacement map*.

A displacement map is a grayscale version of an image saved as a Photoshop file. The Displace filter then uses the displacement map essentially as an applied texture. The black areas are the low points and the light areas are the high points of the contours of the original image.

You create a displacement map of the background image and save it as a Photoshop file. Then you apply the Displace filter to the second image to be placed on top of the background image.

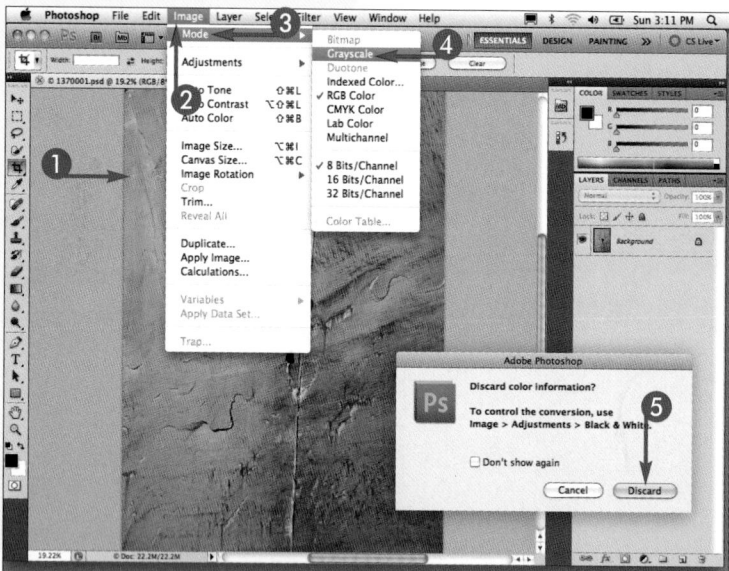

① Open the photo that will be the background image.

② Click Image.

③ Click Mode.

④ Click Grayscale to convert the image to grayscale.

⑤ Click Discard in the warning box that appears.

The image is converted to grayscale.

⑥ Press ⌘+Shift+S (Ctrl+Shift+S).

The Save As dialog box appears.

⑦ Type **Displace** in the name field.

⑧ Click here and select Photoshop.

⑨ Click Save.

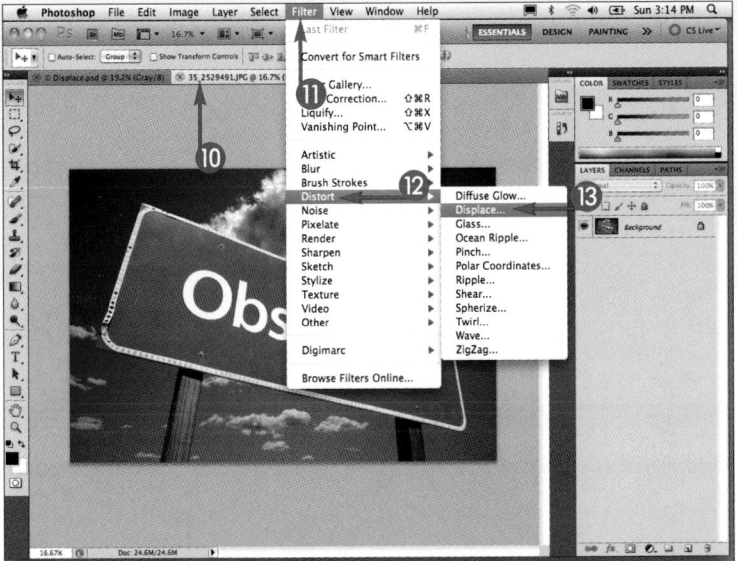

① Open the image that will be blended.

① Click Filter.

② Click Distort.

③ Click Displace.

The Displace dialog box appears.

④ Type a value such as **10** to **30** in both the Horizontal Scale and Vertical Scale fields.

Note: *The scale is the amount the filter shifts the selected pixels to make them wrap to the contours of the base image, based on the brightness values in the displacement map. A low to middle value generally creates a more realistic result for this task.*

⑤ Click Stretch To Fit (○ changes to ⊙).

⑥ Click Repeat Edge Pixels (○ changes to ⊙).

⑦ Click OK.

Did You Know?

If your grayscale image has very strong contrasts, you can reduce the amount of texture in the displacement map image by somewhat blurring the image after changing it to grayscale. Click Filter and select Blur and then Gaussian Blur. Increase the Radius slightly and click OK. Then save the image as the displacement image in the Photoshop (.psd) format.

More Options!

You can add a layer mask to hide the effect on certain areas of the image. For example, you could add a layer mask and paint with black over the rock climber to make the sign appear to be painted on the rocky surface only, and behind the rock climber.

Blend one image into another with a
DISPLACEMENT MAP

The Displace filter applies the displacement map to wrap one image precisely over the other, forcing the top layer to reflect the contours of the base layer. Other Photoshop filters such as Conté Crayon, Glass, Lighting Effects, and Texturizer also load other images or textures to produce their effects. However, not all these filters load the second image in the same way. The Displace filter specifically distorts an image based on the different values of gray in the displacement map image. The greater the contrast in

the gray values, the more texture appears in the blended image.

This technique works best if both original images are the same size and resolution. You can start by clicking Image and selecting Image Size to resize the two photos to match. If the images are not the same size, the Displace filter either resizes or tiles the map, depending on the settings you select in the Displace dialog box. Stretch To Fit resizes the map, whereas the Tile option repeats the map, creating a pattern (see steps 15 and 16).

A dialog box appears.

⑱ Navigate to select the displacement image you saved earlier.

⑲ Click Open.

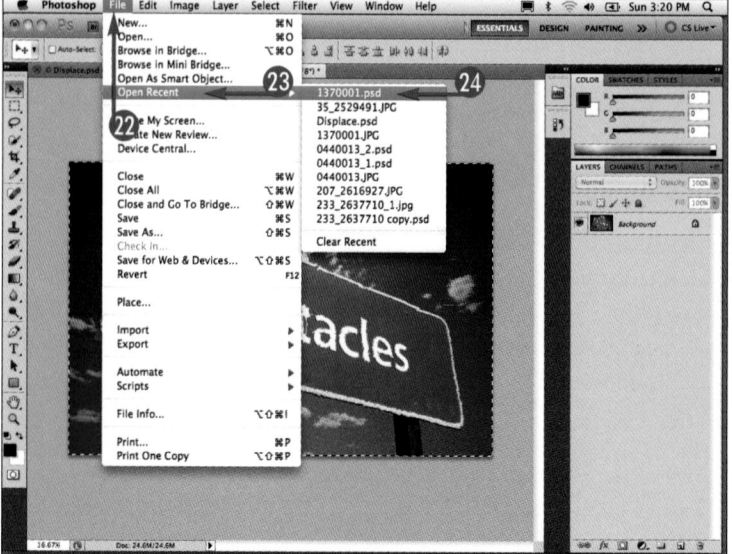

The image is distorted.

⑳ Press ⌘+A (Ctrl+A) to select the entire image.

㉑ Press ⌘+C (Ctrl+C) to copy the image.

㉒ Click File.

㉓ Click Open Recent.

㉔ Click to select the original color image for the background again.

168

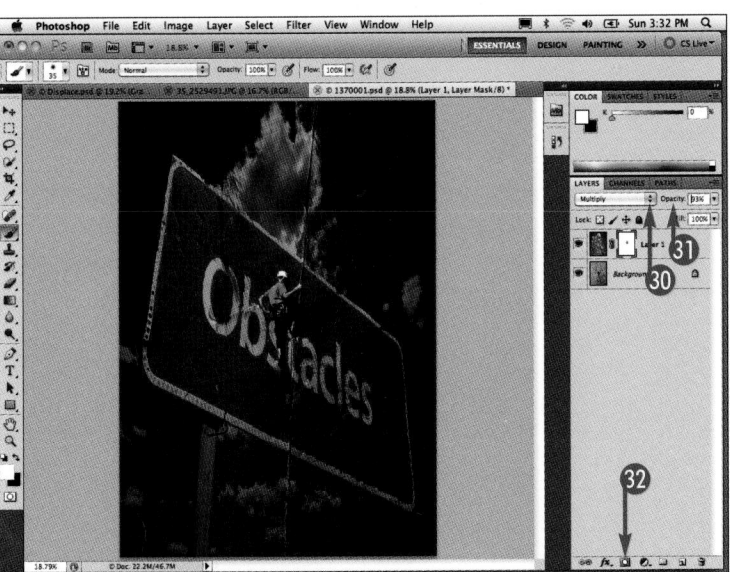

- The background image opens.

25 Press ⌘+V (Ctrl+V) to paste the distorted image as a layer on top of the background image.

26 Press ⌘+T (Ctrl+T).

- The Transformation anchors surround the pasted image.

27 Press ⌘+0 (Ctrl+0) to fit the entire area on screen.

28 Click and drag on the anchors to resize the top image.

29 Click the Commit button to apply the transformation.

The top layer blends into the background layer, wrapping around the contours in the background image.

30 Click here and change the blending mode of the top layer to Multiply.

31 Click Opacity and drag to the left to reduce the layer opacity to fit your image.

32 Click the Layer Mask button to add a layer mask and paint with black to make the subject stand out.

#75
CONTINUED

TIPS

Important!

Photoshop cannot recognize a displacement map image with layers. Be sure to flatten any image you plan to use as the displacement map before saving it as a Photoshop (.psd) file.

Try This!

You can convert the photo to a black-and-white image using the Adjustments panel. Use the sliders to control the amount of dark and light areas for the contours of the displacement map. Flatten the image before saving it as the displacement Photoshop file.

More Options!

You can apply a slight Gaussian Blur filter to the distorted layer to make it blend even more with the underlying background layer.

Design with Text Effects

If a picture is worth a thousand words, then a picture with words has even more persuasive powers. Although Photoshop CS5 is not a page-layout application, you can add text to photographs for impact or to create an original design. You can also create special text effects to give personality to the words or even use the words alone to create the design.

With Photoshop, you can apply effects to text in more creative ways and more quickly than is possible using traditional tools. Not only can you see the end result instantly, but you also have complete creative freedom to make changes without wasting any paper or ink. By combining layer styles, patterns, colors, and fonts, you can create type with just the right look for your project. You can use text on images and make the words appear as part of

the photograph and, conversely, make the photo appear as part of the text.

When you type in Photoshop, the text is placed on a type layer as *vectors,* or mathematically defined shapes that describe the letters, numbers, and symbols of a typeface. You can warp, scale, or resize the words, edit the text, and apply many layer effects to the text while preserving the crisp edges. Some commands, such as the filter effects, painting tools, and the perspective and distort commands and tools, however, require the type to be *rasterized,* or converted to a normal layer filled with pixels. Be sure to edit the text before rasterizing because, once the type layer has been converted, the letters are essentially pixels on a layer and are no longer editable as text.

Top 100

Design
A NEON SIGN

You can give text a neon look using a variety of Photoshop techniques. Although Photoshop does include the Neon Glow and Glowing Edges filters, these colorize and soften the edges of a rasterized image and do not render the traditional neon sign look.

You can apply a neon look to text using layer styles and keep the text editable. You can give letters a simple neon effect using Inner Glow and Outer Glow, or add a double neon glow to give your sign a more realistic appearance.

Type with a double neon glow can be very effective for creating album or Web page titles. Set against a dark background, the glowing letters quickly capture your viewer's attention. You can easily change the way the letters glow on the screen by changing the background layer color or adding a gradient background. The double glow effect surrounding the letters can be altered anytime by simply double-clicking the effect button in the Layers panel to reopen the Layer Style dialog box. You can even save the layer style effect to reapply it for other types of vector shape layers.

❶ Open a new blank document.

❷ Click the Type tool.

❸ Select the font family, style, and size in the Options bar.

   Note: *Select a bold font preferably with rounded corners. This example uses Chalkboard Bold.*

❹ Click in the image and type your text.

❺ Click the Commit button to commit the type.

❻ Click the Layer Style button.

❼ Click Outer Glow.

● The Layer Style dialog box appears with a pale yellow glow color selected.

❽ Click and drag the Spread slider to about 15%, to set the boundaries of the glow away from the text.

❾ Click and drag the Size slider to about 15 pixels to specify the dimensions of the glow.

   Note: *You can reopen any layer style by double-clicking its name in the Layers panel later to readjust the amounts and change the look at the end of the project.*

❿ Click Drop Shadow (☐ changes to ☑).

172

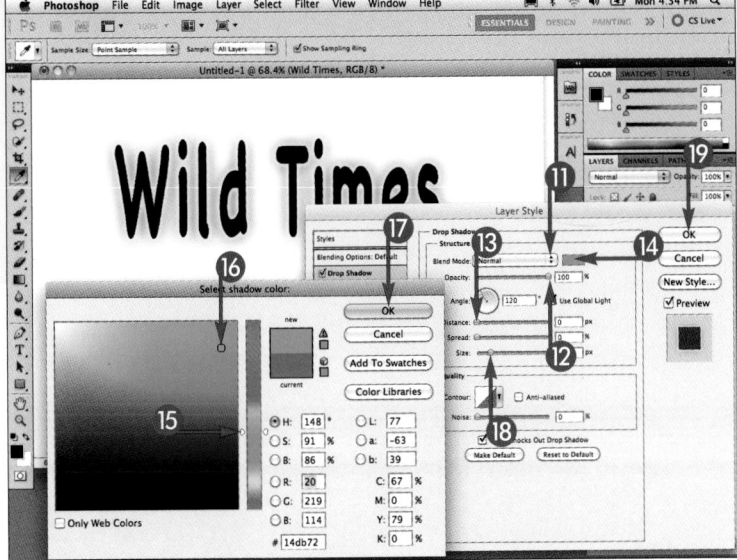

The dialog box changes.

⑪ Click here and select Normal.

⑫ Click Opacity and drag to 100%.

⑬ Click and drag the distance to 0 pixels.

⑭ Click the color box.

The Select Shadow Color dialog box appears.

⑮ Click and drag the color slider.

⑯ Click in the color box to select a shadow color.

⑰ Click OK to close the Select Shadow Color dialog box.

⑱ Click and drag the Size slider until the text looks good in the preview.

⑲ Click OK to close the Layer Style dialog box.

⑳ Press D to reset the foreground color to black.

㉑ Click the Background layer to select it.

㉒ Press Option+Delete (Alt+Backspace) to fill the background with black.

● Double-click the Layer Style button in the Layers panel to alter the neon glow style by changing the sliders or the colors.

The text appears with a neon glow against a dark background.

TIPS

Attention!

Neon looks best on a dark background; however, it does not need to be black. You can also select the Gradient tool (▦) and click and drag across the Background layer to create a gradient color fill.

Keyboard Shortcuts!

With the Type tool (T.) selected, pressing Return (Enter) moves the cursor to the next line; pressing ⌘+Return (Ctrl+Enter) or Enter on the numeric keypad applies the type or any transformations. Pressing Esc cancels the type layer.

Try This!

Type some text with the Type tool. Before clicking the Commit button (✓), press and hold ⌘ (Ctrl) to open the transformation anchor points. Click and drag the anchors while pressing ⌘ (Ctrl) to transform the type.

CREATE A CUSTOM WATERMARK
to protect your images

If you upload your proofs to a Web site for client approval, or if you sell your digital artwork online, you want people to see the images but not to use the files without your permission. You can add a custom watermark with a transparent look to any image to protect it and still keep the image visible.

A custom watermark can be as simple as your name and the copyright symbol. After typing your name on a type layer and adding a large copyright symbol as a

shape layer, you can add any kind of bevel or embossed style to your personalized watermark. You can even copy the two layers to another photo to apply the same custom watermark. To give a transparent look to each layer, you can lower the Fill opacity, which affects only the fill pixels, leaving the beveled areas appearing like a glass overlay. You can also use the same technique to give a transparent look to any text, shape, or other layer on any image.

1. With the image open, click the Type tool.

2. Click Window and select Character to open the Character panel.

3. Select the font family, size, and text options in the Character panel or Options bar.

4. Click in the image and type the text for your watermark, such as your name or company name.

5. Click the Commit button.

6. Click the Layer Style button.

7. Click Bevel and Emboss.

The Layer Style dialog box appears.

8. Click here and select Inner Bevel.

9. Click here and select Smooth.

10. Click and drag the Size slider to increase the effect.

11. Click OK.

12 Click and hold the Rectangle tool and select the Custom Shape tool.

13 Click here and select the copyright symbol.

DIFFICULTY LEVEL

14 Press Shift and click and drag in the photo to create a copyright symbol.

● The copyright symbol appears on the image and as a shape layer in the Layers panel.

15 Press Option (Alt) and click and drag the Layer Style button from the type layer to the shape layer to copy the effect.

The same emboss style is applied to the copyright symbol.

16 Double-click in the Fill data field and type **0**.

17 Click the type layer to select it and repeat step 16.

The name and copyright symbol appear embossed on the image.

TIPS

Caution!
The Custom Shape tool has three options on the Options bar. When you select the Shape tool for the copyright symbol, make sure that the Shape Layer button (⬚) is highlighted on the Options bar rather than the Paths or Fill Pixels button.

Did You Know?
The Layers panel includes two types of sliders. The Opacity slider affects the visibility of both the filled pixels and the layer style. The Fill slider affects only the transparency of the filled pixels without changing any style that is applied.

Important!
Double-clicking the Type thumbnail in the Layers panel selects and highlights all the type on that layer. Double-clicking the blank space next to the name of a layer opens the Layer Style dialog box.

MAKE TEXT WRAP
around a subject

In Photoshop, you can type text in several ways. When you type, the text is placed on a type layer and the words remain editable until you rasterize, convert the type layer to a shape layer, or flatten the layer. You can then scale, skew, or rotate the text to fit a design. You can control the flow of the characters you type within a bounding box by typing text as a paragraph, either horizontally or vertically. For text in a rectangular shape, you can use the Type tool to drag diagonally and define a bounding area and then click and type the text. Typing text as a paragraph is useful for creating brochures, scrapbooks, or various design projects.

Although Photoshop is not a page-layout program, you can still make text wrap around an object by using custom shapes as text bounding boxes or by creating a shape to use as a container for text. You can drag out any solid shape selected from the Custom Shape picker using the Custom Shape tool and type into the shape as a bounding box. You can also use the Pen tool to create an original path to use as the bounding box. You can then fill the shape with paragraph text to create unique visual effects.

① Click the Pen tool or the Freeform Pen tool depending on the intended design.

② Click the Paths button in the Options bar.

③ Click and drag with the Freeform Pen tool to create the text container.

Note: *If you chose the Pen tool in step 1, click along an area with the Pen tool to create the container.*

④ Click the starting point to close the shape.

⑤ Click the Type tool.

⑥ Select the font style, size, color, and alignment.

⑦ Move the cursor inside the shape.

The cursor appears as an *I* in parentheses (⟨I⟩).

⑧ Click inside the shape.

Note: *If you click the shape line rather than inside the shape, the cursor appears as an I with a line across it (I̶) and the text then follows the line rather than stays inside the shape.*

A dotted bounding box surrounds the shape.

⑨ Type the text until the shape is full.

⑩ Click the Commit button.

⑪ Click the Move tool.

⑫ Click and drag in the shape to reposition it on the page if necessary.

⑬ Click the Background layer in the Layers panel to view the text without the outline of the shape.

TIPS

More Options!

You can also select a Custom Shape to fill with text, using steps 12 to 14 in task #77, and selecting the Paths button in the Options bar.

Did You Know?

Click the flyout arrow (▶) on the Custom Shape picker in the Options bar to load more shapes. Select All from the choices in the menu and click Append to add these to the current set.

Try This!

You can copy text from another document and paste it into the shape. Select the text in the other document, and press ⌘+C (Ctrl+C) to copy. Click the Photoshop document. Use the Type tool (T) to click in the shape. Press ⌘+V (Ctrl+V) to paste the text.

WARP TYPE
for a fun effect

You can create many different effects with type by warping the letters into various shapes. Although you can warp text on a rasterized layer, the letters lose their sharp edges and appear fuzzy. Using Photoshop's Warp Text feature gives text a completely new look and keeps the text sharp-edged and editable.

Type the text and then use the Warp Text dialog box to transform it. You can select from a variety of warp styles and use the sliders to alter the look. You can

control the direction of the warp as well as the size of the letters. Because the warp style is an attribute of the type layer, you can change the style at any time by reselecting the layer with the Type tool and opening the Warp Text dialog box. As long as the text is on an editable type layer, you can change the letters and color them individually. With the text on a separate layer, you can apply any layer styles before or after warping the text.

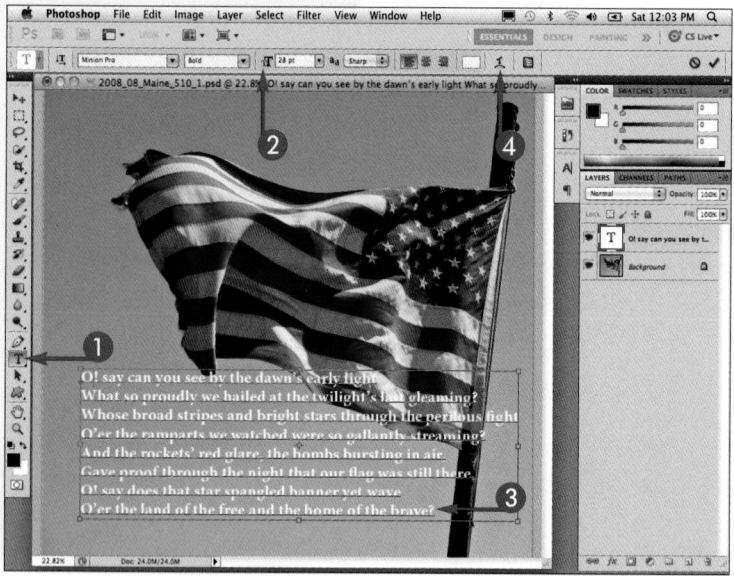

① In a new blank document or on an open image, click the Type tool.

② Select the font family, style, size, alignment, and color.

③ Click in the document and type the text.

④ Click the Warp Text button.

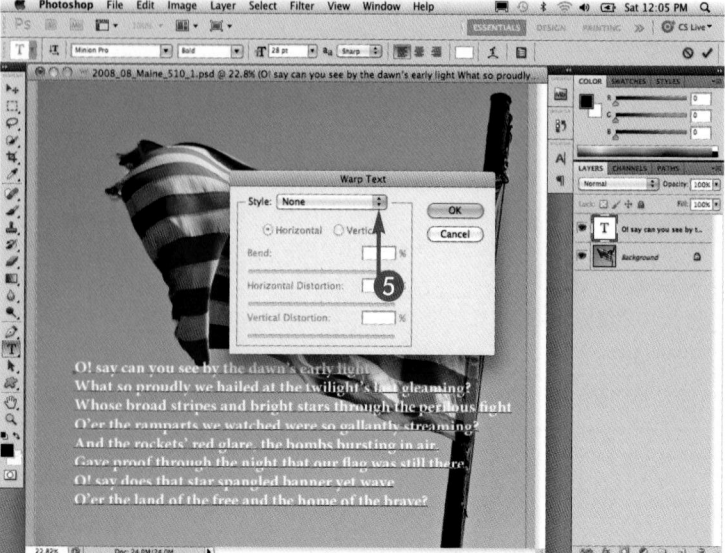

The Warp Text dialog box appears.

⑤ Click here and select a warp style such as Flag.

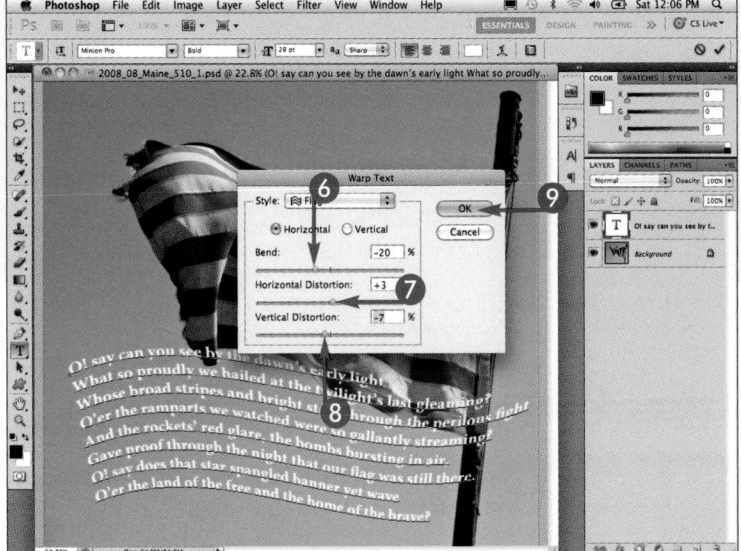

The text in the image changes to match the style selected.

6 Click and drag the Bend slider to change the amount of warp.

7 Click and drag the Horizontal Distortion slider to adjust the direction of the effect.

DIFFICULTY LEVEL

8 Click and drag the Vertical Distortion slider to change the effect.

9 Click OK to commit the warp.

10 Click the Commit button to apply the text.

The style of warp and changes to the text are committed.

● You can change the text color and style; see the tip section for more information.

TIPS

Try This!

You can click the Add a Layer Style button (🖪) at the base of the Layers panel to add effects such as a drop shadow.

Did You Know?

You can change the color of the text after you warp it. Select the Type tool (🅃) and click and drag across the text to highlight it. Click the foreground color in the Tools panel, select another color from the Color Picker, and click OK to close the dialog box. Click the Commit button (✓) in the Options bar.

More Options!

To see the color of the type as you change it, highlight the type. Then press ⌘+H (Ctrl+H), the keyboard shortcut to Hide Extras. The type remains selected but the highlighting is not visible. When you select another foreground color in the Color Picker, you instantly see the color on your text.

ADD PERSPECTIVE TO TYPE
and keep it sharp

When you warp a type layer, the letters always bend the shape to some degree, even if you set the Bend slider to 0 in the Warp Text dialog box. You can use the Edit menu's Transform submenu to scale, rotate, skew, or flip the text; however, the Perspective function is unavailable for a type layer. If you rasterize the layer, turning the letters into pixels, and then use the Perspective function to create the illusion of text disappearing into the distance, the characters blur as you change the angles. You can, however, add realistic perspective to type and

preserve the crisp edges by converting the type layer to a shape layer.

Converting type to shapes changes the type layer into a layer with a colored fill and a linked vector mask showing the outline of the letters. The outline is actually a temporary path and appears in the Paths panel as well. The text is no longer editable, but you can alter the vector mask, modify the paths, add layer styles, and use all the transformation tools to change the look.

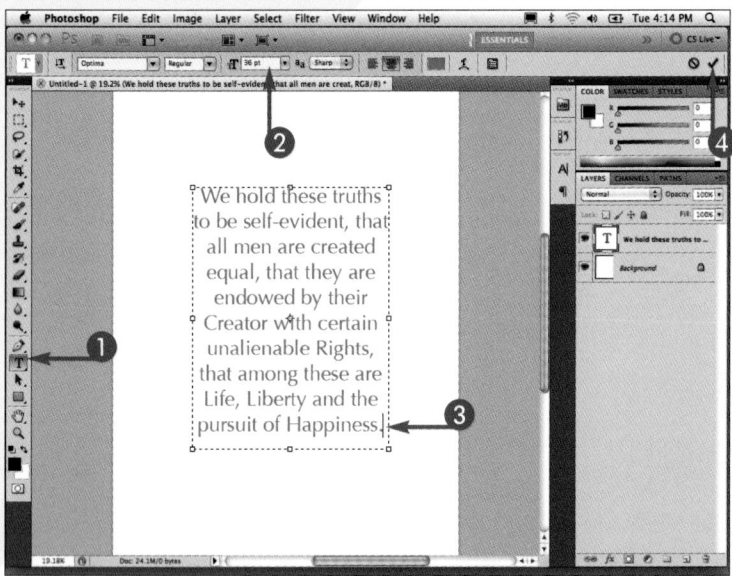

1 In a new blank document, click the Type tool.

2 Select the font family, style, size, justification, and color.

3 Click and drag an area in the image and type the text.

4 Click the Commit button.

5 Click Layer.

6 Click Type.

7 Click Convert to Shape.

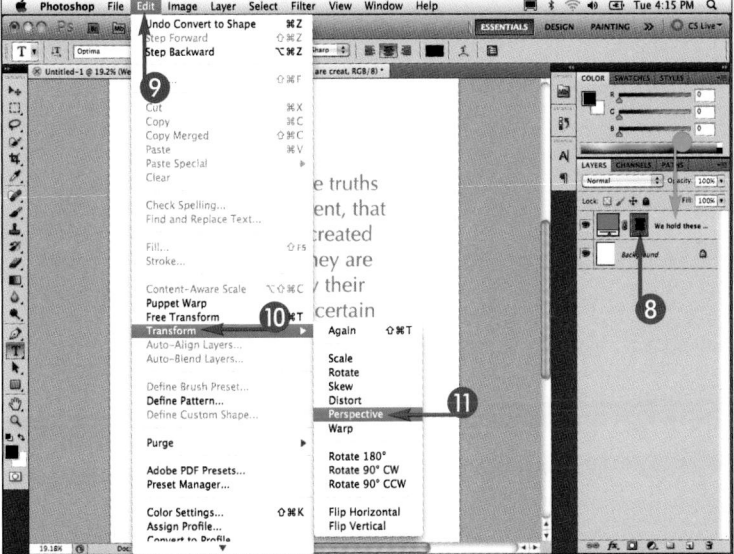

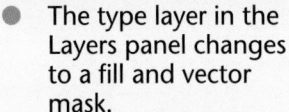

The type layer in the Layers panel changes to a fill and vector mask.

Note: *The type may appear jagged if the vector mask remains selected.*

8 Click the vector mask to deselect it.

9 Click Edit.

10 Click Transform.

11 Click Perspective.

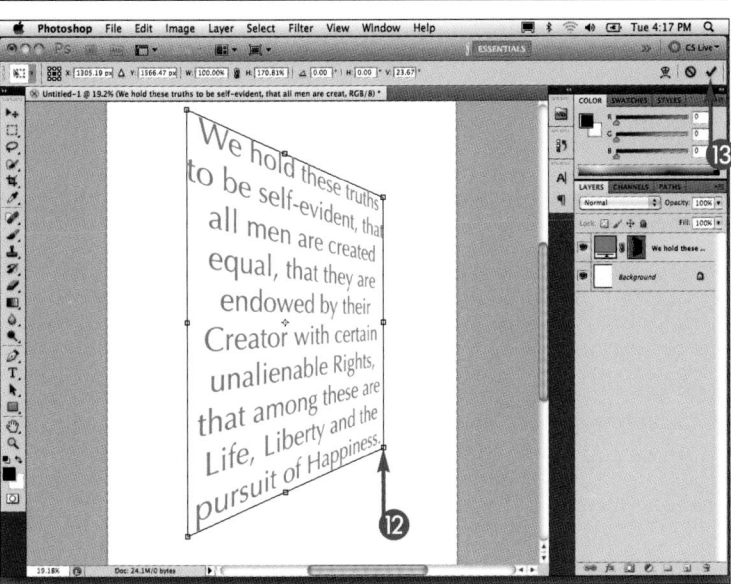

The text has a bounding box with anchor points.

12 Click any of the corner anchors and drag to change the shape of the text.

13 Click the Commit button.

The text retains its sharp edges even as it appears in a perspective plane.

TIPS

Change It!

You can change the look of the type, add a drop shadow or a glow, bevel and emboss, or even add a gradient. Click the Add a Layer Style button (*fx*) at the base of the Layers panel and select any of the options.

Try This!

When you need to select the Type tool to edit type, double-click the *T* in the type layer thumbnail in the Layers panel. The type on the layer is highlighted, and the Type tool is automatically selected.

More Options!

You can also edit type using the Character panel. Click Window and click Character to open the Character panel. You can then make any type changes directly in the panel.

Create a
PHOTO-FILLED TITLE

You can easily create mood-inspiring or memory-evoking titles for a photo or album page by making a photograph fill the letters. Photoshop includes four different Type tools: the Horizontal and Vertical Type tools and the Horizontal and Vertical Type Mask tools. When you use the Type Mask tools, Photoshop automatically creates a selection in the shape of the letters. However, using the regular Type tools to create photo-filled titles gives you more control over the design and makes it easier to see the area of the photo that will be cut out by the letters.

Filling text or any other object with a photograph or other image is one of the many collage and masking techniques in Photoshop. You type text and use a *clipping mask* to *clip* the photograph so that it shows only through the letters and *mask* the rest of the photo. Because the letters are on an editable type layer, you can change the text even after the letters are filled with the image. You can also add a drop shadow or emboss the type layer to make the letters stand out.

① Open a photograph to use as the base photo.

② Click the Type tool.

③ Select the font family, style, and justification. The size will be readjusted when you transform the text in step 5.

Note: *Thick sans serif fonts work best for this effect.*

④ Click in the image and type the text.

⑤ Press ⌘ (Ctrl) and click and drag the transformation anchors to stretch the type.

⑥ Click the Commit button.

⑦ Click and drag the Background layer over the New Layer button to duplicate it.

⑧ Click and drag the Background copy layer above the type layer.

⑨ Click Layer.

⑩ Click Create Clipping Mask.

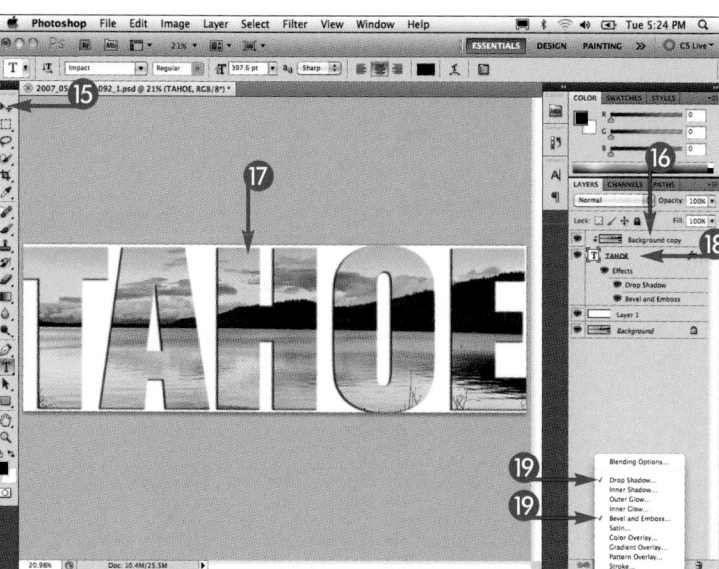

- The Background copy layer is indented with an arrow in the Layers panel, but the image does not change.

⑪ Click the New Layer button to create a new empty layer named Layer 1.

⑫ Click and drag the new empty layer below the type layer.

⑬ Press D to reset the foreground and background colors.

⑭ Press ⌘+Delete (Ctrl+Backspace) to fill the layer with white.

The photo appears to fill the letters on a white background.

⑮ Click the Move tool.

⑯ Click the Background copy layer to select it.

⑰ Click and drag in the image to move the photo into position inside the letters.

The photo is repositioned within the letters, creating an attractive photo title.

⑱ Click the type layer to select it.

⑲ Click the Add a Layer Style button (*fx*) to add a drop shadow and Bevel and Emboss layer effect.

TIPS

More Options!

You can change the background color for the text. Press Option+Delete (Alt+Backspace) in step 14 to fill the layer with black instead of white. Or click in the color box in the Tools panel to open the Color Picker and select a different foreground color. Close the Color Picker and then press Option+Delete (Alt+Backspace).

Important!

Be sure to highlight the Background copy layer, which must be above the type layer, when you create the clipping mask. Changing the stacking order of the layers after a clipping mask has been applied can remove the clipping mask.

More Options!

You can create a clipping mask using two different keyboard shortcuts. Press Option (Alt) and click between the two layers in the Layers panel, or select the layer and press ⌘+Option+G (Ctrl+Alt+G) to clip it to the layer below.

Create a realistic
COLORED SHADOW

When you apply a drop shadow to text using a Layer Style drop shadow, the shadow is gray. Actual shadows of text or other objects are not gray and do not always have the same opacity. Shadows reflect the colors of the objects they cover. If you select another color for the shadow in the Layer Style dialog box, the shadow appears unnatural and uniform in color.

You can add type to a photo and have the shadow appear with the same colors that occur in the real world. Create a selection and add a Brightness/Contrast adjustment layer. Then, link the shadow

layer to the text layer, and reposition the text in the image. The shadow follows the moved text, automatically adjusting itself to the colors in the image below.

You can use the same technique to add a realistic shadow to text or to any object in an image. Add depth to natural-light shadows under a tree or increase the shadow of a person in a sunlit photo. The greater the number of colors and textures affected by the shadow, the more natural your colored shadow appears.

① With an image open, click the Type tool.

② Select the font family, style, size, and color.

   Note: You can click in the Size field and type the size.

③ Click in the image and type the text.

④ Click the Commit button.

   Note: Optionally, press ⌘+T (Ctrl+T) and drag the corner anchors to adjust the type.

⑤ ⌘+click (Ctrl+click) the type layer thumbnail to select the letters.

⑥ Click Select.

⑦ Click Modify.

⑧ Click Feather.

   The Feather Selection dialog box appears.

⑨ Click in the Feather Radius field and type a small amount such as **10**.

⑩ Click OK.

⑪ Click the Type tool.

⑫ Press the right or down arrow keys multiple times.

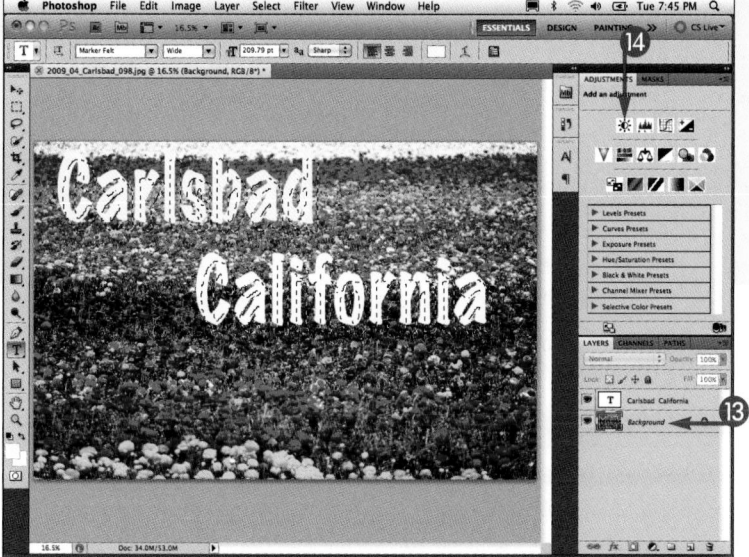

The selection marquee moves down and to the right.

⑬ Click the Background layer thumbnail to select it.

⑭ Click the Brightness/Contrast Adjustment button in the Adjustments panel.

Note: *You can also click the New Adjustment Layer button (*  *) in the Layers panel and click Brightness/Contrast.*

The Brightness/Contrast adjustments appear in the panel, and the selection marquee is hidden.

⑮ Click and drag the Brightness slider to the left to create the drop shadow.

⑯ ⌘+click (Ctrl+click) both the adjustment layer and the type layer in the Layers panel to select them.

⑰ Click the Link Layers button.

The type and its shadow are now linked.

⑱ Click the Move tool.

⑲ Click and drag the text around in the photo.

The shadow follows the text, and the shadow's colors automatically adjust to the colors in the area of the photo below.

DIFFICULTY LEVEL

TIPS

More Options!

You can also keep the type and its shadow separate by not linking them as in steps 16 and 17. You can then move the type and its shadow independently to view the shadow in a new position for a different effect.

Did You Know?

You can quickly change the alignment of type using keyboard shortcuts. Click in the type and press Shift+⌘+L (Shift+Ctrl+L) to align left; press Shift+⌘+R (Shift+Ctrl+R) to align right; and press Shift+⌘+C (Shift+Ctrl+C) to align center.

Did You Know?

The size of the feather radius (see step 9) sets the width of the feathered edge of the selection and ranges from 0 to 250 pixels. A small feather radius in a very large image may not be visible, and a large feather radius in a smaller image can spread too far away from the selection.

WEAVE TEXT AND GRAPHICS
for intriguing designs

You can create a design using type as the central element by changing the letter styles and size, adding layer effects, warping the text, or adding perspective. You can also make the individual letters interweave and interact with each other to add more interest to any project. By converting type layers to shapes and overlapping them, you can make some of the areas transparent to the background, creating new design elements. Add a shape to the text, make the letters intertwine with the shape, and you can create eye-catching logos or page titles.

When you convert a type layer to a shape, the text is no longer editable. However, you can still move individual letters. You can transform, warp, and resize one letter at a time or a group of letters. You can also add layer styles to the grouped design elements and change the look completely. Because the letters and shapes are all on one layer, the color and any layer styles that you use are applied to all the elements on the layer. Flatten the layers as a final step in creating the design.

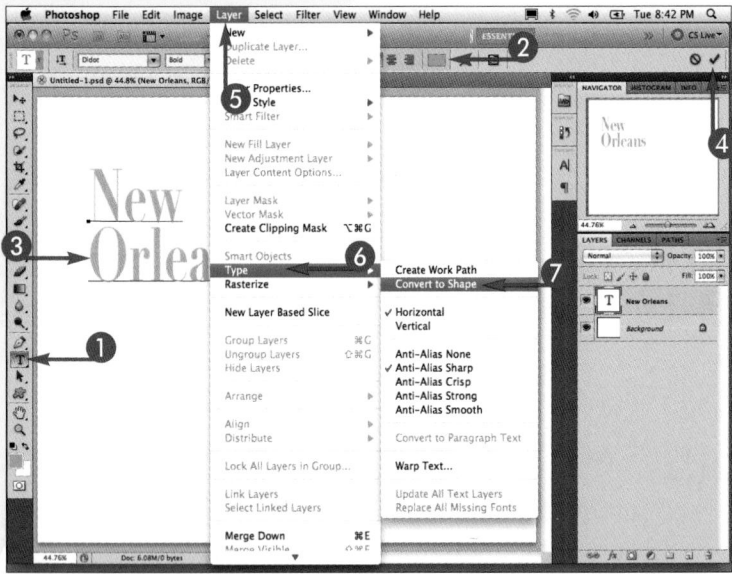

1 In a new blank document, click the Type tool.

2 Select the font, size, and color.

3 Click in the document and type the text.

4 Click the Commit button or press ⌘+Return (Shift+Enter) or Enter on the numeric keypad to commit the type.

5 Click Layer.

6 Click Type.

7 Click Convert to Shape.

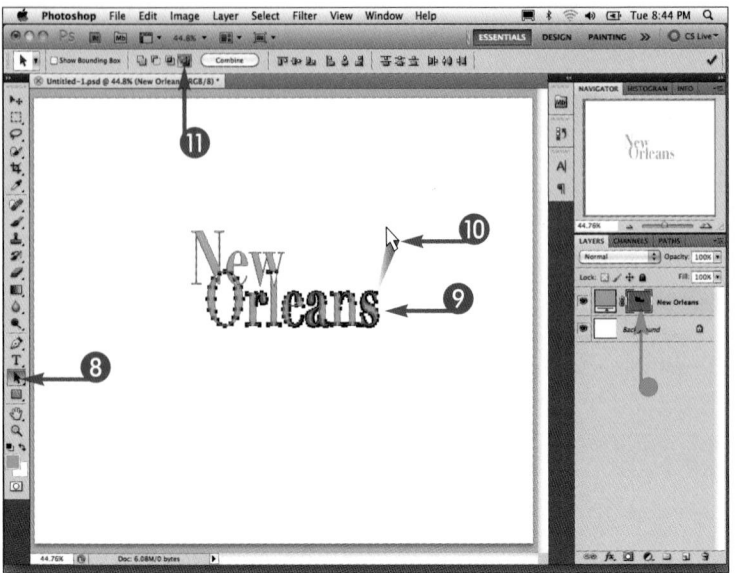

● The type layer changes to a fill layer and a vector mask.

8 Click the Path Selection tool.

9 Click and drag over one line of text to select it.

10 Click and drag the line up to overlap the first line of text.

11 Click the Exclude Overlapping Shape Areas button.

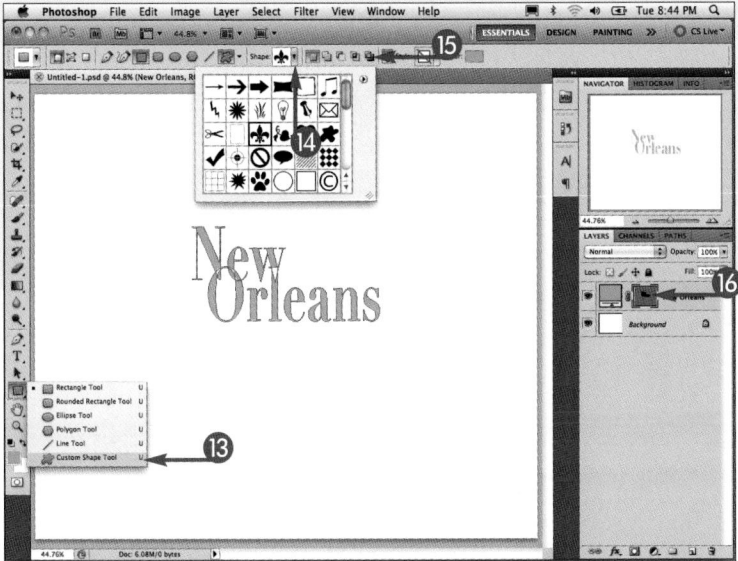

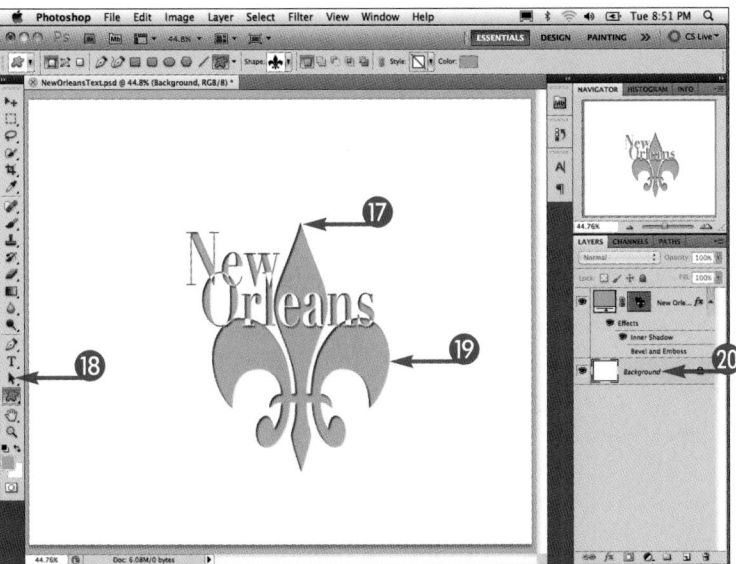

The areas of text that overlap are reversed out.

⓬ Repeat steps 9 to 11 for any other lines of text.

⓭ Click and hold the Rectangle tool and click the Custom Shape tool.

⓮ Click here and click a shape to select it.

⓯ Click the Exclude Overlapping Shape Areas button.

⓰ Make sure that the vector mask thumbnail in the Layers panel is selected.

⓱ Click and drag the shape over the letters.

The areas of the shape and text that overlap are reversed out.

⓲ Click the Path Selection tool.

⓳ Click the shape and drag it to reposition it in the design if necessary.

The shape interacts differently with the type as it overlaps different areas.

⓴ Click the Background layer to view the design.

83

DIFFICULTY LEVEL

TIPS

More Options!

You can apply a layer style to the shapes and letters. Try adding an Inner Shadow or a Bevel and Emboss layer style. Click Texture and select a pattern for the Texture Elements. The pattern is applied to all the colored areas.

Important!

The vector mask layer thumbnail in the Layers panel must be selected before adding the shape in step 15 and all the type and the shapes must be on the same layer for the Exclude Overlapping Shape Areas button (▣) to function.

Did You Know?

The Path Selection tool (▶) is quite different from the Move tool (▶+). You can use the Path Selection tool to move individual letters or the shape separately. Click one letter and move it to create a different look. To undo the move, click the previous state in the History panel.

Chapter 9

Create Digital Artwork from Photographs

Even if you have never tried art in any form or claim you cannot draw a straight line, you can use Photoshop to draw line art, sketch a person or a building, create a painted portrait, or paint with oils and watercolors. You can replicate traditional art materials and techniques and see immediate results on your screen. And if you have worked with traditional materials and know how to draw and paint, you can find a whole new source of creativity as you experiment with different techniques. With digital art media, you can try all sorts of projects without wasting any paper products or paints. You can vary colors, mix media, copy, trace, or draw freehand, and even erase the results before anyone else can see your attempts!

The key to creating digital artwork is to vary the tools and combine different layers, effects, Smart Filters, masks, and blend modes. Each different method produces a different result. When starting with a photograph, the style and the subject matter of the photo also affect the overall look of the finished piece. You can use different techniques to make your work more efficient and at the same time expand your creative horizons. Photoshop CS5 includes even more natural media tools than previous versions. The new Mixer Brush lets you mix colors on your canvas and vary the wetness and length of brush stroke. The new heads-up display, HUD, color picker lets you select color hues and shades right in the document window. You can even use either a strip-styled or color-wheel-styled HUD. Photoshop CS5 enables everyone to create art digitally.

Top 100

Make any photo appear
SKETCHED ON THE PAPER

You can make a photo appear to be sketched onto the page, giving a traditional photograph an entirely new look. You can also apply this technique with a digital drawing or painting for a hand-drawn or -painted look. The main image appears to be applied to the paper using charcoal, soft pencils, or a paintbrush, leaving the edges and brush marks visible.

Starting with any image, you add a new layer filled with white. You then use the Eraser tool with a brush setting to erase through the white, revealing areas of the image on the underlying layer. Using this

technique on a slightly grainy photo even intensifies the hand-sketched look. You can configure the Eraser tool with any of Photoshop's brush settings and change them as you continue sketching the photo onto the page. The greater the number and opacity of the brush strokes, the more of your photograph appears on the white layer. By selecting rough-edged brushes and varying the style of the strokes you use, your photo takes on the characteristics of a sketched image.

1. Click the New Layer button in the Layers panel to add a transparent layer.

2. Click Edit.

3. Click Fill.

   The Fill dialog box appears.

4. Click here and select White.

5. Click OK.

A white layer covers the photo.

6. Click Opacity and drag to the left just enough to see the image underneath.

7. Press E or click the Eraser tool (⌀).

8. Click here to open the Brush picker.

9. Click a brush with a rough-looking edge.

10. Click and drag the Size slider to a large brush size.

DIFFICULTY LEVEL

⓫ Click and drag across the image using several broad strokes.

⓬ Click here to open the Brush picker again.

⓭ Click another brush or drag the Size slider to adjust the size.

⓮ Click and drag across the image to add more brush strokes.

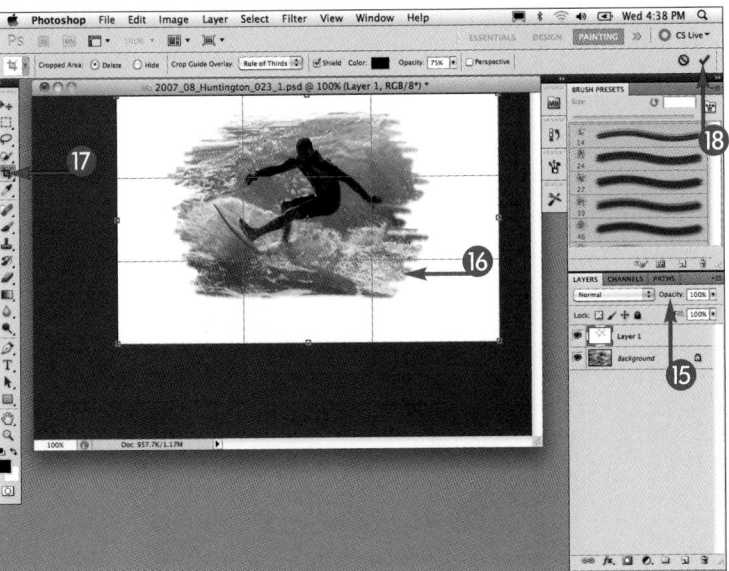

⓯ Click Opacity and drag back to 100%.

⓰ Continue applying just enough strokes until the image looks hand-sketched.

⓱ Click the Crop tool and crop the image if necessary.

⓲ Click the Commit button to apply the crop.

The image appears to be brushed or sketched on a page.

TIPS

More Options!

You can add more brushes to the Brush picker. Click the Brush arrow in the Options bar to open the Brush picker. Click the flyout arrow (▶) to open the Brush picker menu. Click a brush set from the bottom section, such as Dry Media Brushes. Click Append in the dialog box that appears to add the brushes to the existing list.

Customize It!

You can view brushes by name instead of the stroke thumbnail. Click the Brush arrow in the Options bar to open the Brush picker. Click the flyout arrow (▶) to open the Brush picker menu. Click Small List or Large List. You can return to the default brush set by selecting Reset Brushes from the same list.

ADD YOUR OWN SIGNATURE
to any artwork

Fine art prints are generally signed by the artist. You can sign your digital projects one at a time after they are printed, or you can apply a digital signature from within Photoshop. You can create a large-sized custom signature brush and save it in your Brush picker. You can then quickly apply your signature digitally to all your art projects.

You can change the Size slider in the Brush picker to add a signature to your images with any size signature brush, and you can apply the signature in

any color by selecting a specific color as the foreground color before applying the brush.

When you sign your project, add a new transparent layer for the signature. You can then add layer styles and easily change the color of the signature or even create a blind embossed signature effect.

Creating your own signature brush is best accomplished using a Wacom pen tablet because signing your name with a mouse, trackball, or trackpad is difficult.

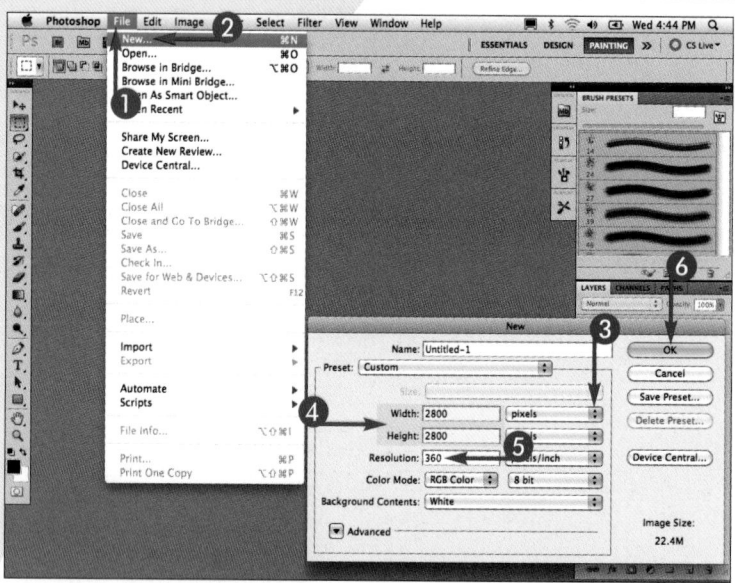

① Click File.

② Click New.

The New dialog box appears.

③ Click here and select pixels.

④ Click in the fields for the width and height and type **2800**.

Note: Starting with a file 2800 × 2800 pixels at 360 ppi gives you the space to make a brush at the largest brush size of 2500 × 2500 pixels. You can then easily resize the brush to fit many different images.

⑤ Click in the field for the resolution and type **360**.

⑥ Click OK.

Note: Make sure Background Contents is set to White, the default.

A new empty document appears.

⑦ Press B to select the Brush tool.

⑧ Click here to open the Brush picker.

⑨ Select a hard-edged brush.

⑩ Click and drag the Size slider to make the brush 35 to 40 pixels.

Note: You can pick any hard-edged brush for your signature. The numbers here are just guidelines.

⑪ Click in the white image and click and drag with the brush to sign your name.

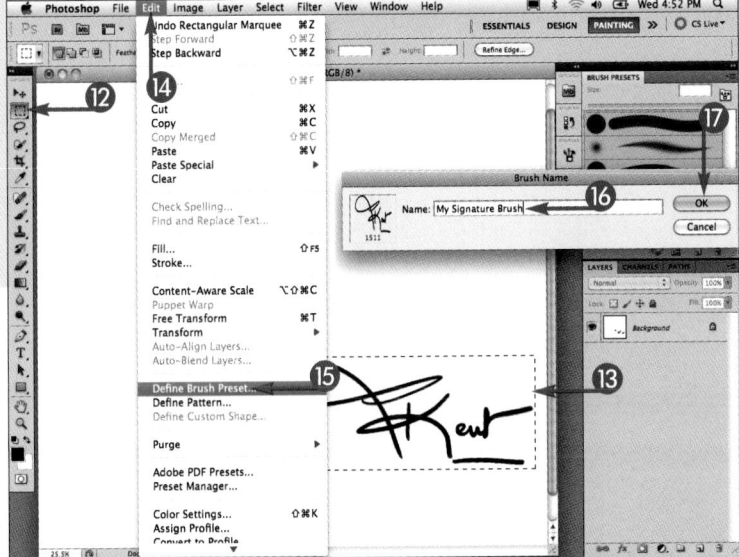

Your signature appears on the white image.

⑫ Click the Rectangular Marquee tool.

⑬ Click and drag just around your signature.

⑭ Click Edit.

⑮ Click Define Brush Preset.

The Brush Name dialog box appears.

⑯ Type a name for your signature, such as **My Signature Brush**.

⑰ Click OK to save the signature brush.

⑱ Open an image to which to add the signature.

⑲ Click the New Layer button to add an empty layer.

⑳ Press B to select the Brush tool.

㉑ Click here to open the Brush picker.

㉒ Select your signature brush and click and drag the Size slider to adjust the size to fit the image.

㉓ Click once in the image.

Your signature appears.

● You can click the Add a Layer Style button to add a drop shadow or bevel.

TIPS

Did You Know?

You can create a custom brush from any signature or any other image up to 2500 × 2500 pixels in size. Signature brushes work best when created with a brush hardness set at 100%.

Attention!

If you create your original signature in color, the custom brush is still created in grayscale. You can change the signature color by changing the foreground color before applying the signature brush or after it is applied to the image on a separate layer.

Try This!

Add a drop shadow and bevel to the signature layer using the Layer Styles dialog box. Then lower the Fill opacity of the layer to 0 to give your signature a blind embossed look.

CONVERT A PHOTO
to a high-contrast stylized image

You can create a unique design using a high-contrast black-and-white image and a gradient background or fill. You can easily transform any photograph into a high-contrast black-and-white image using an adjustment layer. You visually control the maximum contrast in your photo and determine the areas to turn black and the areas to change to white. You can customize the design by adding a solid color or a colored gradient and using a blend mode to combine the effects.

Start with either a color or a grayscale image and add a Threshold adjustment layer to convert the image to a high-contrast black and white. By adding another adjustment layer with a color or a gradient fill and then setting the top layer to either the Lighter Color or Darker Color blend mode, you can give the design a completely different look. All the changes you make are applied using adjustment layers so the image remains completely editable, enabling you to experiment and try different colors and gradients until you find the best design for your project.

① With an image open, click the Threshold button in the Adjustments panel.

Note: Select an image with contrasting areas for the best results.

The color information in the photo is changed to either black or white.

- The Threshold slider and histogram appear in the Adjustments panel.

② Click and drag the slider to the right to make more tonal values shift to black or to the left to change more tones to white.

③ Click the New Adjustment Layer button.

④ Click Gradient.

Note: Clicking Solid Color produces a two-tone stylized effect with only one color and either white or black.

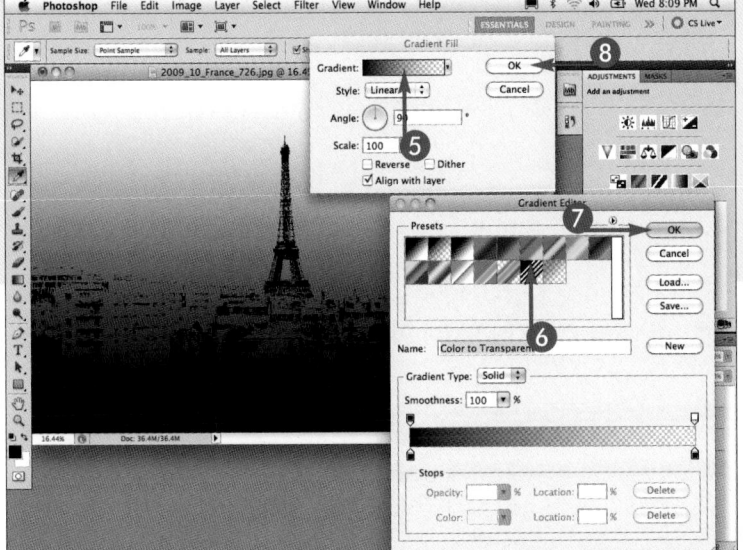

The Gradient Fill dialog box appears.

⑤ Click in the color bar to open the Gradient Editor.

The Gradient Editor appears.

⑥ Click a different preset.

⑦ Click OK to close the Gradient Editor dialog box.

⑧ Click OK to close the Gradient Fill dialog box.

The gradient is applied as a separate adjustment layer covering the image.

⑨ Click here and select Lighter Color to make the gradient cover only the black areas in the image, leaving the other areas white.

The gradient layer blends with the high-contrast of the image.

TIPS

More Options!
You can create your own custom gradient in the Gradient Editor. Double-click in each of the lower color stops under the gradient to open the Color Picker and select a new color.

Try It!
Instead of Lighter Color (see step 9), click the blend mode arrow in the Layers panel and select Darker Color. The image changes, applying the gradient blend to the previously white areas in the image.

Did You Know?
The Darker Color mode displays only the lowest color value from both the blend and base layer; conversely, Lighter Color shows only the highest value color. For example, with the gradient layer in Lighter Color blend mode, only the lightest color value in the image layer below — white in this case — appears through the gradient layer.

POSTERIZE A PHOTO
for a Warhol-style image

Photoshop includes a Posterize command in the Image⇨Adjustments menu that automatically posterizes an image by mapping the Red, Green, and Blue channels to the number of tonal levels that you set. However, to create a posterized image reminiscent of the Andy Warhol style of the 1960s and 70s, you can get better results using three adjustment layers in succession instead. Use a Black & White adjustment layer to convert the photo to a grayscale image. Then apply a Posterize adjustment layer, specifying the levels that correspond to the

number of colors you want in the final image. A lower number of levels limits the number of colors that will be included, making the image more stylized. Finally, use a Gradient Map adjustment layer to map a color to each of the levels of gray. You can edit any of the adjustment layers to change the colors or levels until you get the look that you want. For the best result, select a photo with a main subject on a plain background, or extract the subject and place it on a black background.

① Press ⌘+J (Ctrl+J) to duplicate the Background layer.

② Click the Black & White button in the Adjustments panel.

The image turns to grayscale and the options in the Adjustments panel change.

③ Click Auto to see if the contrast improves.

④ Move the color sliders to enhance the contrast.

⑤ Click the arrow to return to the Adjustments panel list.

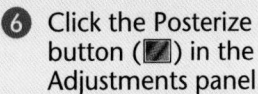

6 Click the Posterize button () in the Adjustments panel.

The options in the Adjustments panel change.

7 Type a low number such as **4** in the Levels data field.

Note: Use a low number to limit the color gradations when creating a posterized effect.

8 Click the arrow to return to the Adjustments panel list.

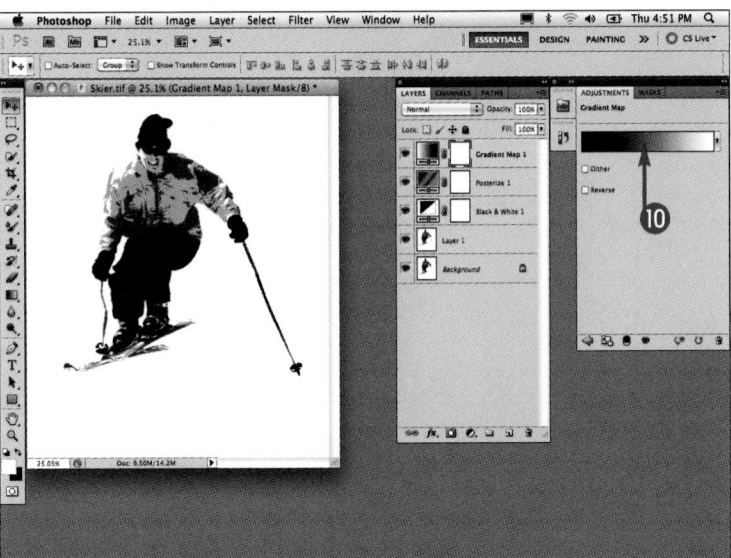

9 Click the Gradient Map button () in the Adjustments panel.

The options in the Adjustments panel change.

10 Click in the gradient.

TIPS

Attention!
You get better results if you match the number of gray levels with the number of color stops in the gradient. To add more gray levels, double-click the Posterize thumbnail in the Layers panel and increase the number of levels. Then double-click the Gradient Map thumbnail and add more color stops.

Try This!
If you want a more realistically colored image, fill the color stops on the right in the Gradient Editor with the lightest colors that you want in the image and the color stops on the left with the darkest colors. The greater the number of color stops and the more colors you use, the wilder the image appears.

Important!
The Poster Edges filter, located in the Artistic filters in the Filter Gallery, creates a completely different look, more like an etching than a posterized print.

POSTERIZE A PHOTO
for a Warhol-style image

After posterizing the first photo by following all twenty-one steps in this task, you can duplicate the steps on four different copies of the original photo. Use different colors for each copy and place them in a new document to replicate the Andy Warhol–like layouts with four posterized and juxtaposed images.

To create the second copy, open your posterized image and click File and then Save As to give the copy another name. Click the Gradient Map thumbnail in the Layers panel to reopen the Gradient Map pane of the Adjustments panel. Click in the gradient to open the Gradient Editor again. Change the colors for

each of the four color stops, always selecting the darkest colors for the leftmost color stops and the lightest colors for the rightmost color stops. Click OK to close the Gradient Editor. Click File and then click Save, saving the second version with all the layers. Repeat this process until you have four different versions of the image.

To finish the project, you can follow the steps in task #31 to create a quadriptych, or just create a new empty document and click File and then Place to place each of the four images on the page.

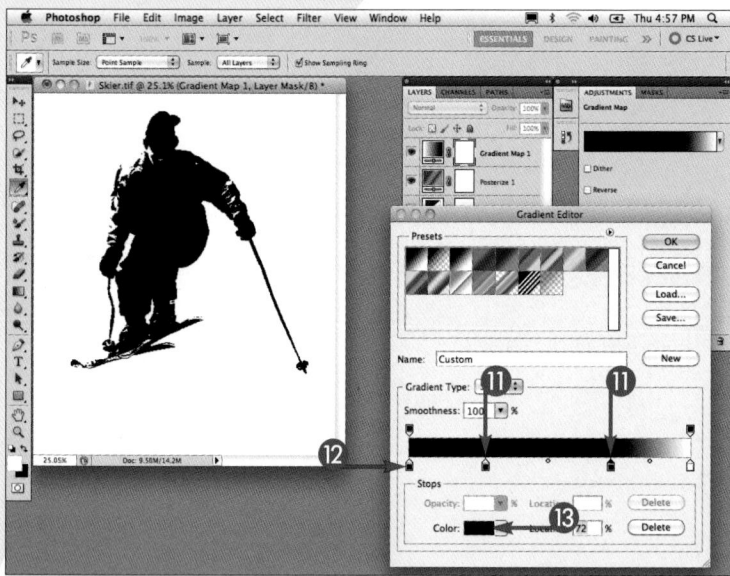

The Gradient Editor appears.

⑪ Click two areas below the gradient bar to add two more color stops.

Note: The number of color stops should match the levels of posterization that you entered in step 7.

⑫ Click the leftmost color stop to select it.

⑬ Click the Color thumbnail.

The Select Stop Color dialog box appears.

⑭ Click and drag the color slider.

⑮ Click in the color selector to select the darkest of the four colors you will use.

Note: If the warning triangle appears, the color is out of gamut for printing and will not print as you see it. Click the small square below the warning triangle to select the closest in-gamut or printable color.

⑯ Click OK to close the Select Stop Color dialog box.

⑰ Repeat steps 12 to 16, selecting each of the other three color stops to change the color.

⑱ Click OK to close the Gradient Editor.

⑲ Click the Black & White adjustment layer in the Layers panel.

The Black & White options appear in the Adjustments panel.

⑳ Click and drag the color sliders to change the amount and areas of posterized colors.

㉑ Press ⌘+S (Ctrl+S) to save the file with all the layers so you can readjust it later.

The final image looks like a posterized and stylized print design from another era.

TIPS

Customize It!

Use the Dodge and Burn tools to change individual areas. Click Layer 1, the Background copy layer, and click the Dodge tool (). Click and drag in the image to make some areas lighter. Click the Burn tool (🖐) and click and drag other areas to make them darker. You can lower the Exposure setting in the Options bar to lessen the change.

More Options!

Instead of using a Gradient Map, you can merge the Background copy with the Black & White and the Posterize adjustment layers. Then add colors individually to gray areas. Select the first gray area using the Magic Wand (🪄) with a tolerance of 0. Click the foreground color and select a new color. Press Option+Delete (Alt+Backspace) to fill the selection.

Set up the Mixer Brush and HUD for
ART PROJECTS

Photoshop CS5 introduces new painting tools with the Mixer Brush and HUD, or heads up display. It also includes a new type of paint brush tip, the Bristle tips. You can use these new tools with any drawing or painting project, whether starting from a reference photo or starting with a blank canvas or paper.

The Mixer Brush let you blend colors together directly on open documents. You can use the Mixer Brush presets to specify the wetness of the canvas and the amount of paint for the brush to pick up. And you can set the brush to sample all the layers or only the one selected.

The Bristle tips are included in the Brush picker. Bristle tips help you paint more natural-looking strokes by defining the length, the thickness, the density, and the texture of the brushes.

The HUD is an on-screen color picker. Pressing ⌘+Control+Option (right-click+Alt+Shift) as you click makes the HUD appear under the cursor. Drag the cursor without lifting the keys to change the hue or lightness/saturation.

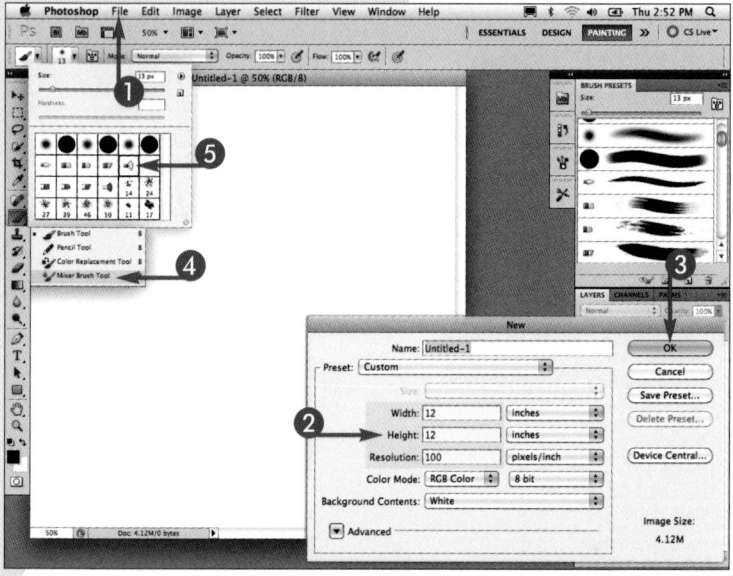

1. Click File and select New.

   The New dialog box appears.

2. Click in the data fields and set the width and height to 12 inches and the resolution to 100.

3. Click OK.

   A new document opens filled with white.

4. Click and hold the Brush tool and select the Mixer Brush tool.

5. Click the Brush picker and select a Bristle tip brush.

   Note: The Bristle tip brushes have icons that look like brush heads.

   The Bristle brush preview appears on the page.

   Note: When using a Wacom tablet, the preview mimics the movement of the pen.

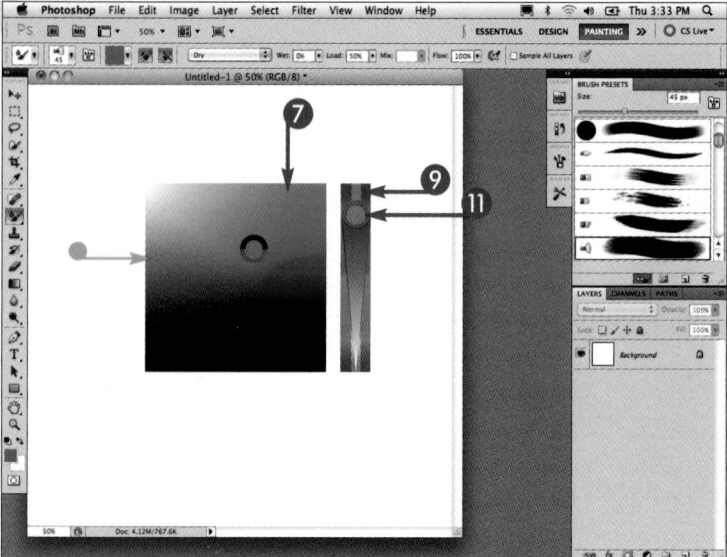

6. Press ⌘+Control+Option (right-click+Alt+Shift) as you click and hold the pen or the mouse button.

● The HUD appears.

7. Release the three keys and drag the cursor to the top right corner of the shade box.

8. Still pressing and holding the pen or mouse button, press the spacebar.

9. Move the cursor over the Hue bar.

10. Release the spacebar without lifting the pen or releasing the mouse button.

11. Drag along the Hue bar to select a hue.

12. Lift the pen or release the mouse button to select the color.

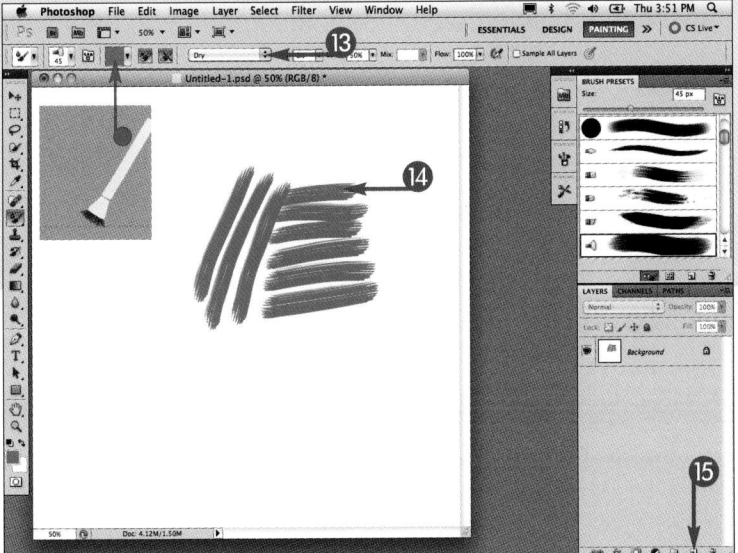

- The Current Brush Load swatch fills with the selected hue and shade.

⑬ Click here and select Dry.

⑭ Click and drag to paint in the blank document.

⑮ Click the New Layer button to add a new transparent layer.

⑯ Repeat steps 6 to 14, selecting a different hue and shade, adding more lines that touch or overlap the original painted lines.

⑰ Click Sample All Layers in the Options bar (☐ changes to ☑).

⑱ Click here and select Very Wet, Heavy Mix.

⑲ Click and drag over the lines to blend the painted strokes.

TIPS

Did You Know?

You can load multiple colors on a tip at one time by pressing Option (Alt) as you click an area. You can change the settings to load the brush after each stroke (🖌), or to clean the brush after each stroke (🗙) with the two buttons in the Options bar.

More Options!

You can set Photoshop's general preferences to view the HUD as a color wheel or a color strip. With the HUD on-screen, you can press the spacebar and release the keys to temporarily lock the HUD in place, and move over the hue selector to change the hue.

Try This!

With a Bristle brush tip selected, a small preview on-screen shows you how the bristles appear. You can minimize the size of the preview box or turn it off directly on the box itself. You can also toggle the preview box on and off using the button on the bottom of the Brushes panel.

Turn a photograph into a
PENCIL SKETCH

Sketching with a pencil is often the beginning step for many forms of drawing or painting. A sketch can be as simple as a line drawing of the subject or as complex as a finely shaded graphite illustration. You can create a pencil sketch with Photoshop CS5 using the pencil or brush tools and drawing on a blank document. You can also start with a reference photograph as an underlying layer and use the Mixer Brush and Bristle tip brushes to draw on a new layer, sampling the photo layer. You can even create a

sketch without really knowing how to draw by using a high-contrast photograph and following the steps in this task.

You start by opening a photo using the File menu and selecting Open As Smart Object. Then you duplicate the layer using the Layer menu to select New Smart Object via Copy. By working on Smart Object layers, you can adjust the filters applied to each layer at any time to change the look.

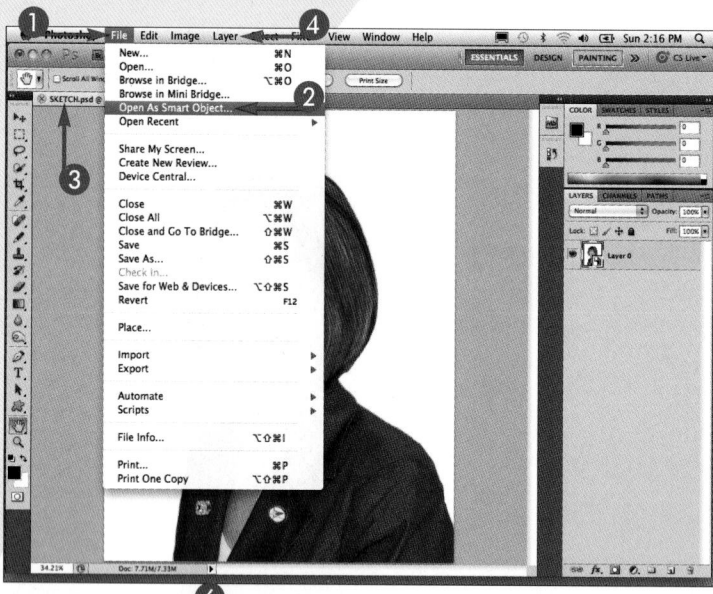

① Click File.

② Click Open as a Smart Object.

③ Navigate to the photo to open it.

The photo opens as a Smart Object layer.

④ Click Layer, Smart Objects, and New Smart Object via Copy.

Note: Duplicating a Smart Objects layer via a copy lets you edit the filters applied to each layer independently of the others.

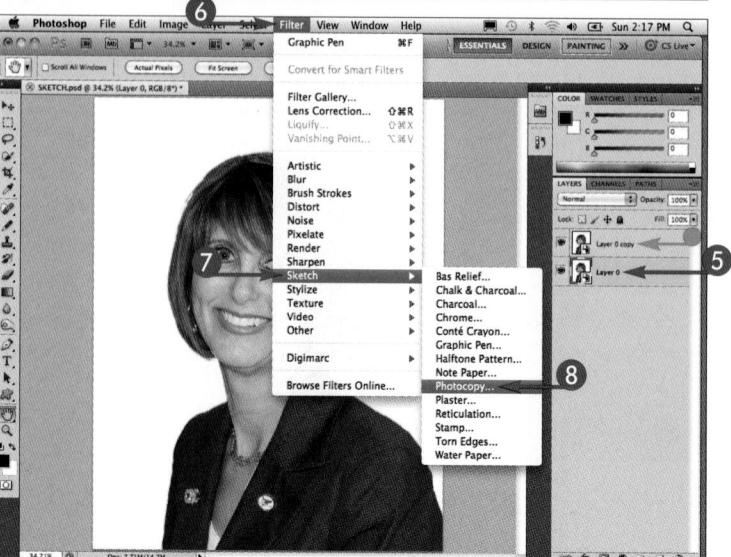

● The second layer in the Layers panel is also a Smart Objects layer.

⑤ Click the bottom layer to select it.

⑥ Click Filter.

⑦ Click Sketch.

⑧ Click Photocopy.

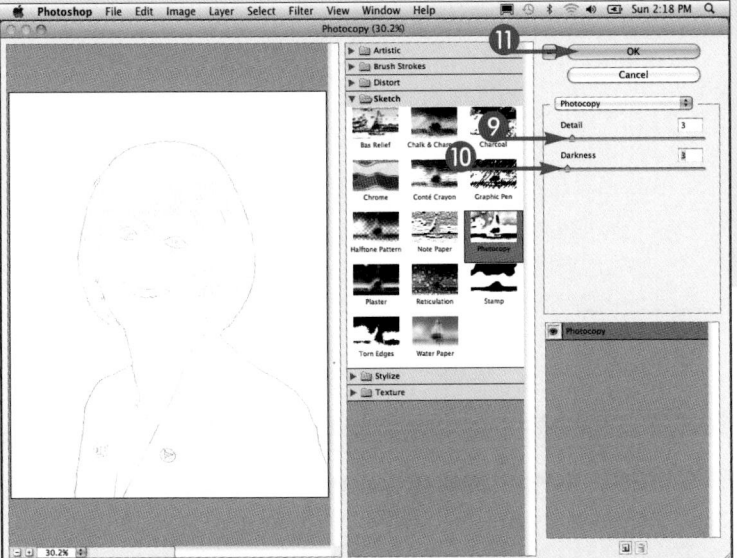

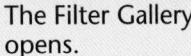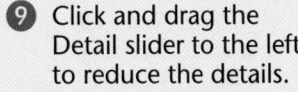

The Filter Gallery opens.

9 Click and drag the Detail slider to the left to reduce the details.

10 Click and drag the Darkness slider to the left to have just a basic outline of the main subject.

11 Click OK.

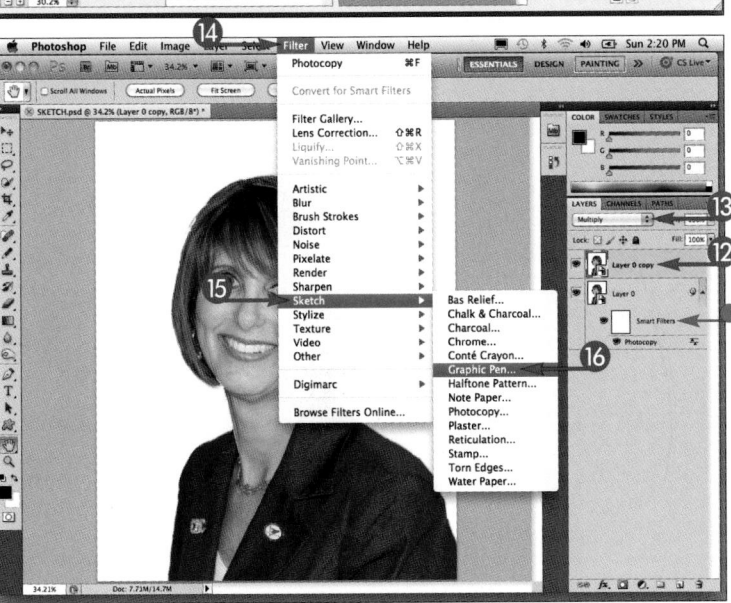

● The Photocopy filter is applied to the bottom layer but not visible on screen.

12 Click the top layer to select it.

13 Click here and change the blend mode to Multiply.

14 Click Filter.

15 Click Sketch.

16 Click Graphic Pen.

17 In the Filter Gallery, adjust the sliders until the subject appears with drawn lines and click OK.

Note: In the Filter Gallery, you can optionally change the stroke direction to right or left diagonal depending on the direction you would normally sketch lines or to mimic the lines in the photo.

TIPS

Did You Know?

Many of the Sketch filters use the foreground and background colors to create the sketched look. You can set the foreground color to a sepia tone or other color before applying the filter for a completely different look.

Caution!

Many filters, including the Sketch filters, only work on 8 Bit images. Set your image to 8 Bits/ Channel before starting the project by clicking the Image menu, Mode, and 8 Bits/Channel.

Try This!

By lowering the brush opacity before you start drawing, the lines appear more like soft pencil lines. To increase the darkness for outlines or shaded areas, paint over the same areas a second or third time.

Turn a photograph into a
PENCIL SKETCH

In the steps that follow, after applying different filters to each layer, you combine the layers into a new layer, and add a plain white layer below the combined layer. You add a black layer mask to the combined layer, which hides the filtered drawing, and then sketch parts of the image back in using white and a rough edged brush.

The key to creating any art with Photoshop is to apply different styles of brush strokes at different opacity settings. Start the sketch with a large, low opacity

brush. Start sketching from the outside edges in toward the center to create the outlines of the subject. By varying the brush size and opacity settings as you sketch, you can vary the lines and shading, and reveal as much detail as you want.

You can give the sketch a finished and more realistic look by adding a top layer filed with a colored paper pattern, and changing the blend mode of the colored paper layer to multiply revealing sketched image.

⑱ Press ⌘+Option+Shift+E (Ctrl+Alt+Shift+E) to create a new layer combining both the other layers.

⑲ Click the New Layer button to add a new blank layer.

⑳ Click Edit.

㉑ Click Fill.

㉒ In the Fill dialog box, click here and select White.

㉓ Click OK.

㉔ Click and drag the blank layer below the combined layer.

㉕ Click the top, combined layer to select it.

㉖ Press D to reset the foreground color to black.

㉗ Option+click (Alt+click) the Layer Mask button.

● A black layer mask is added to the combined sketch layer and hides the sketch.

Note: After a black layer mask is added, the foreground color is automatically changed to white.

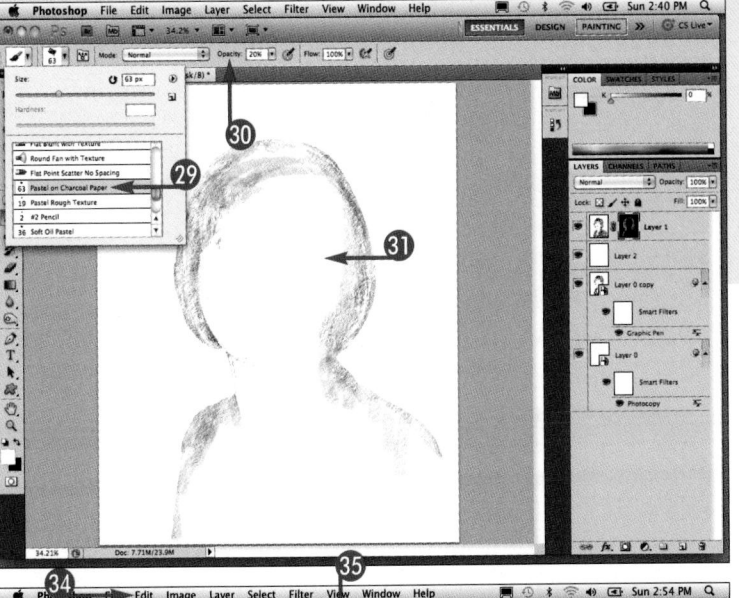

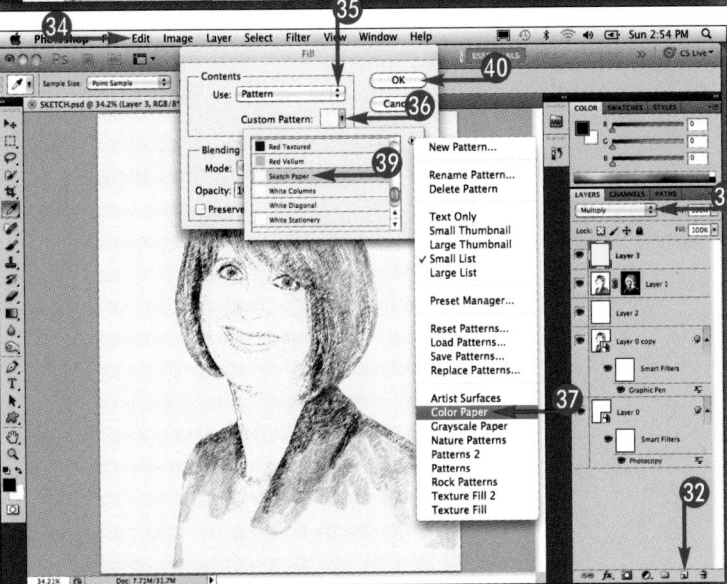

28 Press B to select the Brush tool.

29 Click the Brush picker and select a brush.

30 Click Opacity and drag to reduce the brush opacity to 20%.

31 Click and drag, painting with white to reveal the main shape of the subject.

Note: *Decrease the brush size and increase the brush opacity as you work on details.*

32 Click the New Layer button to add a new top layer.

33 Click here and change the top layer blend mode to Multiply.

34 Click Edit and Fill.

35 In the Fill dialog box, click here and select Pattern.

36 Click here to open the pattern options.

37 Click the pattern menu flyout arrow and select Color Paper.

38 Click Append in the warning dialog box.

39 Click a paper such as Sketch Paper.

40 Click OK.

89 CONTINUED

 **TIPS**

Did You Know?

The Fill dialog box includes a number of options. Once you click the Use arrow and select Pattern, click the Pattern box to see the open patterns. Then click the flyout arrow (▶) to open a submenu. Click a set of patterns such as Artist Surfaces, textures, or paper colors to load them. Be sure to select Append in the warning dialog box so the additional patterns are added to your list without replacing any existing patterns.

More Options!

You can view the patterns by name rather than just the thumbnail. Click Small or Large List in the submenu of the pattern menu to view the paper names.

Important!

Many filter effects require a lot of memory, especially when applied to a high-resolution or a large image. It is generally a good practice to close any unnecessary files and applications to make as much RAM available as possible for Photoshop to process artwork.

Create a digital
PEN-AND-INK DRAWING

You can create the look of a pen-and-ink drawing from a photograph using a variety of methods in Photoshop. Often the method you use depends on the subject matter of the original. Photoshop includes many filters such as Find Edges, which finds areas of contrast and outlines these; however, the filter applies the colors in the image to the edges. By changing a duplicated layer to high-contrast grayscale first and then applying the Smart Blur filter in the Edges Only mode, you get a black image with white lines. You can then invert the image to get black lines

on a white background. Depending on the look that you want, you can apply a filter such as Minimum with a 1-pixel radius to thicken the lines.

Often, the artistic effects do not work well on a large image. If your art project seems too photographic, click File and select Revert, and then click Image and select Image Size to reduce the image size before applying the filters. You can also reduce the amount of detail with a Median or noise reduction filter, before applying Photoshop filters to achieve artistic-looking results.

1 With an image open, click Filter, Noise, and then Median.

2 In the Median dialog box, click and drag the radius to 1, depending on the size of the image, to remove some detail.

3 Click OK.

4 Press ⌘+J (Ctrl+J) to duplicate the Background layer.

5 Click the Black & White Presets disclosure triangle and select a preset such as Infrared to get a high-contrast grayscale image.

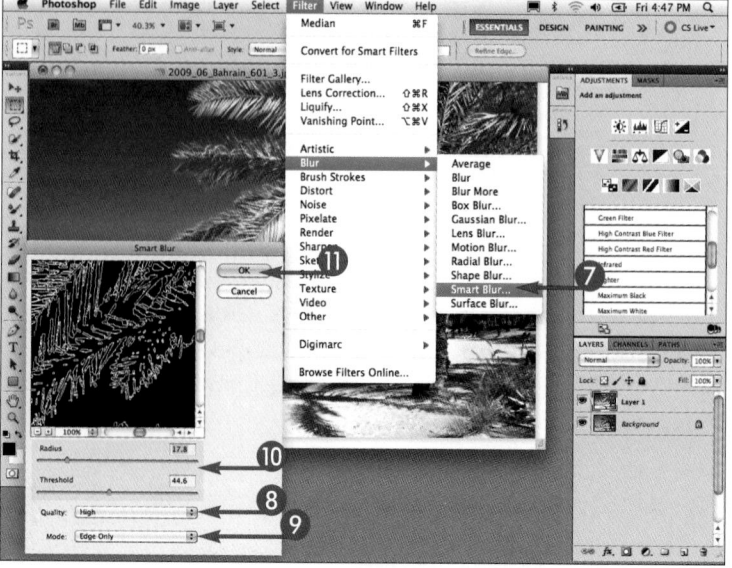

The image appears in grayscale.

6 Press ⌘+E (Ctrl+E) to merge the adjustment layer with Layer 1.

7 Click Filter, Blur, and Smart Blur.

8 In the Smart Blur dialog box, click here and select High.

9 Click here and select Edge Only.

10 Click and drag the Radius and Threshold sliders to see white outlines of the main features of your image.

11 Click OK.

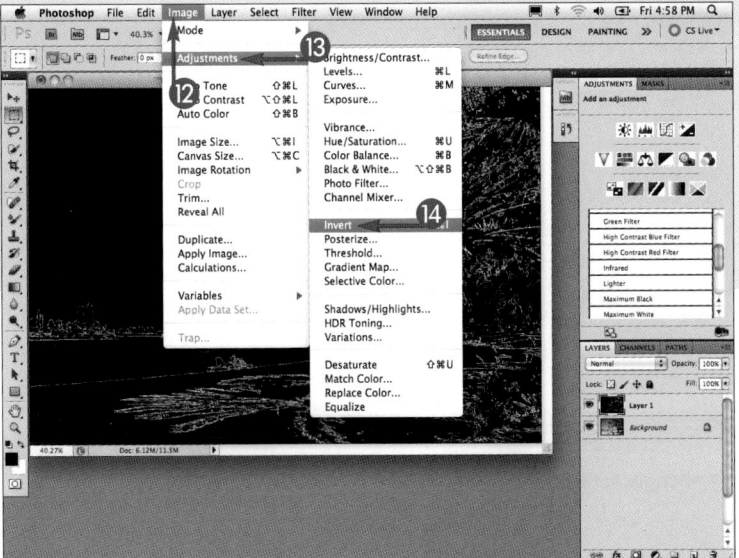

The Smart Blur filter is applied, and the image turns black with white outlines.

⑫ Click Image.

⑬ Click Adjustments.

⑭ Click Invert.

DIFFICULTY LEVEL

The drawing appears as black lines on a white background.

Note: Optionally, to make the lines darker, click Filter, Other, and then Minimum. Set the radius to 1 and click OK.

TIPS

Did You Know?

You can also make the lines thicker and darker by clicking Filter and selecting Artistic, and then Smudge Stick. When the Filter Gallery appears, reduce the stroke length to 0.

More Options!

You can get better results by increasing the contrast in the original image. After the grayscale conversion, click Image, Adjustments, and then Levels. Move both sliders slightly toward the center to increase the contrast.

More Options!

You can put the black lines on a separate layer. Click a white area using the Magic Wand tool (🔲). Click Select and then Similar to select all white areas. Click Select and then Inverse. Then press ⌘+J (Ctrl+J) to copy all the lines onto a new empty layer.

Create a
PASTEL DRAWING FROM A PHOTOGRAPH

Pastels are sticks of colors made from ground pigment and bound with resin or gum. Pastel drawings, popular since the 18th and 19th centuries, show broad painterly strokes, with rich colors blended or smudged in semi-opaque layers. Pastel papers generally have a rough surface texture to capture the pigment, and the paper texture often shows through the pastels in areas on the drawing.

You can re-create the look of a pastel drawing without knowing how to draw using Photoshop and a reference photo. As with most of the Photoshop filters, simply clicking a filter in the Filter Gallery rarely renders the sought-after effect.

The Pastel Drawing technique works best on a photo with a main subject and fewer distracting details. You can also use this technique to create pastel drawings of scenic images by applying many more brush strokes with different amounts of brush Load and Flow.

1. With a photo open, press ⌘+J (Ctrl+J) to duplicate the background layer.

2. Press ⌘+J (Ctrl+J) again to have three identical layers.

3. Click the top layer to select it.

4. Click Filter.

5. Click Stylize.

6. Click Glowing Edges.

The Filter Gallery appears.

7. Click and drag the Edge Brightness slider to 20 or until the edge is as bright as possible.

8. Click and drag the Edge Width slider until it just outlines the main subject.

9. Click and drag the Smoothness slider to around 10 or until the lines appear smooth.

10. Click OK.

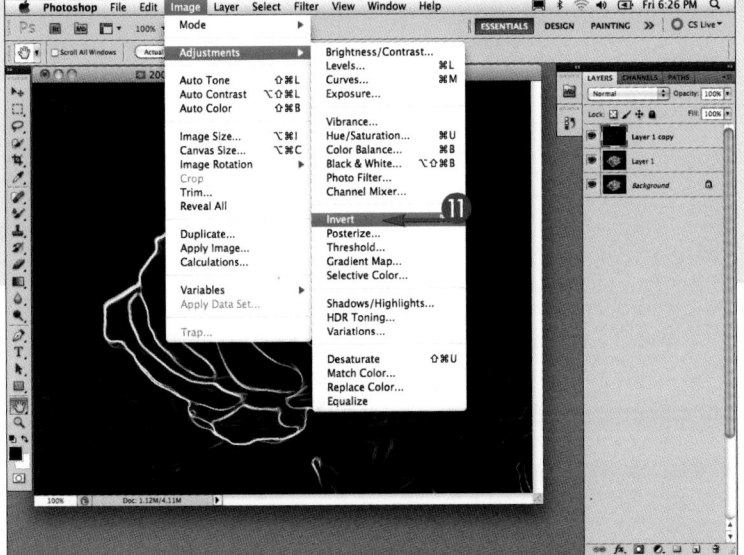

The Filter Gallery closes with the changes applied to the top layer.

⑪ Press ⌘+I (Ctrl+I) to invert the image or click Image, Adjustments, and Invert.

⑫ Press ⌘+Shift+U (Ctrl+Shift+U) to desaturate the image or click Image, Adjustments, and Desaturate).

The image changes to an outline drawing on a white background.

⑬ Click the blend mode for the top layer and change it to Multiply.

⑭ Click middle layer to select it.

⑮ Click Filter.

⑯ Click Blur.

⑰ Click Gaussian blur.

The Gaussian Blur dialog box appears.

⑱ Click and drag the Radius slider to the right to soften edges and detail.

⑲ Click OK.

The image appears fuzzy with a black outline.

TIPS

Try This!

To see the document in full on the screen, double-click the Hand tool (✋) in the Tools panel or click Fit Screen on the Options bar. To zoom to 100%, double-click the Zoom tool (🔍) in the Tools panel.

More Options!

Click the Current Brush Load swatch in the Options bar to select a color to use. You can also Option+click (Alt+click) in an image to select a paint color. The Color swatch fills with the mixture of colors in the sampled area. You can have the brush load only a solid color from the swatch by selecting Load Solid Colors Only.

Did You Know?

You can also load the color in the swatch onto the Mixer Brush by clicking the arrow and selecting Load Brush. Selecting Clean Brush removes all the color from the brush. You can use the Mixer Brush to blend multiple colors on the canvas and vary the wetness of the paint you apply.

Create a
PASTEL DRAWING FROM A PHOTOGRAPH

Depending on the subject matter, you can blur the underlying image more to soften the look. You can also fade the outline layer using the layer opacity slider so the final pastel displays less of a black outline. Or you can eliminate the outline layer for a completely soft pastel work.

To create a natural-looking pastel drawing, you start with a large brush size and very low flow setting just to brush in the main subject. Once the main areas are blocked in and you can see the base image faintly

through the colored paper, you can click and drag your paint strokes to follow the contours of the subject. Continue painting by decreasing the brush size and gradually increasing the flow percentage to cover more areas. Although the Mixer Brush is intended for mixing different paint colors on a canvas, using the Mixer Brush and the settings in the Pastel drawing technique give a more natural pastel-drawn appearance than the regular Brush tool.

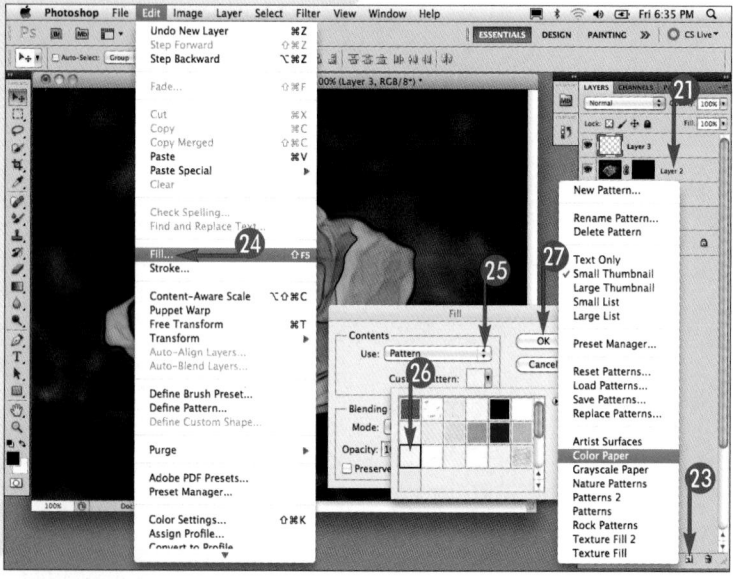

20 Click the top layer to select it.

21 Press ⌘+Shift+E (Ctrl+Shift+E) to combine all the layers onto a new top layer, Layer 2.

22 With the foreground color set to black, Option+click (Alt+click) the Layer Mask button (▣) in the Layers panel to add a black layer mask.

23 Click the New Layer button.

24 Click Edit and Fill.

25 In the Fill dialog box, click here and select Pattern.

26 Click the flyout arrow and select a pattern from the Color Paper custom patterns.

27 Click OK.

The colored paper fills the image on the screen.

28 Click here to change the paper layer's blend mode to Multiply.

29 Click the Eye icons for the bottom two layers to hide them.

30 Click the combined layer's layer mask to select it.

31 Press Shift+B multiple times to select the Mixer Brush tool.

32 Click the Brush picker and select a dry media brush such as Pastel on Charcoal Paper.

33 Click here and select Dry, Light Load.

34 Click here and set the flow to 5%.

35 Click Sample All Layers (☐ changes to ☑).

36 With white as the foreground color, click and drag to paint the image with many broad strokes, revealing the pastel image on the paper.

37 Continue to click and drag, making varied strokes and leaving some areas empty so the paper texture shows through.

38 Press the left bracket key several times to reduce the brush size and continue to paint.

39 Click here to increase the flow for finer details as you paint the image.

TIPS

Did You Know?

When you paint with the Mixer Brush, click and drag with a larger brush at first to cover the main area. Then reduce the brush size and click and drag in other areas to fill them in. With the flow set to 5%, every stroke adds more color to the painted area, so you can create a variegated pastel look.

More Options!

To finish the pastel drawing, click Layer and select Flatten Image. Click OK in the warning box to discard hidden layers. Save the drawing with a new name.

Attention!

You can increase the flow as you paint details. Be sure to leave some areas lighter and not cover the areas uniformly for a more hand-drawn look.

CHANGE A PHOTOGRAPH
into a pen-and-colored-wash drawing

You can easily transform a photograph into a pen-line-and-colored-wash drawing by applying different filters and adjustments to multiple layers. Traditional artists sometimes use India ink and a diluted ink wash to visualize the light and shadow areas before beginning a painting. The technique is also often used in figure studies to create expressive drawings. When applied to a landscape or cityscape, the pen line and diluted ink wash produces an image with a unique look. In the 17th century, Nicholas Poussin and Rembrandt applied such techniques to create rich and varied drawings.

Pen-and-ink-wash drawings are similar to and yet different from traditional watercolors, which generally do not use black lines.

Prepare an image by reducing the noise, brightening the image, and increasing the saturation. Then make multiple duplicates of the Background layer and edit each layer by applying different filters. You transform one of the duplicated layers into a layer of simplified outlines from the edges in the photograph. Then with an added layer filled with white to act as the background, you use the Brush tool to paint the washes.

① Click Filter, Noise, and Reduce Noise.

② In the Reduce Noise dialog box, click and drag the sliders to reduce the noise.

③ Click OK.

④ Increase the brightness and then the saturation if necessary using two adjustment layers as in task #17.

⑤ Press ⌘+E (Ctrl+E) to combine the layers.

⑥ Press D to reset the foreground and background colors.

⑦ Press ⌘+J (Ctrl+J) twice to make two duplicates of the Background layer.

⑧ Click the Background layer to select it.

⑨ Click the New Layer button to create a new empty layer.

⑩ Press ⌘+Delete (Ctrl+Backspace) to fill the empty layer with white.

⑪ Click the top layer, Layer 1 copy, to select it.

⑫ Click the Black and White button in the Adjustments panel.

The top layer changes to a grayscale image and the Black & White options appear in the Adjustments panel.

● You can optionally click and drag the sliders or click Auto to change the style of grayscale image.

⑬ Press ⌘+E (Ctrl+E) to merge the Black & White adjustment layer with the layer below.

⑭ Click Filter.

⑮ Click Stylize.

⑯ Click Find Edges.

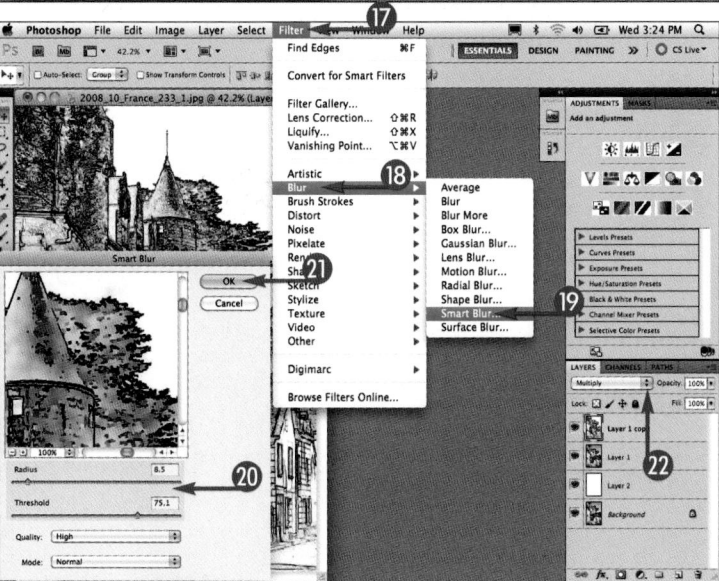

The image resembles a strong line art drawing.

⑰ Click Filter.

⑱ Click Blur.

⑲ Click Smart Blur.

The Smart Blur dialog box appears.

⑳ Click and drag the Radius and Threshold sliders to soften the edges and reduce the details.

㉑ Click OK.

㉒ Click here and select Multiply for the blend mode.

TIPS

Important!

For more artistic results, start by reducing the size of the image. Click Image and then Image Size. Set one of the Pixel Dimensions in the top section of the Image Size dialog box to about 1000 pixels. The filters are more effective on this size of image, and the brush strokes appear more like traditional brush strokes on paper.

Change It!

Change the brush or the brush tip shape as you paint with white on the black mask. With a regular brush selected, you can click the Brushes panel button (▣) in the Options bar. Click Brush Tip Shape and change any of the attributes.

Customize It!

You can also create a dual brush to change the brush strokes even more. Click the Brushes panel button (▣) in the Options bar. Click Dual Brush and click a different brush sample box. Click and drag the sliders to alter the brush style.

CHANGE A PHOTOGRAPH
into a pen-and-colored-wash drawing

The other duplicated layer provides the base for the colors. You use the Noise filter to reduce the details in that duplicated layer even more, so that it has a less photographic appearance. Then you paint on a layer mask to make the colored washes appear. For this digital technique, as with a traditional watercolor painting, you add the washes using large, lighter opacity brushes first, then increase the opacity for the next sets of washes, and finally work with smaller, more opaque brushes to define the details. You can

modify the brush sizes and brush tip shapes for each different wash to add variety and make the result appear less digitally created.

You can use any photo to create the pen-and-colored-wash drawing; however, the results look more like a traditional pen-and-ink wash when the steps are applied to a low-resolution image. As with every project in Photoshop, there are multiple ways you can achieve a similar effect. Each photo also gives you a slightly different result.

㉓ Click Layer 1, the second layer down in the Layers panel, to select it.

㉔ Click Filter.

㉕ Click Noise.

㉖ Click Median.

The Median dialog box appears.

㉗ Click and drag the Radius slider to blur the image and colors.

㉘ Click OK.

㉙ Press Option (Alt) and click the Layer Mask button to add a black layer mask to Layer 1.

● The black layer mask hides the colored Layer 1, and only the outlines are visible in the image window.

㉚ Press B to select the Brush tool.

㉛ Click here to open the Brush picker.

㉜ Select a Bristle tip brush.

㉝ Click and drag the slider to increase the brush size.

34 Click Opacity and drag to the left to reduce the brush opacity to 40%.

35 Click and drag in the image, painting with white on the mask to bring in the colored wash.

Note: Use brush strokes in the direction that fits the objects in the image.

The colors appear as large washes.

36 Press the left bracket key several times to reduce the brush size.

37 Click and drag to paint over more details.

TIPS

Did You Know?
You can make the drawing appear to have multiple layers of washes by starting with a very low brush opacity in the Options bar for the first set of brush strokes, and then increasing the opacity as you brush a second and third time.

Change It!
You can change the blend mode of the top layer after you finish painting in step 37 to change the final look of the pen-and-wash drawing. Try Hard Light or Darken instead of Multiply for totally different looks.

Attention!
To make the washes appear as though they were painted by hand on white paper, be sure to leave some areas around the edges unpainted, letting the white layer show through.

Turn a photo into a
HAND-PAINTED OIL PAINTING

Photoshop CS5 offers new ways to create original artwork. The Mixer Brush tool and Bristle tip brushes give the artist a truly natural way of painting on a computer. You can create a plain white or colored document and start painting with the new brushes using the Color Picker or the Heads Up Display (HUD) to select and change colors. You can also start with an underlying photograph and mix and blend the existing pixels. Photoshop CS5 enables the non-artist to create an oil painting from a photograph with a more naturally painted result than was possible with previous versions. The technique in this task uses the

Pattern Stamp tool and the entire image as a pattern for a base image. The Pattern Stamp tool's Impressionist option breaks up the photographic lines while mixing the photo's colors on the canvas. You can customize the brush settings and use the new Bristle brushes so your brush strokes appear more painterly. You brush the pattern onto an empty layer, and then finish the painting by adding additional brush strokes using the Mixer Brush on more layers so the image appears to be painted rather than digitally generated.

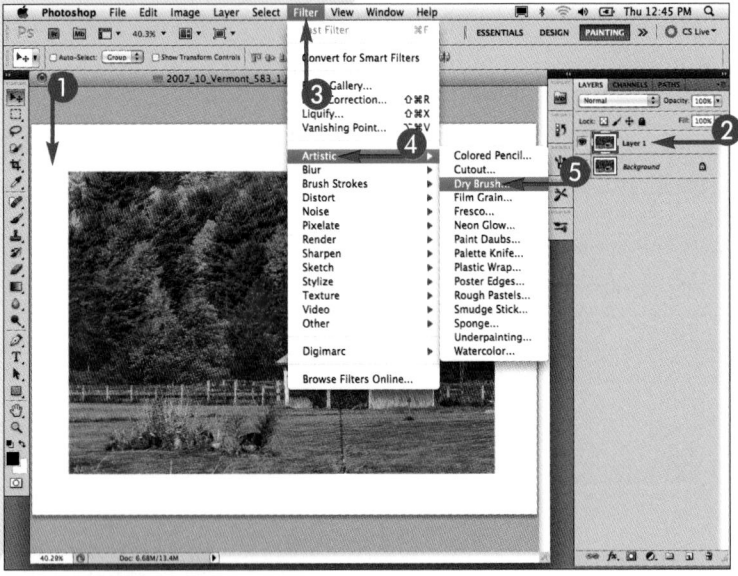

① Open an image and expand the canvas to create a white border around the photo.

Note: *To expand the canvas, use the reverse-crop technique described in task #29.*

A white border appears around the image.

② Press ⌘+J (Ctrl+J) to duplicate the Background layer.

③ Click Filter.

④ Click Artistic.

⑤ Click Dry Brush.

The Filter Gallery appears with the Dry Brush filter applied in the preview window.

⑥ Click and drag the sliders to adjust the Dry Brush appearance for your photo.

Note: *The larger the Brush Size number and the smaller the Brush Detail number, the less photographic the image appears.*

⑦ Click OK.

The filter is applied to the image.

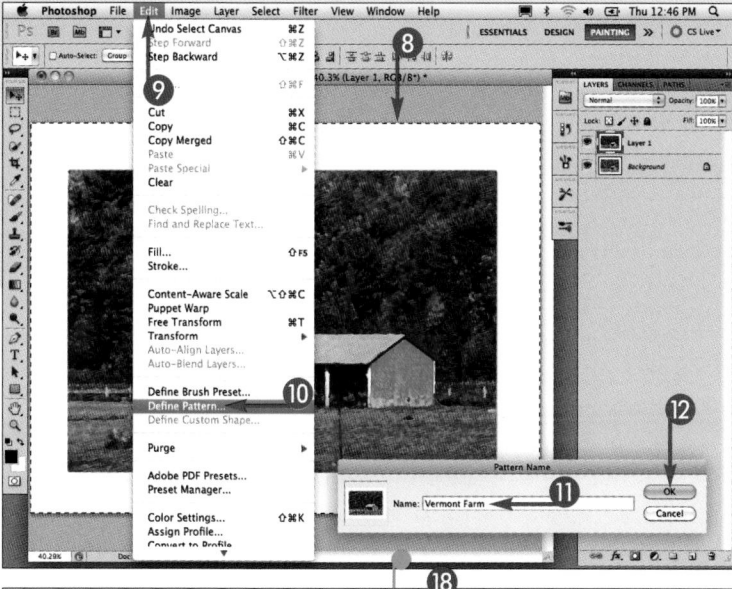

8 Press ⌘+A (Ctrl+A) to select the entire image.

9 Click Edit.

10 Click Define Pattern.

The Pattern Name dialog box appears.

11 Type a new name for the pattern.

12 Click OK.

13 Press ⌘+D (Ctrl+D) to deselect the image.

#93

DIFFICULTY LEVEL

14 Click the Create a New Layer button to add a new empty layer.

15 Click the Pattern Stamp tool.

16 Click the Pattern thumbnail in the Options bar.

The menu of available patterns opens.

17 Click the pattern of the photo that you just created.

18 Click Impressionist (☐ changes to ☑).

● Aligned is selected by default.

TIPS

Attention!
When you first start painting in step 20 using a large brush, click the brush instead of dragging it like a true paintbrush. The effect appears more natural because clicking the brush spreads the paint unevenly.

Caution!
Take your time to make the image appear hand-painted. Change the brush size often. Start with large brushes and make them smaller as you paint details, deselecting the Impressionist option to emphasize the finest details.

More Options!
Using a Wacom pen tablet, you can start with a larger brush and click the Tablet Pressure Controls Size button (☑) in the Options bar to have the tablet pressure control the size of the brush. You can also click the Tablet Pressure Opacity button (☑) in the Options bar to have the tablet pressure control the opacity of the brush.

Turn a photo into a
HAND-PAINTED OIL PAINTING

When trying to replicate a traditionally painted image, you should start with a large brush and paint in more open areas of the photograph. The Impressionist option blends the colors and forms. Then reduce the brush size and continue painting the details. You can compare your painting and the original image as you work by clicking the Eye icon of the top layer off and on. Deselect the Impressionist option and use a very small brush to paint the most important details from the original image. To finish the painting, you can

blend some brush strokes with the Mixer Brush and optionally introduce new colors to highlight areas. You can also add a style effect to certain layers to give the brush strokes an embossed appearance. To finish the oil-on-canvas look, you can add a Texturizer filter using a canvas texture over the painted image, or add a canvas-colored layer as a background to fill in around the edges for a more realistic look.

As with all projects in Photoshop, you can create an oil painting from a photograph in multiple ways.

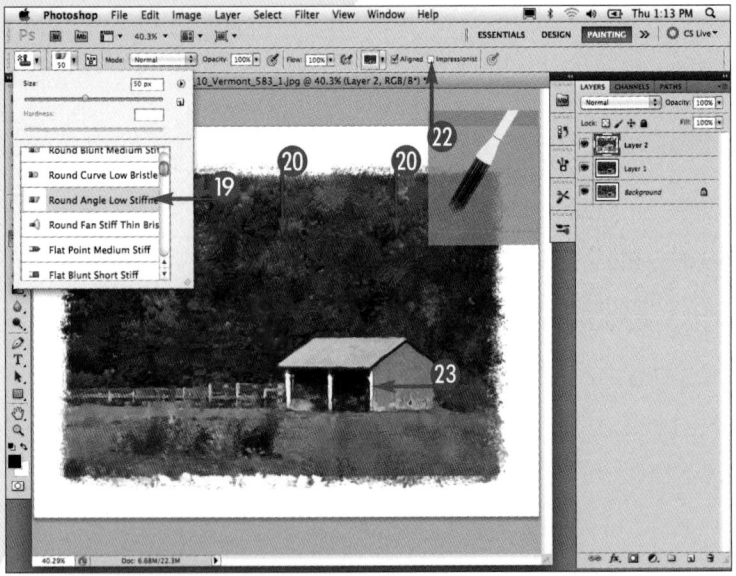

19 Click the Brush picker and select a large rough-edged brush.

20 Click in the layer multiple times to paint the image, covering every area.

Note: Zoom in and out often to check the paint application on different areas.

21 Repeat steps 19 and 20, reducing the brush size or changing the brush shape to paint detailed areas.

22 Click Impressionist to deselect it (☑ changes to ☐).

23 Click in the image to bring back a few photographic details as needed.

24 Click the New Layer button to add a new layer.

25 Click the Mixer Brush.

26 Click the Brush picker to select a brush tip.

27 Click Sample All Layers (☐ changes to ☑).

28 Click and drag to paint on the new blank layer, blending the underlying colors.

29 Repeat steps 24 to 28, creating brush strokes on different layers.

30 Option+click (Alt+click) a color in the image and paint on another layer.

31 Repeat step 30 to add highlights.

Note: You can optionally press ⌘+Control+Option (right-click+Alt+Shift) to bring up the HUD (Heads Up Display) and click to select a new color as an accent color and continue painting.

32 Press ⌘+Option+Shift+E (Ctrl+Alt+Shift+E) to combine all the layers into a new layer.

33 Click Filter, Texture, and Texturizer.

The Filter Gallery Texturizer dialog box appears.

34 Click here and select Canvas.

35 Click and drag the sliders to increase the scaling and relief.

Note: The preview image shows the details at 100%.

36 Click OK.

The Canvas texture is applied to the finished painting.

#93 CONTINUED

Try This!

You can add a canvas-colored layer as a background to fill in around the edges for a realistic look. After step 32, click the New Layer button (🔲) in the Layers panel to create a new layer. Drag the new empty layer underneath the top painted layer. Click Edit and then Fill. Click the Use arrow and click Color. When the Color Picker appears, select a color for the canvas, such as R248, G 242, and B 224, which appears as a natural canvas color. Click OK to close the Color Picker and again to close the Fill dialog box and fill the layer. Click the top painted layer to select it. Then continue with step 33 to apply the Texturizer filter with a canvas texture to the whole image as a final touch.

Paint a
DIGITAL WATERCOLOR

You can use Photoshop CS5 to paint a watercolor starting with a blank document, and painting with the new Mixer Brush, adding colors to the paper. You can also create a digital watercolor from a photograph and make it appear like a traditionally painted image on watercolor paper. Traditional watercolor paintings have transparent colors, minimal transitions of color tones, and loosely defined shapes without black outlines. By applying the Reduce Noise or the Median filter to the photo before starting the painting, your project appears less photographic and more

hand-painted. These filters, found in the Filter menu under Noise, eliminate some of the color changes and sharp edges that make a photograph look like a photograph.

You can start your project by adding white space around the photo and then paint on transparent layers using various brushes and filters. This technique uses the History and Art History Brushes in Photoshop along with multiple layers and other filters. Although the Filter Gallery includes a Watercolor filter, this filter does not render a traditional-looking watercolor.

① Open an image and expand the canvas to create a white border around the photo.

Note: To expand the canvas, use the reverse-crop technique described in task #29.

A white border appears around the image.

② Click the History button or click Window and select History to open the History panel.

③ Click the New Snapshot button to capture this state of the image.

● Snapshot 1 appears in the History panel.

④ Click the left column of Snapshot 1 to set it as the source for the History Brush.

⑤ Click the New Layer button to add a new transparent layer.

⑥ Click the History Brush and select the Art History Brush tool.

⑦ Click the Brush picker and select a large soft-edged brush.

Note: A 50-pixel brush works well on a 3MB file. Use a larger brush for larger images.

⑧ Click Opacity and drag to the left to reduce the brush opacity to 50%.

⑨ Click here and set the style to Dab.

⑩ Click and drag over the photo, covering the layer.

The image appears as a blur of colors.

94

DIFFICULTY LEVEL

⑪ Press ⌘+spacebar (Ctrl+spacebar) and click to zoom in.

⑫ Press the left bracket key several times to reduce the brush size.

⑬ Click and drag to paint over some areas to bring in more detail.

⑭ Repeat steps 12 and 13 multiple times, working with smaller and smaller brushes to increase the details in some areas.

⑮ Click the New Layer button in the Layers panel.

⑯ Click Opacity and drag to the left to lower the opacity to 60%.

⑰ Press D to reset the default foreground and background colors.

⑱ Press ⌘+Delete (Ctrl+Backspace) to fill the layer with white.

The top layer fills with a translucent white.

⑲ Click the Eraser tool.

⑳ Click the Brush picker and select a large rough-styled brush such as Chalk.

㉑ Click Opacity and drag to the left to reduce the brush opacity to 50%.

TIPS

Did You Know?
A true watercolor palette includes only gray and no black paint at all. Photoshop's Watercolor filter in the Filter Gallery adds too much black to replicate a traditional watercolor and also dulls the colors.

Change It!
All the settings for brushes can be applied to the Eraser tool. When using the Eraser tool, click the Toggle the Brushes panel button (🗇) in the Options bar to open the Brushes panel. Click the word *Texture* to highlight it. Make changes to the scale, depth, or pattern to add texture to your brush.

Important!
Photoshop's Artistic filters are applied at a fixed size and work best on files smaller than 5MB. Always view your photo at 100% to see the effect and wait for the effect to process when changing adjustment sliders.

Paint a
DIGITAL WATERCOLOR

After applying paint on multiple layers, you add a white layer and use the Eraser tool to reveal parts of the layers below. You can start with the Eraser tool's opacity set low and vary it as you paint so that the colors look more like traditional watercolor washes, overlapping each other. The strokes appear more realistic if you click and drag in the document, painting vertical objects with vertical strokes and horizontal items with horizontal strokes. Traditional watercolor paintings often leave rough edges around the borders and even some blank areas in the painting, allowing the surface of the watercolor paper to show through the paint. You can simulate this effect by not completely erasing some areas, in effect making those areas appear unpainted.

Traditional watercolors can have a dry brush or a wet look. You can finish the painting by merging the top layers and applying a texture for a dry brush look. Alternatively you can a duplicate the merged layer, blur it, and paint on a mask to make the blur show through in some areas. Finish the watercolor by applying a Texture filter to create the look of rough watercolor paper.

22 Click and drag in the document to reveal the main parts of the image below.

23 Click Opacity and drag to increase the layer opacity to 100%.

24 With a reduced brush size, click and drag to paint more areas.

25 Click Opacity and drag to increase the brush opacity as you work in smaller areas.

26 Press Option+spacebar (Alt+spacebar) and click in the image to zoom out.

27 Press ⌘+Option+E (Ctrl+Alt+E) to merge the layers into a new combined layer.

28 Press ⌘+J (Ctrl+J) to duplicate the combined layer.

Note: For a wet-look style of watercolors, continue with step 29. To keep the dry brush style of watercolors, jump to step 38.

29 Click Filter, Blur, and Motion Blur.

30 In the Motion Blur dialog box, set the angle to 90 degrees.

31 Click and drag the Distance slider to adjust the amount of blur.

32 Click OK.

The top layer shows a vertical blur, simulating running paint streaks.

33 Option+click (Alt+click) the Layer Mask button to add a black layer mask.

34 Click the Brush tool.

35 Click the Brush picker and select a soft-edged brush.

36 Paint with white over the sky and edges or other areas to make the blur show through.

37 Press ⌘+Option+E (Ctrl+Alt+E) to merge the layers.

38 Click Filter, and select Texture and Texturizer.

The Filter Gallery appears.

39 Click here and select Sandstone.

40 Click and drag the Scaling and Relief sliders to achieve the look of rough watercolor paper.

41 Click OK.

The filter is applied to the top layer.

Try This!

You can make the paper look more like watercolor paper by using an off-white color to fill the top layer. Instead of steps 17 and 18, click Edit and then Fill. The Fill dialog box appears. Click the Use arrow and click Color to open the Color Picker. Type **250** for the Red data field, **246** for the Green data field, and **239** for the Blue data field to select an off-white color for the watercolor paper. Click OK to close the Color Picker and click OK again to close the Fill dialog box. Erase carefully over just the objects that you want to show as painted on the image. Areas left blank allow the watercolor paper to show through.

Give Your Images a Professional Presentation

Presentation is so important that most photos or designs can be improved when properly displayed or framed. For professional designers, a powerful presentation can help keep an art director happy. For photographers, an elegant display can make all the difference in securing a new client or keeping a current one. From displaying family snapshots to presenting your portfolio, Photoshop makes it easy to show your images in a professional manner.

You can add frames to enhance any image with minimal effort using the frame actions included with Photoshop. You can also create your own frames, change the frame colors and borders, and add a matte to the photo. Photoshop can

also help you apply an artistic edge to a photo using a sequence of filters from the Filter Gallery, or you can brush an artistic edge onto any images by hand using the Brush tool. You can add space and borders to make a photo look like a gallery print. You can create a contact sheet as a visual index of all the photos in one client folder or on one CD or DVD. You can prepare a custom slide show with professional transitions, burn it to external media, or save it as a PDF document and send it to friends or clients as an e-mail attachment. You can even use Photoshop to design and upload your own photo gallery to a Web site. With Photoshop CS5, you can display all your images with a professional touch.

Top 100

FRAME ACTION

#95

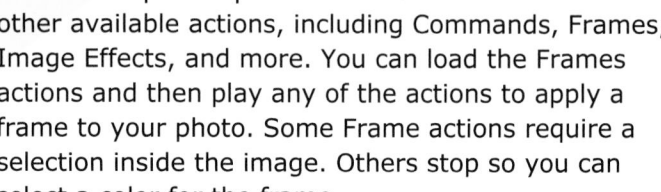

DIFFICULTY LEVEL

You can add interest and give a finished look to your photographs by adding a digital frame to your images. You can apply a variety of designed frames such as a Foreground Color frame easily and quickly using an action from the Actions panel in Photoshop. An *action* is a prerecorded set of commands that are automatically performed in the same sequence when you click the Play button.

Photoshop enables you to record your own actions and also provides a number of predefined actions that are installed with the application. When you first open Photoshop and click the Actions panel tab, you find a

folder called Default Actions. Clicking the panel menu button on the Actions panel opens a list with other available actions, including Commands, Frames, Image Effects, and more. You can load the Frames actions and then play any of the actions to apply a frame to your photo. Some Frame actions require a selection inside the image. Others stop so you can select a color for the frame.

Actions are stored as files with the *.atn* extension in the Photoshop Actions folder in the Presets folder.

① Open an image.

② Press Option+F9 (Alt+F9) to open the Actions panel.

Note: Optionally, click Window and click Actions to open the Actions panel.

③ Click the panel menu button on the Actions panel.

④ Click Frames.

The Frames actions are automatically loaded.

⑤ Click Foreground Color Frame.

⑥ Click the Play button.

Note: If a warning dialog box appears and your image is over 100 pixels wide and tall, click Continue.

Photoshop plays the action and stops so you can select a foreground color.

⑦ Click Continue.

Photoshop places a black frame around the photo.

Note: You can optionally, click Stop in step 7, and select a new foreground color in the Tools panel. Then click the Play button (▶) again on the Actions panel to continue.

MAKE A LINE FRAME
from within a photo

96

You may have a photo with a larger background area than necessary. Rather than crop the photo, you can transform the excess background into a frame to help focus the attention on the main subject. Making a line frame from the photograph itself is a quick way to give a classic and finished look to any image. You make a selection in the photo as if you were going to crop it. You then invert the selection to create the frame. You can even vary the frame shape by using the Elliptical Marquee tool to select the area with an oval frame. To create any style of line frame from within the photograph, place the frame area on its own layer above the Background layer and change the blend mode to Screen to lighten the area that will become the frame.

To separate the frame from the photo even more, stroke the borders of the new frame layer by applying a layer style. You can change the default stroke color to any color that fits your image. As a final touch, add a drop shadow and an inner shadow, and even a bevel-and-emboss look.

DIFFICULTY LEVEL

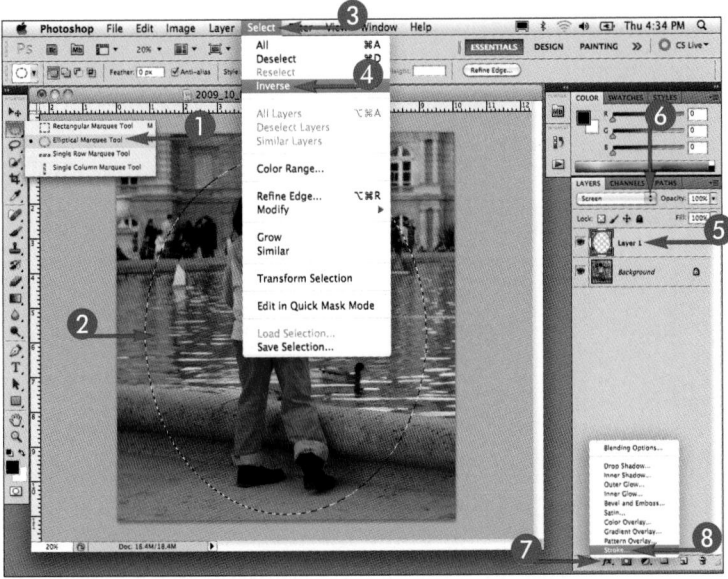

① Click the Rectangular Marquee tool or click to select the Elliptical Marquee.

② Click and drag a large area in the photo to select the main subject.

③ Click Select.

④ Click Inverse.

⑤ Press ⌘+J (Ctrl+J) to place the inversed selection on its own layer.

⑥ Click here and select Screen.

⑦ Click the Layer Style button.

⑧ Click Stroke.

The Layer Style dialog box appears.

⑨ Click the Color thumbnail.

⑩ When the Color Picker appears, set the color to white or another color and click OK.

⑪ Click and drag the Size slider to increase the stroke thickness.

⑫ Click any of the other layer styles such as Drop Shadow, Inner Shadow, and Bevel and Emboss to give the frame a finished look.

⑬ Click OK.

The layer style gives the appearance of a recessed frame.

Apply a filter to give a photo an
ARTISTIC EDGE

You can give any photo an artistic look by adding an irregular edge using the Filter Gallery and the Brush Strokes filters. By duplicating the Background layer and adding a new empty layer filled with white below the top layer, you can create a unique artistic edge. The Filter Gallery enables you to combine the filters in different ways and use the same technique to create a variety of different edges to fit each image. Make a selection on the top layer just inside the edge of the photo and then add a layer mask to delineate the

borders of the photo. The artistic edge starts from the selected area. Open the Filter Gallery and start adding different layers of Brush Strokes filters. The Preview window of the Filter Gallery shows the edge effect in reverse. The white areas represent the photo area, and the black areas represent what will be cut away. Every time you change the various sliders for the Brush Strokes filters, your edge effect changes in the Preview window of the Filter Gallery.

① Press ⌘+J (Ctrl+J) to duplicate the Background layer.

② Click the Background layer to select it.

③ Press D to reset the default colors.

④ Press ⌘+Delete (Ctrl+Backspace) to fill the Background layer with white.

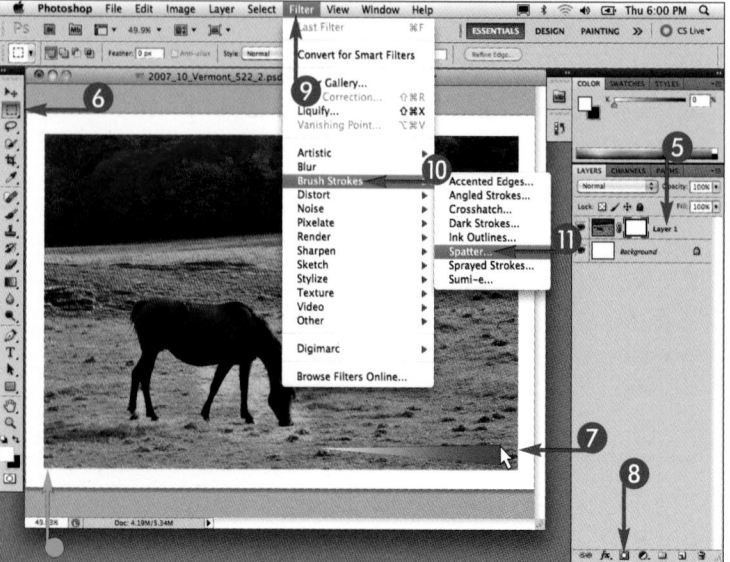

⑤ Click Layer 1 to select it.

⑥ Click the Marquee tool.

⑦ Click and drag a selection just inside the edge of the image.

⑧ Click the Layer Mask button to add a layer mask to Layer 1.

● The image has a small white border.

⑨ Click Filter.

⑩ Click Brush Strokes.

⑪ Click a filter; this example uses Spatter.

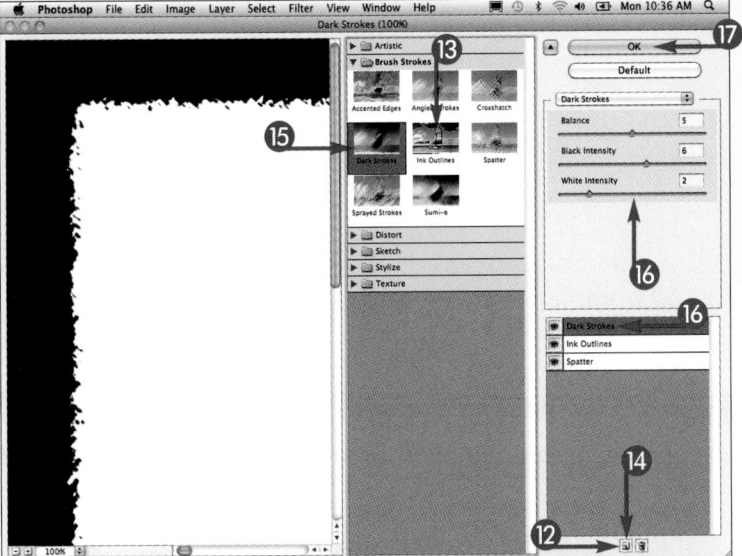

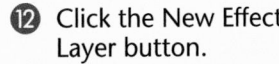

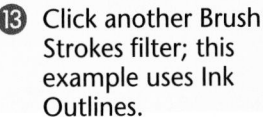

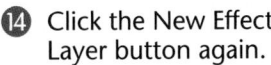

The Filter Gallery opens with the Spatter edge applied.

⑫ Click the New Effect Layer button.

⑬ Click another Brush Strokes filter; this example uses Ink Outlines.

⑭ Click the New Effect Layer button again.

⑮ Click another Brush Strokes filter; this example uses Dark Strokes.

⑯ Click each individual effect layer and adjust the sliders for each effect to get the edge that you want.

⑰ Click OK.

The custom edge is applied to the photo.

97

DIFFICULTY LEVEL

TIPS

Did You Know?
Add as many Filter Effects layers as your computer's memory allows. Each one you add changes the look of the custom photo edge. Change the order of the layers in the Filter Gallery dialog box, and the overall style of the edge changes as well.

More Options!
For a light-colored image, darken the edge for a stronger effect. Click the Layer Style button (📷) in the Layers panel. Click Drop Shadow. Drag the Distance slider to 0. To darken it more, click Inner Shadow and drag its Distance slider to 0.

Try This!
Click the Layer Style button (📷) in the Layers panel. Click Stroke. Click the Color thumbnail and change the default color to black. Click the Position arrow and select Inside. Move the Size slider to get the thickness of line that you want.

Create your own
CUSTOM EDGE

You can let a Photoshop filter draw an artistic edge for you as in task #97, or you can create your own custom edge. You can save your custom edge and apply it to all your images as your personal digital signature. You paint using any rough-edged brush on a separate layer. The default brush set that installs with Photoshop includes various rough-edged brushes; however, you can find many more by clicking the flyout arrow in the Brush picker.

One simple way to create a custom edge without altering any pixels is to place the photo on a separate layer and enlarge the canvas, selecting the Relative option to add white area evenly around the photo for the frame. Then add a transparent layer in between the two photo layers and paint your custom edge on that layer, clicking and dragging around the edges of the photo. You can paint as much or as little of a visible edge as you want as long as the black edges extend underneath the photo. You can save the image with the layers so you can reuse your custom edge on other images of the same size. You can also flatten the image to permanently apply the custom edge.

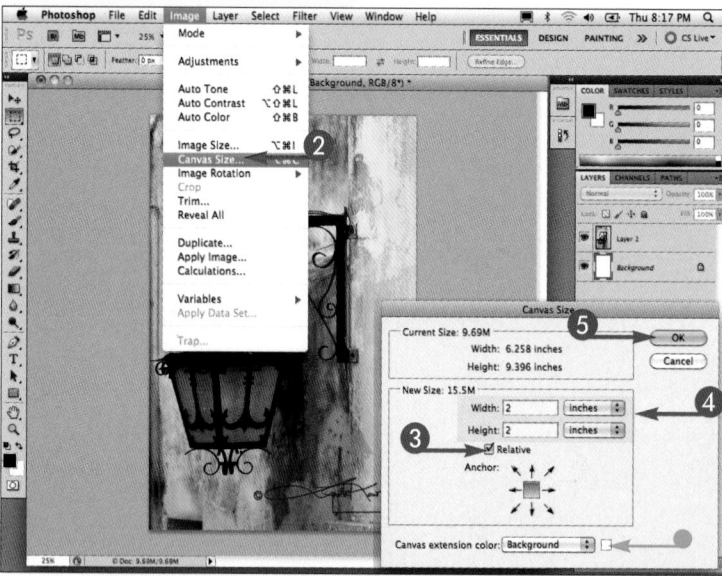

① Follow steps 1 to 4 in task #97 to put the image on Layer 1 with a white Background layer below.

② Click Image and then Canvas Size.

③ In the Canvas Size dialog box, click Relative (☐ changes to ☑).

Note: Selecting Relative adds a specific amount of additional canvas.

④ Type **2** in the Width and Height fields to add 2 inches to the canvas in each direction.

● You can click in the color box to select a different color for the canvas extension.

⑤ Click OK.

A white border appears around the photo.

⑥ Double-click the Hand tool to fit the image to the screen.

⑦ Press B to select the Brush tool.

⑧ Click here to open the Brush picker.

⑨ Click a rough-edged brush.

⑩ Click the New Layer button to add a new empty layer.

⑪ Click and drag the empty layer between the other two layers.

⑫ Using the Brush tool, click and drag to paint on the empty layer along the visible edge of the photo.

Note: *Make sure to paint partially over the edge of the photo. The overlap will not be visible because the photo layer is above the painting layer.*

⑬ Click here to open the Brush picker.

⑭ Click another brush such as Hard Pastel on Canvas.

⑮ Continue painting brush strokes around the edge of the photo to add variety to the edge.

The photo appears with a custom border, giving it a unique look.

98

DIFFICULTY LEVEL

More Options!

You can gradually blend the photo into the custom edge by clicking the top photo layer and using the rectangular marquee to make a selection just inside the edge of the photo. Then click Select and Inverse. Next click Select, Modify, and then Feather. Type a number such as **10** pixels for the Feather Radius and click OK. Press Delete to soften the edge of the photo and blend it into the custom border.

Did You Know?

You can change the brush angles by clicking the Brushes Panel button (▣) in the Options bar and clicking Brush Tip Shape in the Brushes panel. Click and drag on the Brush Angle and Roundness thumbnail to narrow the circle. Change the Brush Tip Shape for each side.

Try This!

Save your custom edge as a separate file. Click the Background layer, press ⌘+A (Ctrl+A), ⌘+C (Ctrl+C), and then ⌘+N (Ctrl+N) to create a new same-size document. Click back on the original image. Press Shift as you click and drag the edge layer onto the new document so it fits in the same exact position. Click File and click Save to name and save the new custom edge file.

Make a photo look like a
GALLERY PRINT

You can give your photograph a professional finish by making it look like a gallery print. This technique is effective for both color and grayscale photographs. Gallery prints generally have wide white, black, or even gray borders depending on the tones in the image. The photo is placed in the top portion of the border or frame area, allowing the name of the gallery, artist, and artwork to fit under the image in stylized type.

After making a selection of the photo and cutting it out onto its own layer, you enlarge the canvas size by about 3 inches using the Relative option to add the space evenly all around the photo. You then add more space below the photograph, to extend the area for the text. You can add a stroke or even a double stroke around the outside edge of the photo to give a finished look to the gallery print. The strokes can be the same or different colors, and each stroke can have a different pixel width.

① Press ⌘+J (Ctrl+J) to duplicate the Background layer.

② Click the Background layer to select it.

③ Press D to reset the default colors.

④ Press ⌘+Delete (Ctrl+Backspace) to fill the Background layer with white.

⑤ Click Image.

⑥ Click Canvas Size.

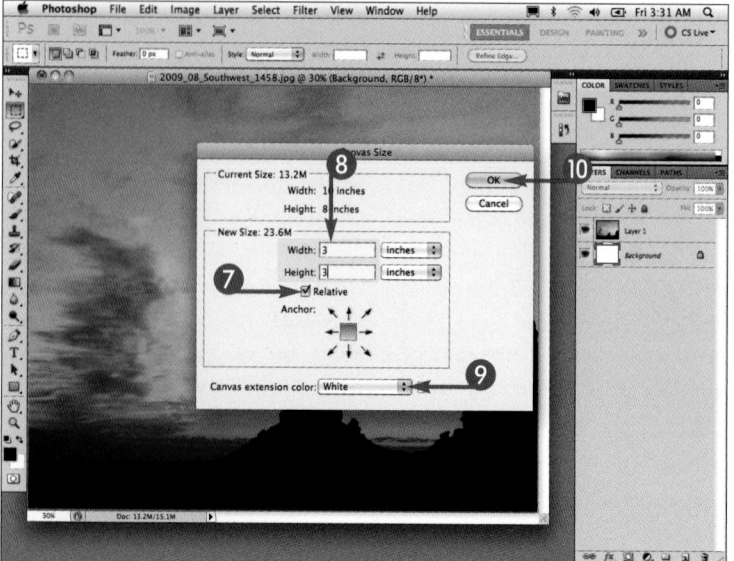

The Canvas Size dialog box appears.

⑦ Click Relative (☐ changes to ☑).

Note: Selecting Relative adds the exact typed amount of width and height to the existing image.

⑧ Type **3** in both the Width and Height data fields to add 3 inches to the canvas in each direction.

⑨ Click here and select White.

⑩ Click OK.

⓫ Double-click the Hand tool to fit the image to your screen.

The image is centered in a wide white border.

⓬ Repeat steps 5 and 6 to open the Canvas Size dialog box again.

Note: *Relative remains selected.*

⓭ Click the top center arrow of the Anchor grid.

⓮ Click in the Height data field and type **2** to add 2 inches to the bottom of the white border.

⓯ Click OK.

The photo is offset in the white border.

⓰ Double-click the Hand tool to center the image on the screen.

⓱ ⌘+click (Ctrl+click) the photo thumbnail in the Layers panel to select the photo.

⓲ Click the New Layer button to add a new empty layer.

● The new layer is automatically selected.

⓳ Click Edit.

⓴ Click Stroke.

TIPS

Change It!

Set the canvas color to black in the Canvas Size dialog box for a dramatic effect. Use white for the inside border stroke color and gray for the outside border stroke color, and type the text using white or gray.

Try This!

For a realistic look, type a print number or the words **artist's proof** on the left side under the border using black for the color and a script-styled font. You can then make the stylized letters appear to be written in pencil by lowering the opacity of the Type layer. Using the Type tool (Ⓣ), click the center title under the image, and click the Horizontal Scale button (Ⓣ) in the Character panel to widen the overall spacing, or the Tracking button (Ⓐⓥ) to extend the space between all the letters. (See the next pages of this task to add text.)

Make a photo look like a
GALLERY PRINT

By placing the strokes on separate layers, you can adjust the opacity of each stroke individually and change the look of the gallery print. You ⌘+click (Ctrl+click) the photo layer to have an active selection the exact size of the photo. You add a new empty layer above the photo layer and, with the selection active, apply a stroke on the new layer. The stroke makes the photo stand out. With the selection still active, you make the selected area slightly wider and higher, add another empty layer, and then apply a stroke on the second empty layer.

Gallery prints often have the name of the gallery, the artist's name or studio, or the name of the image set in a serif-styled font in all capital letters. Type the name and click Window and then Character to open the Character panel. Use the tracking options to increase the space between the letters. Select a script font to sign your work under the outside stroke and add a print number to complete the gallery print look.

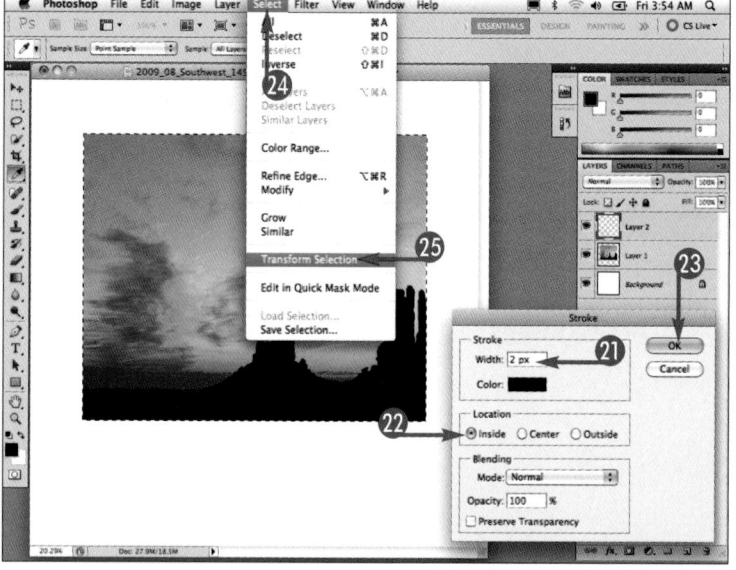

The Stroke dialog box appears.

㉑ Type **2 px** in the Width data field.

㉒ Click Inside for the location (○ changes to ◉).

㉓ Click OK.

A thin, black stroke is applied to the image on the top layer.

㉔ With the marquee still around the image, click Select.

㉕ Click Transform Selection.

● Anchor points are added to the selection.

㉖ Type **103** in the W data field and **104** in the H data field.

㉗ Click the Commit button to commit the transformation.

㉘ Click the New Layer button.

㉙ Repeat steps 19 to 23, increasing the stroke width to 6 px, to add a black stroke outside the border of the photo on the new layer.

㉚ Press ⌘+D (Ctrl+D) to deselect the border.

31 Click the Type tool.

32 Click Window and select Character to open the Character panel.

33 Select a size and a handwriting-styled font.

34 Click one side of the image, type a title, and press Enter (Ctrl+Enter) or click the Commit button.

35 Click the other side of the image, type your name, and press Enter (Ctrl+Enter) or click the Commit button.

36 Select a serif font such as Adobe Garamond Pro and a font style such as Regular.

37 Type a font size in the data field.

38 Click in the center of the gallery frame and type a title, studio, gallery, or print series.

39 Click the arrow or type a number into the field to change the space between the letters.

40 Press Enter (Ctrl+Enter) to commit the type.

The image now appears like a traditional gallery print.

99 CONTINUED

 **TIPS**

Did You Know?
The size of the stroke that you apply to the borders depends on the size and resolution of the image.

Important!
Selecting Inside for the stroke location in the Stroke dialog box gives the stroke sharp corners. Selecting Outside applies a stroke with rounded corners.

More Options!
Because each stroke border is on its own layer, you can use different colors for the stroke for different effects. If the photo is light in color, try using a shade of gray to stroke the inner border instead of black, or lower the opacity of the layer if the color of the stroke appears too bold.

MAKE A CONTACT SHEET
of your photos

Whether you use photos from a digital camera or scans of traditional prints and negatives, the first file downloaded or scanned is the original. You should always keep a duplicate set of the photos on a separate hard drive or burn a CD or DVD of the originals before you enhance them or use them in projects. You can create a contact sheet to help you identify and keep track of the images on the external drive or other removable media using the Output module in Bridge CS5. You can also create a photo index of all the images in one project folder to help

you identify and catalog groups of images using the same steps.

Use the Output button in Bridge to open the appropriate options on the right panel. Select a contact sheet template, define the layout of the images and spacing you prefer, and select the font, size, and color of the text captions, or *overlays*, for each photo on the sheet. Bridge CS5 runs a script and builds the contact sheet as an Acrobat PDF file you can save or print as a visual reference.

1 In Photoshop, open Bridge by clicking the Bridge button (**Br**) on the Application bar or the Mini Bridge, or by clicking File and then Browse in Bridge.

Bridge launches.

2 Click Folders.

3 Navigate to the folder of images to use for the contact sheet.

4 Click Output.

The interface and options change.

5 In the Output section, click PDF.

6 Click here to select a contact sheet template, such as 4*5 Contact Sheet.

7 In the Document section, click here and select U.S. Paper.

Note: You can optionally select International Paper.

8 Scroll down to view the next sections.

- In the Overlays section, you can change the font, size, and color for the file names and extensions that will print on the contact sheet.

⑨ Click View PDF After Save (☐ changes to ☑).

⑩ ⌘+click (Ctrl+click) the photos in the Content pane to use on the contact sheet.

- The number of items selected is updated and the thumbnails appear in the Preview pane.

⑪ Click Refresh Preview to view the contact sheet.

The Output Preview pane displays the contact sheet as it will print.

⑫ Click Save.

The Save As dialog box appears.

⑬ Type a name for the contact sheet.

⑭ Click Save.

Bridge builds the contact sheet, saves it as a PDF, and launches your default PDF reader. You can then print the contact sheet or open it with Photoshop to print it.

TIPS

Did You Know?
The size of the thumbnails is constrained by the number of rows and columns. More columns and rows result in smaller thumbnail images. You can generally select Low Quality in the Document section for printing a contact sheet because a higher resolution does not make a noticeable improvement.

More Options!
To make a contact sheet fit a CD/DVD jewel case, use these settings:
In the Document section, type **4.688** inches in both the Width and Height fields. The page preset changes to Custom.
In the Layout section, type **5** in both the Columns and Rows fields. Select Use Auto-Spacing.
In the Overlays section, click the Size arrow and select 6-point type to fit the text under the thumbnail.

CREATE A SLIDE SHOW
presentation

If you want to e-mail photos to friends or your portfolio to a prospective employer or send a client some images for review, you can use Photoshop and Bridge CS5 to help you create a slide show and save it as a PDF presentation. You can then attach the PDF slides show to an e-mail or burn it to a CD or DVD. You can use any images from Bridge to create the slide show. You determine the layout of the images, and

you can add a watermark or copyright to each image. You can select a complete folder of source images or individually select the images to include in the slide show. You determine the amount of time that each slide appears on-screen and decide if the slide show should stop after the last image or continue in a loop. You can even select from a number of slide transitions to give your presentation a professional look.

① Repeat steps 1 to 5 in task #100 to open the PDF Output options for Bridge.

② Click here and select Photo.

③ Click here and select Landscape, 2 × 3 to create small sized PDF slide show for attaching to e-mail.

④ Click here and select a resolution.

⑤ Click and drag the Quality slider.

Note: Set resolution and quality settings high for displaying on a large screen.

⑥ Click here and select Black.

⑦ Click Layout.

⑧ Type **1** in the Columns and Rows fields.

⑨ Click Use Auto-Spacing (☐ changes to ☑).

⑩ Click Repeat One Photo per Page (☐ changes to ☑).

⑪ Click the first two check boxes (☐ changes to ☑).

● You can optionally type a different slide duration.

⑫ Click here and select Fade.

13 ⌘+click (Ctrl+click) the photos in the Content pane to use in the slide show.

● The thumbnails of the selected images appear in the Preview pane.

14 Click Refresh Preview.

The Output Preview pane displays one slide of the slide show.

15 Click View PDF After Save (☐ changes to ☑).

16 Click Save.

The Save As dialog box appears.

17 Type a name for the slide show.

18 Click Save.

Bridge builds the slide show, saves it as a PDF, and launches your default PDF application.

TIPS

Customize It!
You can change the transition style to any of the transition options. You can change how many seconds each image appears on the screen by typing the number in the Advance data field in the Playback section. If you want the presentation to repeat in a continuous loop, click Loop After Last Page (☐ changes to ☑).

Did You Know?
You can view the slide show with Acrobat or Acrobat Reader, or even Apple's Preview application, and set the slide show to fill the screen. To stop the slide show presentation, press Esc.

Try This!
To protect the images from being printed without permission, click Permissions Password (☐ changes to ☑) in the Document section. Type the password in the data field and click Disable Printing (☐ changes to ☑).

Create a
WEB PHOTO GALLERY

In addition to PDF slide shows and contact sheets, you can build a Web photo gallery using Bridge CS5. You can easily create a Web site home page with your images displayed both as thumbnails and full-sized images. You can select from a variety of Web gallery styles and personalize your Web page. Bridge CS5 includes many different templates, including Flash and HTML galleries. The steps to creating a Web photo gallery are similar to those for creating a contact sheet or a PDF slide show presentation. You

select the images in Bridge CS5, determine a template and a style, and add a gallery name, your name, your e-mail, and whether or not to display the filenames as image titles. You can select your own set of colors to use on the Web gallery to customize your site's appearance even more. You can preview your Web gallery inside Bridge as you create it and also preview how it will appear in a Web browser. You can even upload your Web gallery directly to an FTP server from within the Bridge CS5 application.

Create a Web Gallery

1 Repeat steps 1 to 4 in task #100 to open the Output options for Bridge.

2 Enlarge the Preview pane by clicking and dragging the separator bar to the left.

3 In the Output section, click Web Gallery.

4 ⌘+click (Ctrl+click) some images in the Content pane to select them.

The images appear in the Preview pane.

5 Click Refresh Preview.

Bridge builds a Web gallery and displays it in the Output Preview pane.

6 Click here and select a different template such as Left Filmstrip.

7 Click here and select a style such as Large Thumbnail.

8 In the Site Info section, click in each text field and type all the information for your gallery.

9 Type your name.

10 Type your e-mail address.

11 Click Refresh Preview.

Bridge builds the Web gallery in the selected style and displays it in the Output Preview pane.

● You can optionally click the Play button in the Output Preview pane to view the Web gallery slide show.

⑫ In the Color Palette pane, click a color box, such as the Text color box under Title.

⑬ Click a different color In the Colors dialog box.

⑭ Close the Colors dialog box.

⑮ Click Refresh Preview to view the color changes.

⑯ Click Preview in Browser to see how your Web gallery will appear in your default Web browser.

Upload Your Web Gallery to an FTP Site

⑰ Type your gallery name.

⑱ Type your FTP server address, username, password, and a folder name.

⑲ Click Upload.

Bridge CS5 creates the Web gallery and uploads it to your FTP site.

Try This!

You can design your Web gallery and click Save in the Create Gallery section to save it to your hard drive or removable media such as a DVD. You can then upload it to an FTP site or publish it to a WebDAV server such as Apple's MobileMe when it is more convenient, or even host it on your own computer through Personal Web Sharing (Mac).

Did You Know?

If you include your e-mail in the Site Info section, a viewer can click on your name on the Web gallery site and automatically open a new mail message with your e-mail address in the address field. Try using an e-mail address you do not use anywhere else to avoid excess spam.

Plug In to Photoshop CS5

Although you can completely edit your images using Photoshop CS5, you can generally adjust your images more quickly and easily and often with better results using third-party plug-ins. Plug-ins exist for nearly every project and for every user level.

You can improve your images with the most professional results using Nik Software's filters. You can sharpen and reduce noise with better results using Nik Software's Sharpener Pro 3 and Dfine 2. Nik Software's Color Efex Pro 3, Viveza 2, and Silver Efex Pro help you adjust the colors and tones in your photos more precisely and visually than using Photoshop's tools alone. AKVIS creates plug-ins and stand-alone applications for all types of image editing, from enlarging images to poster size prints, to

masking and creating artwork. AKVIS Coloriage even enables you to accurately colorize black-and-white photos. Alien Skin's plug-ins help you improve, mask, and enlarge photographs, and change photos into art. Alien Skin's Eye Candy helps you create magical effects. You can paint colors and tones into your photos selectively with Auto FX plug-ins, or easily give a finished look to your images by applying a sophisticated action from Kubota Image Tools. You can improve any portrait with Imagenomic Portraiture, add a frame with OnOne, or make quick and simple adjustments with Topaz Labs products.

Third-party plug-ins can enhance the way everyone uses Photoshop.

Top 100

Control digital noise with
NIK DFINE 2

Digital noise is inherent in digital photographs. Noise can appear as bright, colored specks called *chrominance noise* or as dark spots called *luminance noise*. Various factors can affect or create noise, including the light, length of exposure, and temperature when the photo is taken, as well as the peculiarities of individual cameras and sensors. You may also see more noise in photos taken using high ISO speeds and in low-light situations. Although you can reduce digital noise in a general manner with the built-in filters in Photoshop CS5, using Nik Dfine 2

enables you to control how and where you reduce the noise, and optimize the detail. Dfine 2 reduces luminance noise, chrominance noise, and JPEG artifacts; improves contrast; and adjusts colorcasts while taking into account the effects of the noise reduction. You can reduce the noise for the whole image, for specific color ranges, or by setting control points. The large preview screen enables you to see the improvements as you try them. You can try Nik Dfine 2 on your own images by downloading the trial software from www.Niksoftware.com.

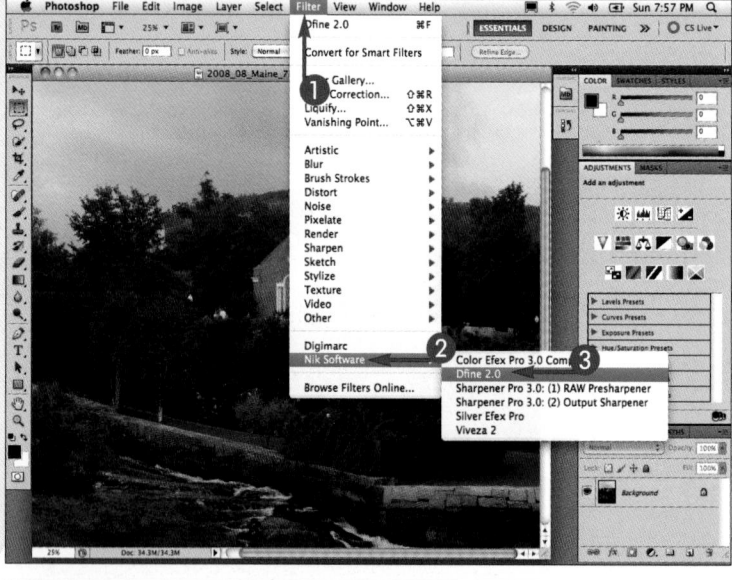

Reduce Noise in Automatic Mode

① Click Filter.

② Click Nik Software.

③ Click Dfine 2.0.

Dfine 2 opens, analyzes the image, and applies an automatic profile.

④ Click and drag the resize corner if necessary, to get the most screen space.

⑤ Press ⌘+Option+0 (Ctrl+Alt+0) to view the image at 100%.

⑥ Click the Pan tool.

⑦ Click and drag in the image to view different areas.

● You can click and drag the red navigator box over different areas to view the noise.

⑧ Click a preview button to view a split or a side-by-side preview.

⑨ Click OK to apply the noise reduction.

Reduce Noise by Color Range

1. Repeat steps 1 to 8.

2. Click Reset.

3. Click Reduce.

   The panel expands, showing the Control Point method.

4. Click here and select Color Range.

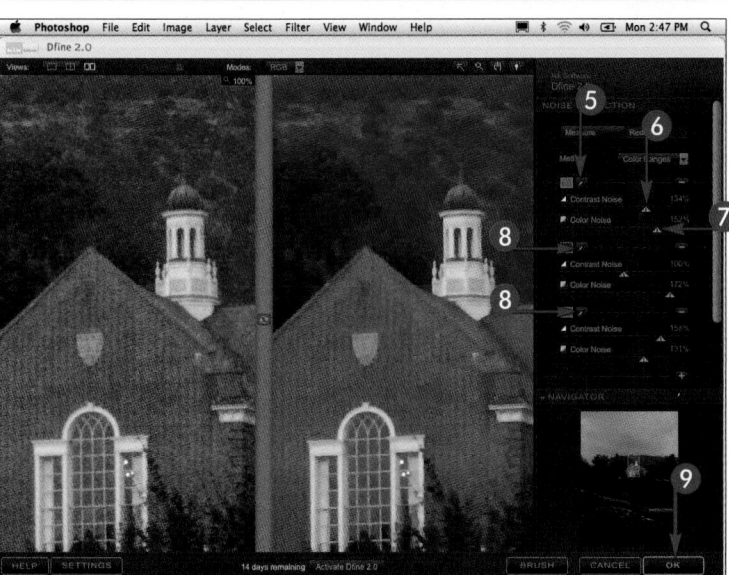

The panel expands, showing the Color Range options.

5. Click the Eyedropper and click in the image to select the first color range.

6. Click and drag the Contrast Noise slider for that color range.

7. Click and drag the Color Noise slider for that color range.

8. Repeat steps 5 to 7 using the Eyedropper for the other two color range options.

9. Click OK to apply the noise reduction.

TIPS

More Options!

Instead of clicking OK in step 9, click Brush to reduce the noise in specific areas. A layer mask is added to the Dfine 2 layer in the Photoshop Layers panel. Click Paint in the Dfine 2 Selective tool. Use the Brush tool to paint selective noise reduction on specific areas.

Try This!

You can also reduce the noise selectively using control points. Click Reduce and click the Control Points button to add points in the image. The top slider controls the range of pixels affected. The Contrast and/or Color Noise sliders reduce the noise in the selected area.

Did You Know?

Noise reduction is more effective when applied early in the image-editing workflow, right after importing images or converting from the RAW format.

Sharpen photos with finesse using
NIK SHARPENER PRO 3

Sharpening is an essential step in digital imaging. Photoshop's built-in filters apply the sharpening based on the screen image. The various output methods and devices, such as displays and different types of printers and papers, require specific kinds of sharpening. Using Nik Sharpener Pro 3 (www. Niksoftware.com), you can sharpen your images for all types of output. Sharpener Pro 3 analyzes the image and sharpens according to the type of detail in the image and the output device.

You can sharpen the whole image or apply sharpening to specific areas using Nik's Selective tool and a

Photoshop brush to paint over areas, or you can control the areas to be sharpened with Nik's U Point technology by placing *control points* directly on an area you want to edit. You then click and drag the points to change specific sharpening attributes that Nik calls output sharpening strength, structure, local contrast, or focus sharpening.

You can also use Nik Sharpener Pro 3 for a creative effect. For example, you can use a Nik control point and increase the focus sharpening amount to slightly sharpen a particular area and draw the viewer's eye to that point.

① Click Filter.

② Click Nik Software.

③ Click Sharpener Pro 3.0: (2) Output Sharpener.

The Sharpener Pro 3 interface appears.

④ Press ⌘+Option+0 (Ctrl+Alt+0) to view the image at 100%.

Apply General Output Sharpening

⑤ Click here and select a type of output, such as Inkjet.

⑥ Click here and select Auto.

⑦ Click here and select a paper, such as Luster.

⑧ Click here and select the resolution of your printer, such as 2400 × 2400.

⑨ Scroll down.

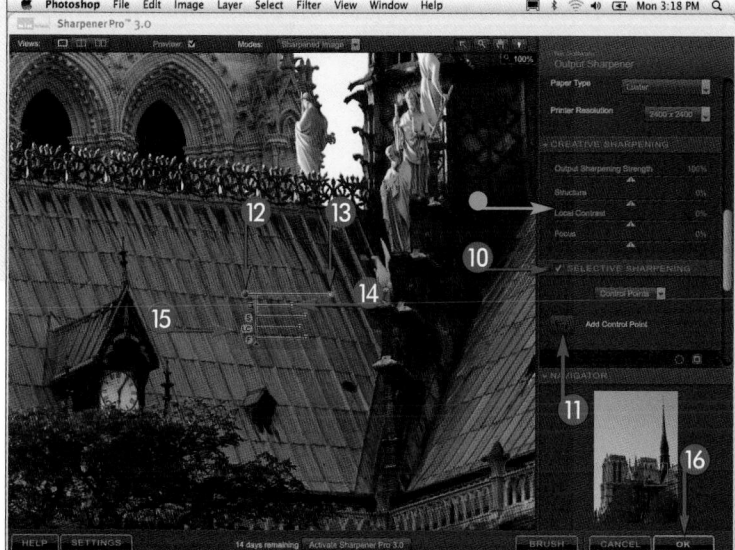

⑩ **Click Selective Sharpening** (☐ changes to ☑).

⑪ **Click the Add Control Point button.**

⑫ **Click an area in the image to add a control point.**

⑬ **Click and drag the top line to control the size.**

⑭ **Click and drag the Output Sharpening Strength slider.**

⑮ **Click the triangle to expand the controls, and click and drag the control point lines to change the type of sharpening.**

Note: Structure sharpens areas of texture under the control point. Local Contrast sharpens small edges or details under the control point. Focus adapts to sharpen out-of-focus areas more than the areas in focus under the control point.

● You can click Selective Sharpening (☑ changes to ☐) and move the Creative Sharpening sliders to sharpen the overall image.

⑯ **Click OK.**

● Nik Sharpener Pro 3 adds a layer with the specific type of sharpening applied.

TIPS

Important!

The order in which you apply image enhancements affects the quality of the final print. Apply noise reduction first, adjust the image for tone and color, and then resize the image. Output sharpening should be the final step in the editing process to avoid introducing unwanted details in the image.

Did You Know?

Although JPEG and TIFF images have some sharpening applied automatically when the camera processes the capture, RAW files do not. Sharpener Pro 3 includes a RAW Presharpening filter to sharpen RAW image files at the beginning of the editing process, without increasing noise or introducing artifacts. Be sure to turn off any sharpening in the camera's settings and in the Camera Raw processing software. Apply Nik's RAW Presharpener so you can better view your photos on your monitor.

Apply photo filters digitally using
NIK COLOR EFEX PRO 3

Professional photographers often carry a selection of lens filters and light reflectors to take advantage of every lighting condition they might encounter. You can achieve similar effects using Color Efex Pro 3 from Nik Software. Nik filters can help you enhance images better than using Photoshop alone. Based on photographic filter technology, these filters consider the existing color and light in an image and apply the effect accordingly. The filters can adapt to any previous adjustments in the photo, so you can apply multiple filters in a different order and achieve more

natural-looking photographic enhancements. Color Efex Pro 3 can also be applied to a Smart Object photo layer so you can readjust images even after the effects have been applied. You can even save your settings to apply them to a range of photos for a consistent workflow and increased productivity.

The Indian Summer filter shown in this task is just one of the many filters. It gives the foliage the appearance of late fall colors. You can see samples of the many Color Efex Pro 3 filters at www.Niksoftware.com.

1 Click Color Efex Pro 3.0 in the Selective tool.

Note: If the Selective tool is not open, click File, Automate, and Nik Selective Tool.

Note: You can optionally click Filter and select Nik Software and click Color Efex Pro 3.0 to open the NIK Color Efex interface.

2 Click the Dy-I tab.

3 Click Indian Summer.

The Indian Summer filter interface appears.

4 Click the Lock Loupe Position button.

5 Click in the image to lock the position of the loupe.

6 Click either of the two Split preview buttons to select a before and after preview.

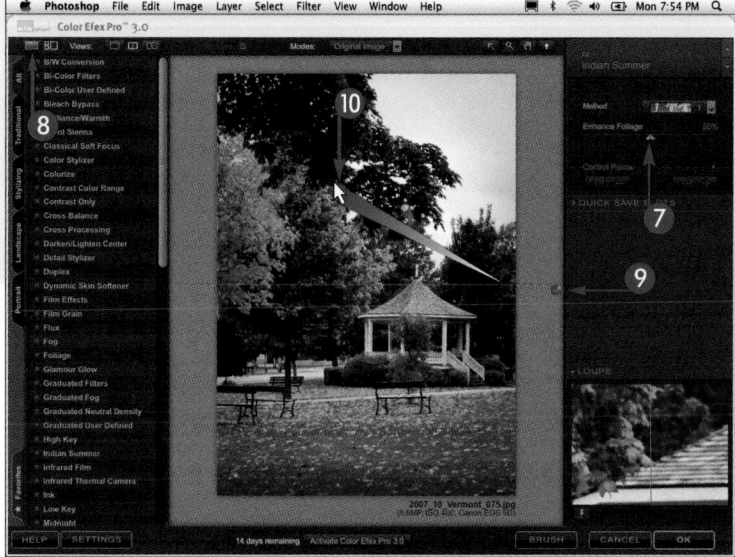

7 Click and drag the Enhance Foliage slider to control the intensity of the colors.

8 Click the Show Image Only button to enlarge the preview window.

9 Click the Rotate Preview button to change the Split preview.

10 Click and drag the red divider line to compare different areas.

11 Click OK.

Color Efex Pro 3 applies the filter to a separate layer.

#105

DIFFICULTY LEVEL

TIPS

Try This!
You can click Brush instead of OK and paint any filter into your image using a brush to easily control the location and amount of the effect. The filter is automatically applied to the layer mask of a new layer so you can paint the effect directly on the photo. Use a pen tablet for even greater control.

More Options!
In addition to applying the filter to the entire image, apply the filters to specific areas using Nik's patented U Point technology for even more control. Click a Control Point button and click in the image. Click and drag the sliders to increase or decrease the areas affected and the intensity of the color change.

Did You Know?
Nik Color Efex Pro 3.0 Complete edition includes 52 conventional film emulation and special effects filters. Nik Color Efex Pro 3 Select and Nik Color Efex Pro 3 Standard editions include 35 and 15 filters, respectively.

Enhance colors and light selectively with
NIK VIVEZA 2

You can edit the color and light in your images using Photoshop's filters; however, to do so to specific areas requires selections, feathering, layer masks, and an in-depth knowledge of the tools in Photoshop. You can easily enhance the color and light in your images and do so with greater control using Nik Software's Viveza 2 plug-in. You can darken the background and lighten the main subject, or modify the tones in specific areas visually using interactive sliders. Like other Nik plug-ins, Viveza 2 includes the U Point technology so you can create multiple control points in the image and change how the filter is

applied to each area individually. As you move the point sliders to control the brightness, contrast, and saturation, Viveza 2 edits the colors of the objects under the points and automatically blends the tonal changes as it applies them. You can also choose to paint the edits directly on the image using the Brush option in the interface.

If you apply Viveza 2 to a Smart Object layer, you can fine-tune any edits after they have been applied. Viveza 2 is also available as part of a complete collection bundle of Nik software plug-ins available at www.Niksoftware.com.

① Click Filter and then Convert for Smart Filters.

● The Background layer is changed to a Smart Object layer.

Note: Nik's Brush option is deactivated when using a Smart Object layer.

② Click Viveza 2 in the Selective tool.

Note: If the Selective tool is not open, click File, Automate, and then Nik Selective Tool.

Note: You can optionally click Filter, Nik Software, and Color Efex Pro 3.0 to open the Nik Color Efex Pro 3 interface.

The Viveza 2 interface appears.

③ Click the Side-by-Side preview button to select a before and after preview.

● You can also click the Split preview button to display a split preview.

④ Click Add Control Point.

⑤ Click an area in the photo to adjust it.

● A control point appears.

⑥ Click and drag the top slider to adjust the circle so it covers the area to be changed.

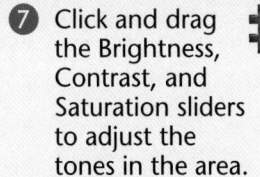

#106

7. Click and drag the Brightness, Contrast, and Saturation sliders to adjust the tones in the area.

8. Repeat steps 4 to 7 to add more adjustment points.

9. Click OK.

Viveza 2 applies the changes to the colors and light in the image as a Smart Filter.

● You can double-click the Viveza 2 Smart Filter to reopen the interface and readjust the sliders.

TIPS

Did You Know?

When you view the full image in the preview window, the Loupe tool shows the image at 100%. When you click the Zoom tool to preview the image at 100%, the Loupe tool shows the whole image and acts as a navigator.

Try This!

You can click the Settings button in the Viveza 2 interface to set how the interface functions. You can select the default zoom size, change the default preview style, change the control point size and the types of sliders, and choose to always have the filter applied to a separate layer.

More Options!

Each time you add a Viveza 2 control point, there are four sliders visible. Click the arrow below the fourth slider. More lines are added to the control point so you can individually adjust the hue, red, green, blue, and warmth of the selected area.

Create a dynamic black-and-white image with
NIK SILVER EFEX PRO

Photoshop CS5's Adjustments panel includes many presets and adjustments for converting a color photo to black and white nondestructively. Nik Software's Silver Efex Pro is a sophisticated and yet easy-to-use tool for converting color images to grayscale and re-creating the different techniques for traditional darkroom photographic film processing. As with other Nik plug-ins, Silver Efex Pro enables you to selectively control the tones and contrast in the image with the U Point technology. Silver Efex Pro conversions have the look of traditional film black-and-white images because the Nik plug-in re-creates the film grain from

the pixels in the photo, instead of overlaying a grain pattern as with other digital conversions. You can also select a black-and-white film type so your final image more closely emulates the look of a grayscale photo shot with film.

Silver Efex Pro includes a number of presets, including tints and toners, so you can vary the resulting conversion in numerous ways. You can add a vignette or burned-in edges, and you can even save your own settings as presets. You can download a trial version to use with your images at www.Niksoftware.com.

① Click Silver Efex Pro in the Selective tool.

Note: If the Selective tool is not open, click File, Automate, and then Nik Selective Tool.

Note: You can optionally click Filter, Nik Software, and then Color Efex Pro 3.0 to open the Nik Color Efex Pro 3 interface.

② Click any of the preset styles in the left panel to view the preset conversion in the main preview window.

③ Click and drag any of the sliders to adjust the overall tones in the image.

Note: Increasing the Brightness slider increases the lightness of the image. Increasing the Contrast slider increases the contrast in the image. Increasing the Structure slider makes finer details more noticeable. Decreasing the Structure slider gives the area a smoother appearance.

● You can click Add Control Point; click in the image to add a control point and drag the sliders to adjust the tones in a specific area.

④ Click the Show Image Only button to hide the style browser and make the image in the preview area larger.

⑤ Click a color filter, such as the red filter.

The preview enlarges and the color filter changes the grayscale composition.

6 Scroll to view more options.

7 Click Stylizing (■ changes to ☑).

8 Click the Toning arrow.

9 Click the Presets arrow to view the presets.

10 Position the cursor over each preset to view the results.

11 Click a preset to apply it.

12 Click the Vignette arrow or the word Vignette.

The Vignette options appear.

13 Scroll to view the sliders.

14 Click and drag the Amount and Size sliders to adjust the vignette.

15 Click and drag the slider under Rectangle to create a rectangular vignette as in this example, or under Circle for a circular vignette effect.

16 Click OK.

The black-and-white filter is applied to the image as a separate layer.

TIPS

Did You Know?

You can select a different location for the center of the vignette by clicking the Place Center button (■) in the Vignette pane and then clicking the image in the area you want for the center.

More Options!

Stylize a black-and-white image by clicking one of the presets, such as Copper Toner as in step 11. Then move the Strength, Balance, and Paper Toning sliders to customize the look.

Try This!

Click the Burn Edges arrow or the words Burn Edges at the bottom of the Stylizing pane. Click one of the four edge buttons to adjust the left, top, right, or bottom edge. Then click and drag the Strength, Size, and Transition sliders to digitally burn one edge of your image for a unique look.

Colorize a black-and-white photo with
AKVIS COLORIAGE

You can add color to a grayscale photo in Photoshop using adjustment layers, masks, and brushes; however, the Coloriage plug-in from AKVIS makes colorizing a black-and-white photograph quick and automatic. You can easily add color to a variety of images from antique photos to hand-drawn sketches and cartoons and still maintain a very natural look. You can even use Coloriage to replace the colors in a color image.

Your image must be in RGB mode for the Coloriage filters to be applied. Click Image in the menu, and then click Mode and RGB before selecting AKVIS Coloriage from the Photoshop filters.

You can colorize an image with Coloriage by clicking different colors from the Colors palette or use the Color Library for difficult colors such as skin, hair, and lips. Paint over the areas in the photo with loose brush strokes. When you click the green forward button, the software determines the borders of the various areas and applies the color based on the grayscale values.

You can find Coloriage along with other AKVIS filters at http://AKVIS.com.

1 Press ⌘+J (Ctrl+J) to duplicate the Background layer.

2 Click Filter.

3 Click AKVIS.

4 Click Coloriage.

The Coloriage interface appears.

5 Click and drag the slider to reduce or enlarge your preview.

6 Click a color you want to apply to one area, such as the skin in this example.

7 Click the Pencil tool to make the size slider appear.

8 Press the left or right bracket keys to adjust the pencil size.

9 Click and drag to draw in the image with the first color.

⑩ Repeat steps 5 to 9 to set all the colors to be used.

⑪ Click the Eraser tool.

⑫ Click and drag to correct any stray marks.

⑬ Click the Run button to see a preliminary colorization.

● AKVIS determines the blends, and the colorized image appears in the After pane.

⑭ Click the Before tab and repeat steps 6 to 12 to change any colors as needed.

⑮ Click the Run button again to view the corrections.

⑯ Click the Apply button.

The final colorization is applied to the image.

Note: If the colors are too vibrant in the Background copy layer, you can lower the opacity of the layer.

TIPS

Did You Know?

If you want to change one particular color in a color image and not alter the rest of the colors, use the Pencil tool (🖉) and draw on the object. Then use the Keep-Color Pencil tool (🖉) and draw a closed outline around the object.

Try This!

When you colorize a black-and-white photograph, select the less saturated colors in the Color palette to make the colorization appear more natural. The less saturated colors are at the bottom of the palette.

More Options!

You can save the color strokes to edit colors later or vary different colorization schemes. Click the Save Strokes button (🖾) after drawing all the strokes but before applying them and closing the interface.

Create a graphite drawing with
AKVIS SKETCH

In addition to Coloriage, AKVIS makes a number of other plug-ins for Photoshop to restore, retouch, and enhance your photographs. AKVIS art-styled plug-ins are the best for creating natural-looking art from photos.

You can easily turn a photo into art using AKVIS Sketch or AKVIS Artwork. Both these plug-ins give you control over the style and thickness of lines and brush strokes, as well as other artistic attributes in a preview mode. You can change a setting, run a new preview, and make changes before applying the

effects. By creating the art version of your photo on a separate layer, you can create multiple artistic versions of the original Background layer for comparison or to blend together for different effects. You can also use Photoshop CS5's new Bristle tip brushes and the Mixer Brush tool to further customize the sketch or painting on another, separate layer.

Using a photo-to-art plug-in from AKVIS alone or in combination with Photoshop CS5's art tools enables you to unleash your creativity, learn to draw and paint, or improve your artistic skills.

① Press ⌘+J (Ctrl+J) to duplicate the layer.

② Click Filter.

③ Click AKVIS.

④ Click Sketch.

The Sketch interface appears with a default sketch sample selected in the center of the image.

⑤ Click to maximize the interface.

⑥ Click and drag the selection area around to view different parts of the sketch.

⑦ Click and drag the Sketch Effects and the Strokes sliders to adjust the sketching style.

⑧ Click and drag here to zoom in on the image.

9. Click the Edges tab.

10. Click and drag the Edge Strength, Sensitivity, and Edge Width sliders to increase or decrease quality of the lines.

11. Click the Run button to preview the changed settings.

#109

AKVIS redraws the image as a sketch.

12. Click here and select Fit Image to view the whole image at once.

13. Click and drag any of the sliders to readjust the drawing.

14. Click the Run button to preview the new settings.

15. Click the Apply button to apply the sketch to the layer in Photoshop.

● You can optionally click Save to save the settings as a preset.

DIFFICULTY LEVEL

TIPS

Try This!

AKVIS Artwork is one of the best plug-ins available to turn a photo into a painting. The sliders and settings are very similar to those in Sketch, and you can select the style of paint, thickness of brush strokes, and more to make your painting look more as though it were done with natural media.

Did You Know?

AKVIS makes plug-ins to create special lighting and other effects. With AKVIS LightShop you can even add reflection to shiny objects. AKVIS Magnifier can help you change the size of an image without loss of quality, and AKVIS Noise Buster helps in noise reduction. You can try any of the AKVIS plug-ins or stand-alone applications with the trial software at www.AKVIS.com.

More Options!

Selecting areas and masking are often easier to accomplish with a plug-in such as AKVIS SmartMask. Using technology similar to Coloriage, you draw over areas to keep with a blue pencil and then draw with a red pencil to define the areas that should be cut away. SmartMask finds the borders and removes the unwanted areas in the photo.

USE ALIEN SKIN SNAP ART 2
to change your photos into art

Turning a photograph into a fine-art piece such as an oil painting or a pencil sketch using Photoshop's actions and brushes can be a lot of fun. It can also be time-consuming. By using the Snap Art 2 plug-in from Alien Skin Software, you can transform a photograph into art that looks as though it was done with traditional art tools with just a few clicks. You can apply the Snap Art 2 filter settings and then move the various sliders and controls and view your painting or sketch as it builds in the large preview window.

The Snap Art 2 interface includes several split screen previews so that you can see both your photo as a reference and the effects as you apply them. By applying different types of art media filters on multiple layers and changing the blending modes, you can completely alter the results and make your artwork unique. The plug-ins work best on smaller images with defined contrast areas.

You can find many other powerful plug-ins at www.alienskin.com.

Create a Stylized Drawing

① Press ⌘+J (Ctrl+J) to duplicate the Background layer.

② Click Filter.

③ Click Alien Skin Snap Art 2.

④ Click a filter such as Stylize.

The Alien Skin Snap Art 2 interface for that media appears.

⑤ Click the Basic tab.

⑥ Click to apply the filter to a separate layer (☐ changes to ☑).

⑦ In the small preview window, click and drag the red box over the main subject.

⑧ Click here and select a preview split.

⑨ Click and drag any of the sliders to adjust the look.

A progress bar appears briefly, and the large preview image displays the results.

⑩ Click OK.

The filter is applied to a new layer named for the type of filter (Stylize in this example).

Change the Look by Adding Another Filter

⑪ Click Layer 1 to select it.

⑫ Click Filter.

⑬ Click Alien Skin Snap Art 2.

⑭ Click another filter such as Impasto.

⑮ Repeat steps 5 to 10 to apply the other art media filter on a separate layer.

The filter is applied to a new layer named for the type of filter (Impasto in this example).

Note: You can change the order of the layers to change the blended effect.

⑯ Click the top layer to select it.

⑰ Click here and select a layer blend mode such as Soft Light or Overlay.

⑱ Click Opacity and drag slightly to the left.

⑲ Double-click the Zoom tool to view the image at 100%.

Note: Optionally, to vary the effect more, repeat steps 11 to 18 using different Alien Skin Snap Art 2 filters in step 14.

The final image looks more like artwork than a photograph.

TIPS

Did You Know?

Snap Art 2 uses edge detection to outline the objects in the photo. It uses this outline to place the natural media strokes and fill areas with colors. Snap Art 2 uses an advanced paint engine to transform your photo into an artistic composition, preserving enough detail while giving the piece a loose and artistic appearance.

Try This!

Each filter in Snap Art 2 has many sliders and options. Move a slider to try a different look. To undo a change, press ⌘+Z (Ctrl+Z) or, to redo the change, press ⌘+Y (Ctrl+Y). You can return to the default settings anytime by clicking the Settings tab in the Snap Art 2 interface and clicking Factory Default, or by pressing ⌘+R (F5) to reset the filter to the original settings.

Create special effects with
ALIEN SKIN EYE CANDY 6

Eye Candy 6 from Alien Skin helps you create a diverse range of designs and specialty effects. You can easily build glass-like buttons for a Web interface, add depth to stylize a logo, design custom titles, or even simulate natural phenomena, such as fire and smoke. You can create metal, gel, or animal fur textures simply by moving the sliders. You can even add a drop shadow to text and make it converge in perspective. Eye Candy 6 includes 30 filters you can use and combine to make designs come to life. The

filters perform complex simulations to render detailed images, and the results are easier to accomplish and often more realistic than using the filters built into Photoshop.

You can start with text or a flat logo and then add texture to extrude it and add a shadow that makes the design pop off the page. Experimentation is key to designing with Eye Candy 6. Eye Candy 6 includes 1,500 presets that you can use or visually edit to fit your particular design.

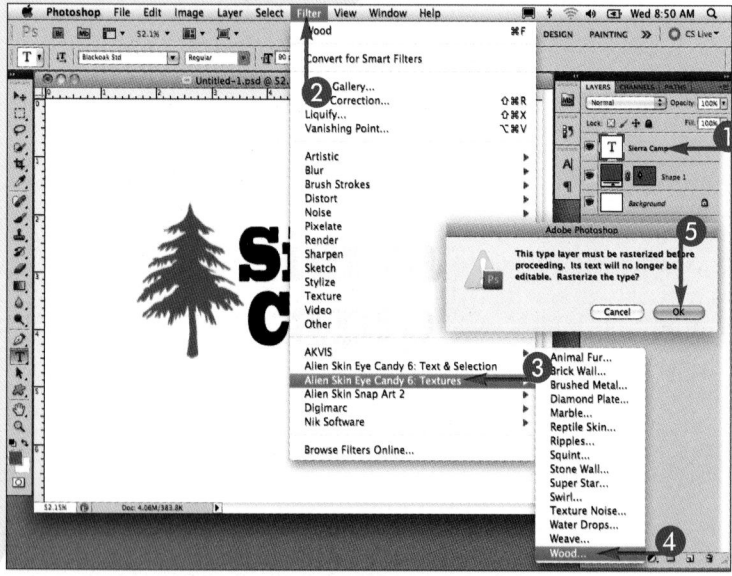

Note: This task starts with a shape on one layer and text on a type layer.

1 Click the type layer.

2 Click Filter.

3 Click Alien Skin Eye Candy 6: Textures.

4 Click a texture such as Wood.

Note: The type layer will be changed to a pixel layer and the text will no longer be editable.

5 Click OK in the warning dialog box.

The Alien Skin interface appears.

6 Click any of the Natural Wood types in the Settings window.

● You can optionally click any of the other tabs — Basic, Knots, or Grain — to customize the wood look.

7 Click OK.

111

DIFFICULTY LEVEL

The Wood texture is applied to text on a layer above the rasterized black text layer.

⑧ Click the Eye icon of the white Background layer to deselect it.

⑨ Press ⌘+Opt+Shift+E (Ctrl+Alt+Shift+E) to combine the layers into a new one with a transparent background.

⑩ Click Filter, click Eye Candy 6: Text & Selection, and Perspective Shadow.

Note: You can also or optionally click Filter, Eye Candy 6: Text & Selection, and Bevel to add a bevel to the shape and text.

⑪ In the Alien Skin interface, click any of the perspective shadow options in the Settings pane.

● You can optionally click and drag on the anchor points to alter the perspective shadow.

● You can optionally click the Basic tab to make changes to the offset, opacity, blur, or fade of the shadow.

⑫ Click OK to apply the perspective shadow to the layer.

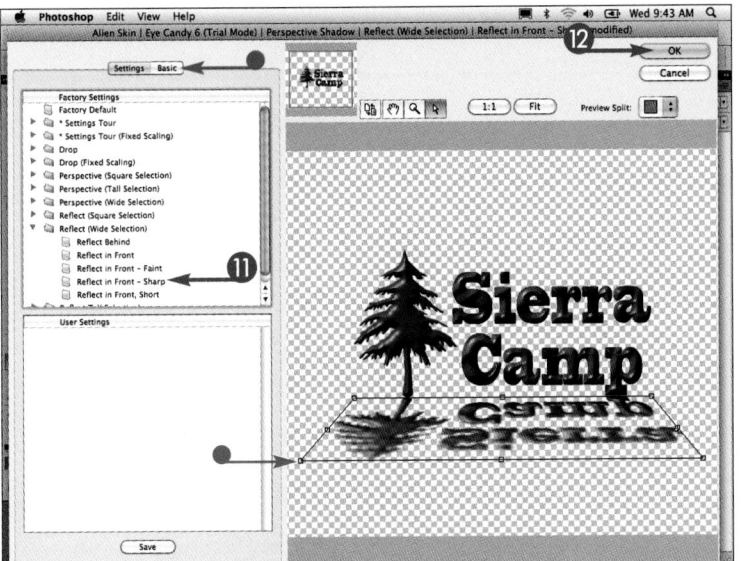

TIPS

Did You Know?

The Eye Candy 6 Filters work with CMYK files and 16-bit per channel images. They can be used on very large files because they work in the 64-bit version of Photoshop. And because they can be applied to Smart Objects and can be built on separate layers, the filters are nondestructive.

More Options!

Alien Skin offers a number of plug-in filters to help the photographer as well as the professional graphic designer. Alien Skin Blow Up helps resize images, and the Bokeh filter gives the photographer the ability to selectively change the depth of field after capture. Image Doctor and Exposure help with image restoration and film simulation. The photo-oriented plug-ins are also available as a bundle at www.alienskin.com.

Explore colors and tones visually with
AUTO FX SOFTWARE

The colors in your images can express moods and messages that transcend the subject matter. Using software plug-in filters such as Mystical Tint, Tone, and Color (MTTC) from Auto FX Software makes it easy to visually explore color tones and reinterpret your images in an artistic way. MTTC includes many different visual effects and presets. You can apply the changes to your images globally, or you can apply them to specific regions of the image by brushing them on, using gradients, effect masks, or an effect ellipse to apply different tones to different areas. Auto

FX plug-ins let you work nondestructively to transform images with dynamically adjustable layers so you can combine multiple effects and still control the settings for each one. You can try the layer presets from a visual gallery or explore the results with any number of the individual special effects, experiment with various settings, and watch the results in a large display. When you see the results you want, you apply the filters to the image.

You can find other visual imaging solutions for creative effects on the gallery pages at www.AutoFx.com.

① With an image open in Photoshop, press ⌘+J (Ctrl+J) to duplicate the Background layer.

② Click Filter.

③ Click Auto FX Software.

④ Click Mystical Tint • Tone • Color.

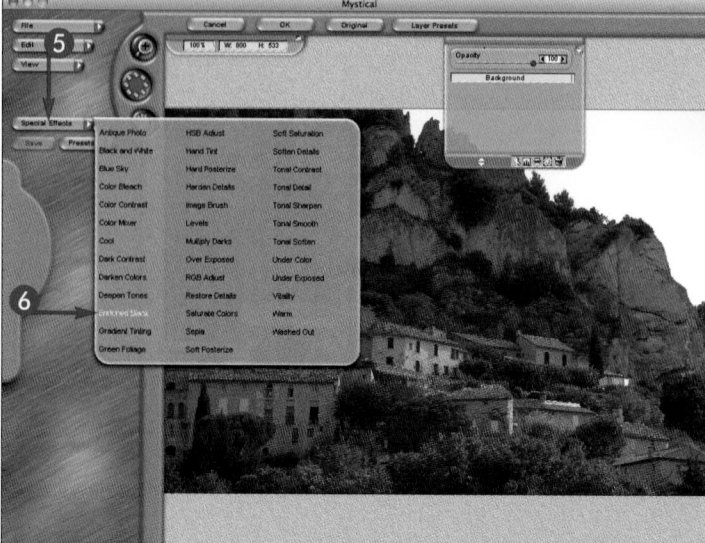

The main Mystical 2.0 interface fills the screen.

⑤ Click Special Effects to open the menu.

⑥ Click an effect such as Enriched Black.

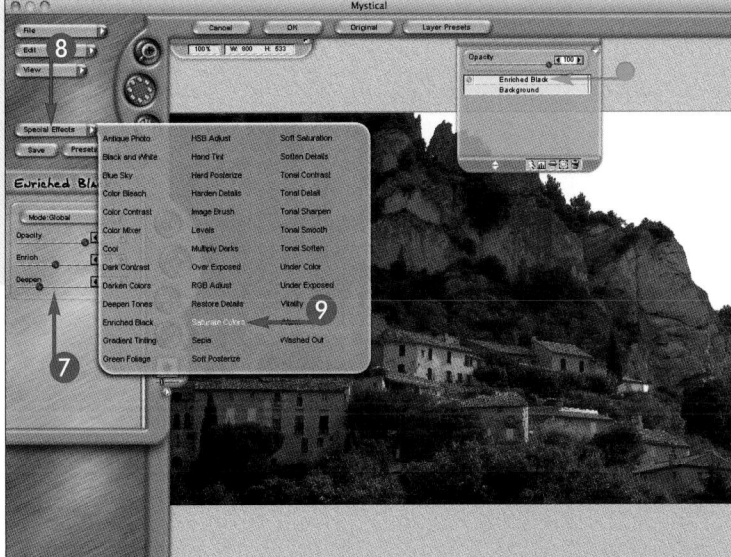

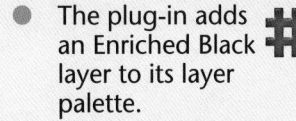

- The plug-in adds an Enriched Black layer to its layer palette.

7 Click and drag the sliders to change the effect.

8 Click Special Effects again.

9 Click an effect from the menu such as Saturate Colors.

112

DIFFICULTY LEVEL

The plug-in adds a Saturate Colors layer.

10 Repeat steps 7 to 9, selecting another effect such as Deepen Tones.

11 Click and drag the sliders to change the effect.

Note: You can optionally click and drag a layer and move it to a different position in the Auto FX layer palette to alter the effect.

12 Click Mode Global.

13 Click Brush On from the menu.

The overall effect reverts to the previous look.

14 Click the Brush button.

15 Click and drag in the image to change the effect.

16 Click OK to apply the filters.

The image reopens in Photoshop with the filter applied to Layer 1.

TIPS

Did You Know?

Mystical Tint Tone and Color includes portrait-enhancing filters to smooth skin, edit skin color, naturally brighten the eyes, enhance the hair, and even enlarge eyes and lips.

Try This!

After applying an effect in the Global mode as in step 12, click the Auto FX Eraser tool (⊘). Change the size, feathering, and opacity using the small sliders in the thumbnail below the Eraser. Click and drag in the image to remove the effect from specific areas.

More Options!

Auto FX provides other creative plug-ins such as Photographic Edges for adding edges and effects to images, and Mystical Lighting and Ambience to change the lighting and shading of your image with complete visual control. You can use Mystical Lighting and Ambience to create both photo-realistic and surrealistic effects.

Enhance your portraits with
IMAGENOMIC PORTRAITURE

Retouching portraits and softening skin in Photoshop involves many different tools and techniques, and multiple masks and steps. You have to make detailed selections of areas such as hair and eyelashes to protect them when you apply softening effects to the skin. Using Imagenomic's Portraiture plug-in, you can smooth skin and remove imperfections without making selections or manually creating masks.

Portraiture's algorithms work differently compared to standard Photoshop tools. The plug-in includes an Auto Mask feature that automatically selects only the range of skin tones in the image so you can build an effective

mask without selecting the hair, eyelashes, or other detailed areas. You can adjust the auto mask and then select from different tones to give your particular image the most natural-looking results. You can refine the corrections using the Enhancement sliders.

Portraiture includes presets you can use as a starting point. You can tailor any preset and save the modified version as your own custom preset to speed up your processing time. Imagenomic also makes Noiseware, an excellent plug-in for noise reduction, and RealGrain for adding grain to digital images. www.imagenomic.com

① With a photo open in Photoshop, click Filter, Imagenomic, and Portraiture.

● The Portraiture interface fills the screen and the default smoothing is applied.

● Portraiture remembers the last settings you applied. You may need to click here and select Auto if it is not selected.

② Click a Split Preview Window button to see a before and after preview.

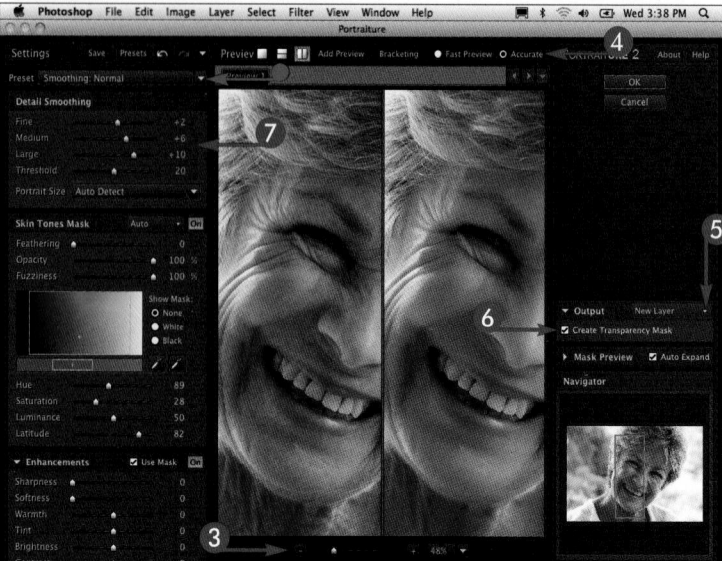

③ Click the slider to zoom in or select 100%.

④ Click Accurate to see the most accurate preview (⬛ changes to ⚫).

⑤ Click here and select New Layer.

⑥ Click Create Transparency Mask to apply the adjustments on a transparent layer (⬛ changes to ☑).

⑦ Click and drag the Detail Smoothing sliders to increase or decrease the effect.

● You can optionally click here to select another preset, such as Smoothing: Normal.

8 Click White to see the current Auto Mask (⬛ changes to ◙).

9 Click and drag the Hue, Saturation, Luminance, and Latitude sliders completely to the left.

10 Click the left eyedropper.

11 Move the cursor over the skin tones to see the mask selections in the Mask Preview window.

12 Click the most representative area of skin in the image.

● A new mask appears in the after view.

13 Click None to hide the mask and show the preview of the smoothed image (⬛ changes to ◙).

14 Click in the image and drag to preview other areas.

15 Click OK.

The smoothing appears on a separate layer above the Background layer in Photoshop.

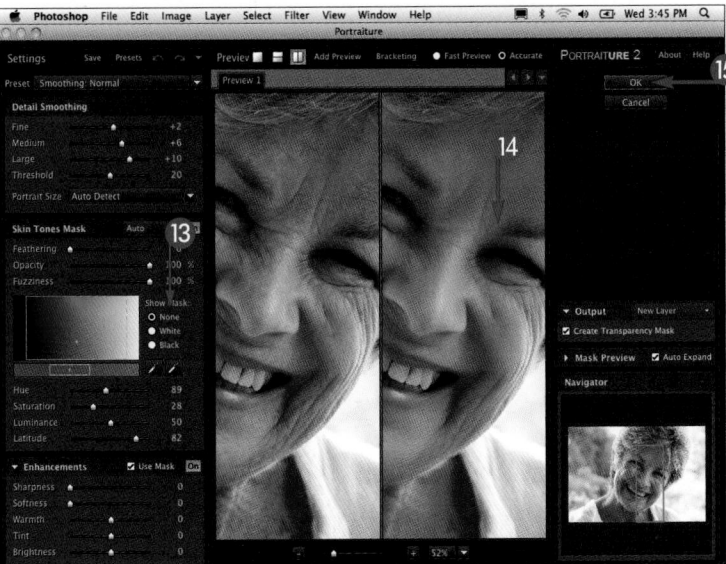

#113

DIFFICULTY LEVEL

TIPS

Try This!
You can apply Portraiture's Auto Mask even when batch-processing images. The masks are built based on each image's unique skin tone range, so even in a group of photos every skin type is handled individually.

More Options!
You can add a glamour effect to a portrait quickly by using the sliders under Enhancements to change the sharpness, softness, warmth, brightness, and contrast for a different effect.

Did You Know?
The area on the forehead between the two eyebrows is generally a good representation of the overall skin tone in the portrait and a good area to select from with Portraiture's eyedropper tool.

Transform an image with an action from
KUBOTA IMAGE TOOLS

Kubota Image Tools designs image-enhancing tools to help photographers process images quickly. The various tool packs include an assortment of Photoshop actions you can use to change an image with one click. You can increase the strength of the colors, add overall contrast, lighten shadow detail, sharpen, resize images, add frames, and more without working through the steps in Photoshop. Kubota Image Tools uses a customizable Dashboard interface with all the Kubota actions either listed alphabetically or grouped by the type of effect. You can add your own custom actions to the Kubota dashboard and even create

favorites so you can access them more quickly. Because actions are a series of prerecorded steps, some actions stop and ask you to adjust a selection for your photo or enter values in a dialog box before the transformation is complete.

To apply a Kubota Image Tools enhancement, you click the desired action in the Kubota Dashboard and click the Apply button. You can process multiple images with a single action using the batch command in Photoshop to increase your productivity. You can view the results of many of Kubota Image Tools actions at www.kubotaimagetools.com.

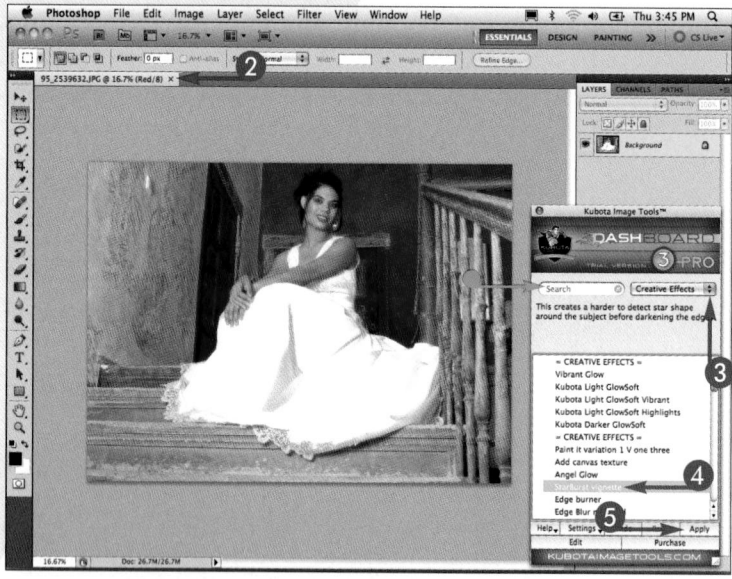

Apply a Starburst Vignette with the Dashboard

1. Load the Kubota actions and Dashboard following the step-by-step instructions.

   Note: Some instructions are also available in the Kubota Dashboard.

2. Open a photo in Photoshop.

3. In the Kubota Action Dashboard, click here and select an action type.

● You can optionally type the name of an action to search for it.

4. Click an action from the list such as StarBurst Vignette.

5. Click Apply.

6. Click Continue in the dialog box that appears.

   The action creates a custom shape layer and stops so you can adjust the starburst shape to fit your photo.

7. Click and drag the anchors to adjust the shape.

8. Click and drag the shape into position over the main subject, if necessary.

9. Press ⌘+Return (Ctrl+Enter) or click the Commit button to apply the shape.

266

- The action applies a blended starburst vignette-shaped layer and mask to the photo.

#114

DIFFICULTY LEVEL

Apply a Frame with the Dashboard

⑩ Type a word, such as **border**, into the search field of the Kubota Dashboard.

The corresponding actions are listed in the menu.

⑪ Click a border, such as Border Black with White Vertical.

⑫ Click Apply.

- The action applies a new layer with a black frame and a white keyline on the photo.

- Depending on the action selected, a dialog box may appear with more instructions. Close the dialog box by clicking Stop.

⑬ Click Layer and then Flatten Image to finish the enhancement.

TIPS

More Options!
Kubota Image Tools also makes a separate Border and Textures Dashboard. Using the actions listed in this Dashboard, you can apply different styles of colors, patterns, or edges and have them blend automatically into the image. You can easily add a texture over the whole image and then erase the texture using a layer mask where the added texture hides the main subject.

Try This!
Using the search field in the Dashboard, you can type the first letters of the name of an action, and the list of corresponding actions appears in the main Dashboard section.

Did You Know?
Once installed, you can open either of the Kubota Dashboards by clicking the Photoshop File menu, Automate, and Kubota Dashboard 3 Palette or Kubota Bor-Tex Dashboard Palette.

Add a frame for a finishing touch with
ONONE PHOTOFRAME

OnOne software makes a variety of plug-ins for Photoshop, as well as stand-alone products for enlarging images, creating photographic effects and frames, selective masking, adjusting tone, and changing the focal point. OnOne's Plug-In Suite 5 includes 6 separate plug-ins for Photoshop, including PhotoFrame.

PhotoFrame contains a complete library of instant frames, edges, backgrounds, textures, and ornaments you can add as a finishing touch to your images. You can also use PhotoFrame's predesigned album pages

to lay out your own photo books. You can browse the library of frame styles and pages, and preview the designs on your image to find the one that best fits your design and the photograph. PhotoFrame even includes authentic film and darkroom looks, including film and Polaroid edges, and you can control the size, colors, and blending of the effect.

PhotoFrame also includes a number of textures, backgrounds, and ornaments you can use to completely customize a photo frame or a complete photo album at www.ononesoftware.com.

① Open the image to frame.

② Click OnOne in the menu.

③ Click PhotoFrame 4.5 Professional Edition.

④ Click PhotoFrame 4.5 Professional Edition to view the entire library, or click an individual designer frame style.

The PhotoFrame Library opens.

⑤ Type **acid** to find acid-burn-styled frames.

⑥ Scroll to find the style to work with.

⑦ Click a frame style to apply it.

⑧ Click Add Frame.

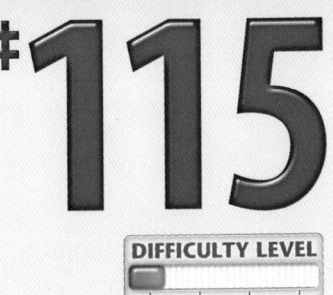

The image appears in the selected frame.

⑨ Click and drag on the anchor points to resize the image inside the frame.

⑩ Click Apply.

● The image opens in Photoshop with the frame parts as layers above the image.

TIPS

Did You Know?

Adding a frame with PhotoFrame is one of the last steps in editing your images. You should add the frame after all the color and tonal corrections are completed but before resizing and sharpening for final output.

Try This!

You can stack individual design elements to create your own custom preset and save it, so you can easily apply it to other images with one click.

More Options!

In addition to PhotoFrame, the OnOne Software suite also includes Genuine Fractals for resizing images, PhotoTune for color-correcting photos, FocalPoint for changing the point of focus, and PhotoTools for enhancing the overall image. The Mask Pro plug-in helps you remove backgrounds without complicated selections.

Give a photo greater color depth with
TOPAZ ADJUST

The various Photoshop plug-ins from Topaz Labs enable photographers to easily adjust images to fit their creative vision. You can improve image quality, reduce noise, manipulate details, smooth and stylize a photograph, or change a photo into unique artwork, effectively reinterpreting photographic realism with an artist's brush. And by applying Topaz plug-ins to a Smart Object layer, you can change the settings even after they are applied. From artistic exposure effects to edge manipulation, Topaz plug-ins make many complicated photo-editing tasks easy.

Topaz Adjust helps you intensify your images and includes many presets for different styles from mild exposure enhancements to dynamic photographic effects. You can create a simulated HDR look without having multiple exposures and make the final image look natural or extreme. You can apply a variety of presets and then customize the look to fit your photo. The Topaz Adjust plug-in includes separate adjustments for exposure, detail, color, and noise so you have complete control over the way your photo appears at different settings or for unique effects. www.topazlabs.com

① With a duplicated layer converted to a Smart Object in Photoshop, click Filter, Topaz Labs, and then Adjust 4.

The Topaz Adjust interface opens.

② Click a preset such as Clarity.

③ Click here to open the right panel if necessary.

④ Click the Exposure tab.

⑤ Click and drag the sliders to change the exposure settings.

⑥ Click the Details tab.

7 Scroll down.

8 Click Process Details Independent of Exposure (■ changes to ✓).

Note: *The details will now be adjusted without affecting the exposure and reducing the overall image noise.*

9 Click and drag the sliders to change the Details settings.

10 Repeat steps 4 to 9 for the Color and Noise tabs.

11 Click OK.

● The adjustments are applied to the Smart Object layer.

#116

DIFFICULTY LEVEL

TIPS

Did You Know?

Topaz ReMask offers simple steps for extracting detailed selections, and Topaz Detail gives images a sense of depth by enhancing details without creating edge artifacts.

More Options!

Topaz Simplify gives you many options for transforming a photo into art. You can create paintings in different artistic styles, as well as shaded line-art sketches. You can apply the presets or modify these and save the edited versions as a custom preset so you can reapply the tool to another image.

Important!

Topaz plug-ins work on both 8- and 16-bit images so you can take advantage of the larger color space. And because the plug-ins work on Smart Object layers in Photoshop, they are completely nondestructive.

Index

D

Index

Index

Index